ELIZABETHAN MINOR EPICS

ELIZABETHAN MINOR EPICS

Edited
with Introduction
by
ELIZABETH STORY DONNO

New York: Columbia University Press
London: Routledge & Kegan Paul
1963

*Library of Congress
Catalog Card Number:* 63-20343

722

Printed in Great Britain

For Sylvia and Peter Allen

CONTENTS

INTRODUCTION

NASO MAGISTER ERAT

Ars Amatoria III. 812

WITH THE derisive phrase 'amorous scholemaister' Stephen Gosson in 1579 dismissed the claim of the *praeceptor amoris*, but, in point of fact, Gosson's phrase aptly describes the role of Ovid in the sixteenth century when familiarity with his writings, stemming from the schoolroom, was in due course to elicit the warmest of responses—literary imitation.

The most important of Ovid's works were staples of the curriculum, valued for their content, their style, and their language. The *Metamorphoses*, that vast repository of myth, the *Fasti*, with its store of information about the 'rytes and ceremonies which were observed after the Religion of the Heathen,' and the *Tristia*, their varied elegiacs useful for versification, were all widely used in the grammar schools. The *Heroides*, appealing because of their psychological range, had been recommended by Erasmus as an aid to letter writing.[1] Even the *Ars Amatoria* (translated in 1513 as *The flores of Ovide de arte amandi with theyr englysshe afore them*) might take its place among the 'how to' books and, in conjunction with the *de Remedio*, serve as a hortatory example of vice reproved. In any case, works of such questionable import as the *Amatoria* and the *Amores* became familiar through the various *flores poetarum*.

The sixteenth-century system of education was such that students became exceedingly familiar with selected authors. Memorization both of the Latin original and of English equivalents was standard practice; this was followed by close analysis, by imitation, and lastly by variation. 'Congruent epithetons,' 'choice Phrases, acute Sentences, wittie Apophthegmes,' and 'livelie Similitudes' were duly recorded in the students'

[1] For a full discussion see T. W. Baldwin, *William Shakspere's Small Latine and Lesse Greeke* (Urbana, 1944), particularly II, 239 ff; 418-19; 453.

commonplace books, while analysis of language and structure led to a similar familiarity with and reservoir of effective rhetorical devices. Well-stocked with such raw material, the student was then encouraged to imitate and vary his model, to seek out the 'flowers of fancy, the jerks of invention.' This school habit was to linger in the minds of many future writers and be put to apprentice use.

Ovid's role as an esteemed model was not a Renaissance innovation but rather the carry-over of a pattern established several centuries earlier. Lost in the Dark Ages, texts of Ovid were gradually recovered. By the eleventh century circulation of his works had begun to increase markedly, reaching such a peak in the twelfth and thirteenth centuries that the period has been called the *aetas Ovidiana*. Writers of the period, imitating both 'matter and manner,' attest to the widespread habit of using him as a poetic model. In reading lists of the period, the *Metamorphoses*, the *Fasti*, the *de Remedio* all receive endorsement, but R. R. Bolgar has pointed out that an analysis of quotations suggests no works of Ovid were 'more widely read and more lovingly remembered' than the *Heroides* and the *Ars Amatoria*.[1] Imitations during the medieval period range from the infectious songs of the goliards to the chivalric romances of the courtly poets who 'refined and etherialized' Ovid's theory of love. For Chaucer, as for Dante, Ovid claimed a revered place with Homer, Horace, Lucan, and Statius.[2]

Concurrently with this response to the power and persuasiveness of Ovid's art was the need to defend his writings from detractors, and for the thirteenth and fourteenth centuries an easy means was at hand. Moral passages had long been culled to make up *florilegia*; scholia, glosses, and commentary then followed; finally, the moralizing was attached to the stories themselves. Thus in the thirteenth century Ovid's mythological tales became metamorphosed into the 70,000 verses known as the *Metamorphoses Moralisées*.[3] In the fourteenth century the same justifying technique appeared in the *Reductorium Morale*

[1] *The Classical Heritage and Its Beneficiaries* (Cambridge, 1954), pp. 189 and 430, n.
[2] For an engaging account of Ovid in the Middle Ages, see E. K. Rand, *Ovid and His Influence* (New York, 1928), pp. 114–49.
[3] This pattern is fully traced in L. K. Born's 'Ovid and Allegory,' *Speculum* IX (1934), 362–79.

of Petrus Berchorius. It was to persist, summarized in appendices and prefaces, capsuled in handbooks of mythology, and ultimately transmogrified into a strange blend of alchemical and cabalistic lore. But there was to be an interlude at the end of the sixteenth century when Ovid stepped out of these medieval trammels a free spirit.

For the English Renaissance we begin with that Janus figure William Caxton, who on 22 April 1480 finished his translation of *Ovyd, Hys Booke of Methamorphose*. Although he refers to it in his prologue to the *Golden Legend* (1483), only books X–XV are extant, and it is uncertain whether all copies of a printed edition have completely disappeared or whether something prevented its ever being printed. For his translation Caxton had used a French text enriched with the moralizings of Berchorius as well as additions from the Troy legend. The latter digressions he followed faithfully, but, curiously,[1] he included little of the moralizing. Only at the end of Book X did he append 'thexposicion of the fables to fore wreton by sens hystoryal.' These interpretations vary from the moral to the astrological ('Jupyter is a planette sette above other and more hoote than other') to the natural ('the Mirre desireth & requyreth the hete of the sonne & swete humeur'). An example of the naïve moralizing is the exposition of Pygmalion and his ivory statue:

This is to saye that some grete lord myghte have a mayde or a servaunt in hys hows. Whiche was pouer. nacked & coude no good. but she was gent & of fayr fourme. but she was Drye & lene as an ymage. This ryche man that saw he[r] fayr Clothyd. norysshyd and taughte her so moche, that she was wel endoctryned. And whan he sawe her drawynge to good maneres he lovyd her so moche that it plesed him tespowse her & take her to hys wyf. of whom he hade after a fayre sone. prudent. wyse & of grete renomee.[2]

[1] His most recent editor says 'happily.' See the introduction to the edition by S. Gaselee and H. F. B. Brett-Smith (Oxford, 1924).

[2] *Ovyde, Hys Booke*, p. 26. For an example of the 'unedifying' moral tradition, see the interpretation of that 'good harper & synger' Orpheus, p. 24 f. That it was common is shown by the fact that the same interpretation is given in the allegorical treatise assigned to Giovanni Del Virgilio (P. Wicksteed and E. G. Gardner, *Dante and Giovanni Del Virgilio*, Westminster, 1902, p. 319). In 1567 Golding, on the other hand, interpreted Orpheus also as one who reduced the 'wyld,' 'feerce,' and 'rude' people to a good order, living in 'reverent awe/Like neybours in a common weale,' *Shakespeare's Ovid*, ed. W. H. D. Rouse (Carbondale, 1961), p. 11, ll. 521–26.

3

Other translations of Ovid to supplement knowledge of the originals do not appear (apart from the *Ars Amatoria* mentioned above) until the 1560's when a steady stream begins: the anonymous *Fable of Ovid treting of Narcissus* (1560), with moral appended; Thomas Peend's *Pleasant Fable of Salmacis and Hermaphroditus* (1565), with moral appended; George Turbervile's *Heroycall Epistles* (1567), straight; and the most important, Arthur Golding's translation of the complete *Metamorphoses* (1565-67).

Golding's translation is an influential work: in his two prefaces he deploys much of the artillery of the later defences of poetry. Books I–IV were published in 1565 with a short prose dedication to the Earl of Leicester in which he affirms that this work which outwardly purports 'moste pleasant tales and delectable histories' is inwardly fraught 'with most piththie instructions and wholsome examples' and that both contain 'moste exquisite connynge and deepe knowledge.' For the complete edition he expanded his dedication into an epistle of some six hundred lines. After referring to the natural philosophy in the *Metamorphoses*, Golding cites moral examples from each of the fifteen books and then asserts that it would be 'labor infinite, and tediousness not small'[1]—both to the Earl and to his other readers—to expound the meaning of all of them, especially since 'a booke of many quyres' could scarcely contain them. He then shows how the first book of Ovid may be reconciled with Christian doctrine. A preface to the reader (so as not to offend 'the simple sort') of 222 lines follows; here Golding explains what the deities symbolize, acknowledging, however, that since these names 'oft may and must' have other significances, he will again not be so 'tedious' as to declare them all, leaving them rather to the construction of the reader (ll. 77–80). (This acknowledging of multiple significances should be noted.) He then turns to defending the poet's art and that of Ovid in particular, for its 'darke and secret misteries,' its 'counselles wyse and sage,' its 'good ensamples,' its 'reprooves of vice,' and its 'fyne inventions' (ll. 185–88). These eight

---

[1] A comment echoed by Sir John Harington in 1591 in his 'Apologie of Poetrie' where having given one fourfold interpretation of a story from the *Metamorphoses*, he adds: 'the like infinite Allegories I could pike out of other Poeticall fictions, save I would avoid tediousnesse.'

4

hundred-odd prefatory lines constitute the whole of the moral justification; he leaves the tales untouched.

As the adversaries of poetry became more vociferous, the methods of defence became more diverse. The Horatian dictum of *utile* and *dulce* provides a common base, but the means of 'enterlacing profit wyth pleasure' is viewed in different ways. For example, when Sidney mocks the over-ingenious interpreters who are accustomed to turn 'others' children' into 'changelings' (Sonnet 28), he is not merely offering a poetical *jeu d'esprit*, nor is he countering the pleasure-profit doctrine. Rather, he is being consistent with his own critical theories, upholding Golding's 'good ensamples' instead of 'allegory's curious frame.'

Having shot a bolt in 1589 at the 'ragged Rimes' that were being 'slubberd up,' Thomas Nashe took care to explain that *poetry* is a 'hidden & divine kinde of Philosophy' and that 'the fables of Poets must of necessitie be fraught with wisedome & knowledge.' This 'hieratic' view of poetry obviously had particular appeal for the deep and searching wits of the period. But we may wonder whether the general cultivated reader (in contrast to the 'simple sort' whom Golding had addressed) did not, like the oft-cited bee, speed, unerring, to the sweetest honey among the bitter flowers and sharp nettles. For Nashe too mocks the 'mis-interpreting' of 'this moralizing age':

There is nothing that if a man list he may not wrest or pervert: I cannot forbid anie to thinke villainously, *Sed caveat emptor*, Let the interpreter beware; for none ever hard me make Allegories of an idle text.[1]

Thus defenders of 'peerlesse Poesie' might make use of one weapon from their arsenal at one time while resorting to a different one at another; the point was that it should be well stocked. Using whatever means appealed to individual taste and temperament, the Elizabethans built up a considerable body of apologetic material to oppose both the Poet-whippers

[1] *Works*, ed. R. B. McKerrow (Oxford, 1958), I, 24–25; 26; 154–55. Cf. his account of the 'Gentleman well studied in Philosophie' who 'trotted over all the Meteors bredde in the highest Region of the ayre' to reconcile I Cor. 3 with '*Ovids* fiction of *Phaetons* firing of the world,' p. 89; for other examples, see I, 259–60; III, 235.

and the 'rakehelly rout of ragged rhymers.' It ranged from the traditional allegorizing and moral instancing to the dark and secret mysteries of poetry so often asserted but so rarely adumbrated.

Thus by 1589, the year in which Thomas Lodge's *Scillaes Metamorphosis* appeared, the Elizabethans had been exposed in theory to the excellence of poetry and in practice to the 'ragged Rimes' of which Nashe had complained. It is true that both the *Shepheardes Calender* (1579) and Peele's *Arraignment of Paris* (1584) had been published,[1] that manuscripts of Sidney were in circulation among the elect, and that the soaring rhetoric of *Tamburlaine* had stirred play-goers; but when from his quarters at Lincoln's Inn, Lodge rushed his small volume of 'unperfit Poems' to the printer, he inaugurated not only a new Elizabethan genre but also a new standard of poetic achievement.

Perhaps written when he was still a student at Oxford (since the Isis provides the setting),[2] the main poem is an Ovidian narrative of love, a genre that was to spur the efforts of youthful poets for at least three decades. Although Lodge's attempt at a new form has been thought somewhat tentative (the volume is eked out with 'The Discontented Satyre' in addition to sonnets and complaints), nonetheless he introduces many of the elements that were to become typical of the erotic-mythological verse narrative.[3] There is, first of all, a personal framework:

[1] Nashe commended Spenser 'the miracle of wit' and Peele 'the Atlas of Poetrie' in his preface to Greene's *Menaphon* (1589) which had appeared before his own attack on 'ragged Rimes' in the *Anatomie of Abuses*.

[2] N. Burton Paradise, *Thomas Lodge, The History of an Elizabethan* (New Haven, 1931), p. 82.

[3] The term 'epyllion' or 'minor epic' gained currency following the publication in 1931 of M. M. Crump's *The Epyllion from Theocritus to Ovid*. But scholars have pointed out that it was not a literary type recognized by the ancients and that its critical usage stems from the nineteenth century. See, for example, the comments of Walter Allen, Jr., 'The Epyllion: A Chapter in the History of Literary Criticism,' *Transactions and Proceedings of the American Philological Association* LXXI (1940), 1–26; John F. Reilly, 'Origins of the Word "Epyllion",' *Classical Journal* XLIX (1953–54), 111–13; Paul W. Miller, 'The Elizabethan Minor Epic,' *SP* LV (1958), 31–38 (answered by Allen, pp. 515–18). Whatever its propriety for certain examples of classical poetry, it is a particularly useful term for classifying the Elizabethan genre with its mingling of disparate elements. L. P. Wilkinson, acknowledging that it is found only once in its modern sense in an ancient writer, also makes ample use of it in *Ovid Recalled* (Cambridge, 1955). The most valuable guide to this poetry is Douglas

the poet, unhappy on account of love, encounters an equally unhappy Glaucus who, resting his head on the poet's knee, tries to console him by speaking of his own greater grief. Then '(loe) a wonder':

> Upon the silver bosome of the streame
> First gan faire Themis shake her amber locks,
> Whom all the Nimphs that waight on Neptunes realme
> Attended from the hollowe of the rocks.

And the tale begins. The personal element is lightly touched on here and there and emerges in the envoy where the moral is stressed:

> That Nimphs must yeeld, when faithfull lovers straie not.[1]

About one-half of the poem sets forth the 'complaint' of Glaucus as he and the poet are encircled by sympathetic water nymphs like stars from Ariadne's crown. Thetis then appears and, hoping to ease her son's grief, invokes the aid of the goddess of love who arrives in all her pomp. Cupid shoots a furious dart, and the sea-god is cured. While all are rejoicing at his change of mood, Scilla appears, vaunting her beauties. Cupid then directs a dart at her. At once enamoured of her former lover, she becomes the wooer. Both the 'complaint' motif and the feminine wooer become popular elements in the epyllia.[2]

Lodge's choice of setting, the 'lovely Streame' the Isis, represents the tendency to localize myth and to transport the whole gorgeous panoply of pagan deities, nymphs and sylvan creatures to the Elizabethan world. His adorning of the narrative with literary (stt. 24–27) and mythological allusions—

> He that hath seene the sweete Arcadian boy
> Wiping the purple from his forced wound
> . . . . (stt. 21–23)—

[1] This personal framework is most strongly paralleled by Fletcher in *Venus and Anchises* but there are personal and topical allusions in Drayton and Edwards, where lines 763–66 of *Cephalus and Procris* are perhaps a tribute to Marlowe.

[2] Both have a basis in Ovid: see the complaint of Narcissus (III, 407 ff.) and the story of Byblis (IX, 454 ff.). Wilkinson also cites (p. 123) the *Ars Amatoria* I, 277–340 for parallels of the forward female taken from the animal kingdom and myth.

Bush's *Mythology and the Renaissance Tradition in English Poetry* (Minneapolis, 1932); see also the relevant chapters in M. C. Bradbrook, *Shakespeare and Elizabethan Poetry* (London, 1951) and Hallett Smith, *Elizabethan Poetry* (Cambridge, 1952).

is a technique repeated by others who often incorporate a complete secondary tale, either borrowed or invented. His dedication to 'the Gentlemen of the Innes of Court and Chauncerie' makes clear the kind of sophisticated readers he (and later poets of the genre) had in mind. And overriding these elements are the opulent imagery and delicately cadenced verse in a six-line stanza form:

> Borne of the Sea, thou Paphian Queene of love,
> Mistris of sweete conspiring harmonie:
> Lady of Cipris, for whose sweete behove
> The Shepeheards praise the youth of Thessalie:
> Daughter of Jove and Sister to the Sonne,
> Assist poore Glaucus late by love undone.
>
> So maist thou baine thee in th'Arcadian brookes,
> And play with Vulcans rivall when thou list,
> And calme his jealous anger by thy lookes,
> And knit thy temples with a roseat twist
> If thou thy selfe and thine almightie Sonne,
> Assist poore Glaucus late by love undone.   (stt. 81–82)

On 28 September 1593, Marlowe's *Hero and Leander* was entered in the Stationers' Register, but the first edition extant is that of 1598. The numerous parallels, echoes, and re-echoes of it that blaze out in the mid-1590's confirm its having been ardently read and remembered, whether in manuscript or in an edition that has been lost. For his narrative Marlowe turned both to the epyllion of Musaeus and Books XVIII and XIX of the *Heroides*,[1] but he infused his work with a distinctly Ovidian spirit. As with Ovid there is the same infectious response to his material (countered by a knowing detachment), the same capricious fancy (shaped into highly stylized expression), the same speedy rush of narrative (kept in bounds by the smooth hard couplets). The most distinctive Elizabethan (and Ovidian) quality in *Hero and Leander* is its artifice: the constructing of something that exceeds the merely natural. Artifice demands admiration for achievement, not empathy.[2] Chapman expresses

---

[1] From the parallels between Musaeus' poem and the two books of Ovid, Hermann Fränkel (*Ovid*, Berkeley, 1956, pp. 196–97) concludes that both poets had evidently used the same model.

[2] A short stimulating article analysing Elizabethan aesthetics and styles of poetry, and one to which I am much indebted, is 'Elizabethan Decoration: Patterns in Art and Passion,' *TLS*, 3 July 1937, pp. 485–86.

this idea in his letter to Royden prefacing *Ovids Banquet of Sence*:

It serves not a skilfull Painters turne, to draw the figure of a face onely to make knowne who it represents; but hee must lymn, give luster, shaddow, and heightning; which though ignorants will esteeme spic'd, and too curious, yet such as have the judiciall perspective, will see it hath motion, spirit and life. (A2)

This delight in the *artificial* explains why the writers of epyllia frequently use only the core of a myth for their story line[1] and why the narrative is the least important element. They attend rather to embroidering and ornamenting their poems with all the power of rhetorical devices and ingenious invention (*Ut nectar, ingenium*).[2] This explains the stress on myth-making, sometimes lightly tossed off (e.g., why Cupid is blind; why the dawn blushes; why roses are red or white); sometimes fully developed into a second tale (e.g., Mercury and the country maid, *Hero and Leander* I, 386–484; Jove's infatuation with Salmacis, *Salmacis and Hermaphroditus*, ll. 103–360).[3]

In fact, the appeal of myth as source material was its endless variety and adaptability: the whole teeming multiplicity of divinities, greater, lesser, of sky, earth, and water, embodied in myriad tales, often stamped with quite disparate associations. In a literary age like the Renaissance, the coupling of an epithet with a classical name was enough to start ripples of association; and, as Douglas Bush has observed, the use of a figure in one context did not preclude its use in another. Elements typical of one story adhere to another; aspects of the gods and goddesses

---

[1] Lodge, for example, depends on two facts from Ovid: that Glaucus loved Scilla and that she became a monster; everything else in the poem is shaped by his invention. On the other hand, Beaumont invents freely for 650 lines and then concludes *Salmacis and Hermaphroditus* with 300 lines very close to Ovid (IV, 285–388).

[2] Critics who object to the lack of psychological realism—the character of Hero and Leander, at one moment naïve, the next sophisticated—or the rhetorical emphases or the decorative effect of this highly wrought poetry are like Aesop's cock looking for his barley corn.

[3] An Ovidian trick: Wilkinson points out 'it was fashionable to insert in an epyllion a secondary tale which might have no bearing on the main theme.' He cites the Ericthonius inset in Callimachus' *Hecale* and the inset story of Ariadne on Naxos as embroidered on the bridal coverlet in Catullus' *Marriage of Peleus and Thetis* and adds that 'of some fifty episodes in the *Metamorphoses* which are long enough to rank as epyllia about a third contain one,' p. 147.

become conflated. Thus when great Phoebe (hailed in all her titles—Diana, Delia, Luna, etc.) appears in triumph to Endimion, she is accompanied by the (proper) companions of Venus and Apollo, the Graces and the Muses.[1] The infinite seas of evocative associations that myth afforded are sounded by the writers of epyllia—to heighten an image or inject a touch of wit or humour. A mocking attitude towards the gods, seen as infinitely human (a quality found in Ovid and, of course, in Lucian), provides an astringent to offset the languor and sweetness.

At one sweep Marlowe had mastered the form; imitators could only hope to capture his witty, ironic strain. But if the dominant tone of Marlowe's poem has insured its generic acceptance by critics, the same cannot be said for Shakespeare's contribution to the vogue. Addressing the young (and wanton) Earl of Southampton in 1593 with the first heir of his invention, Shakespeare offered a poem quite different in effect from that of Marlowe, with the result that *Venus and Adonis* (with all the parallels and echoes and re-echoes of it) became the second prototype of the erotic epyllion. Where Leander had wooed like a 'bold sharpe Sophister,' Venus was given the *suasoria* and became the wooer, a pattern established, as we have seen, by Scilla and followed by Oenone, Aurora, Phoebe, Salmacis, Venus (in *Venus and Anchises*), and Echo. As the nymph Salmacis puts it:

> Ages are bad, when men become so slow,
> That poore unskilfull mayds are forc't to woo.

Shakespeare's alternating of fresh outdoor scenes with highly sensuous imagery has often been commented on; his rhetorical tricks have likewise been noted; that they lead to realistic humour has not so often been noted.[2] We can conclude that the heirs of his invention understood him well, since it is precisely the sensuous quality, the naturalness, and the comedy that they

[1] Their *numbers*, it is true, provided Drayton with a transition to his mystical doctrines, but see Edgar Wind (*Pagan Mysteries in the Renaissance*, New Haven, 1958, pp. 74–75) for examples of the Renaissance merging of Diana and Venus and the iconographical and literary interpretation of the Graces as Pulchritudo-Amor-Voluptas, Chaps. 4, 5.

[2] An exception is Rufus Putney, 'Venus and Adonis: Amour with Humor,' *PQ* xx (Oct. 1941), 533–48.

imitate. Impressionable Elizabethan poets, essaying the 'first fruits' of their endeavours, turned either to Marlowe or to Shakespeare and, very frequently, to both.

The contribution of Spenser to the genre, albeit indirect, must also be recognized, as Douglas Bush has pointed out in an instructive chapter. With the publication of the first three books of the *Faerie Queene* in 1590, the sage and serious poet[1] had naturalized the lush Italianate style. In addition to decking out his heroic narrative with a wealth of mythical allusions (The hangings in the house of Busyrane, for example, serve as an admirable gloss to Marlowe's 'gods in sundrie shapes,/Committing headdie ryots, incest, rapes'.), Spenser had developed a pattern for a long riming stanzaic form. And when writers of short verse narrative did not turn to the sixains of Lodge and Shakespeare or the couplets of Marlowe, they turned to an eight or nine-line stanza, intricately rimed (Chapman, Fletcher).

Once the possibilities and pattern for the epyllion had been recognized, its vogue developed with amazing rapidity. As Ovid had varied the mood and tone of his tales, so the configuration and colouring of each poem was determined by the individual poet's taste, temperament, and talent. Among the earliest imitators was young Thomas Heywood[2]; his *Oenone and Paris* appeared in 1594 and bore the clear impress of Shakespearean influence, so much so that older critics harshly called it both a 'plagiarism' and a 'travesty' of *Venus and Adonis*. Taking material from the *Heroides* and Lucian's *Dialogue of the Gods*, Heywood invented his central situation but his language recalls both Shakespeare and Marlowe: on Mt. Ida Paris has paused from the chase to sit by a fountain and muse, leaning his elbow on a mossy stump; here the deserted Oenone finds him and utters a long complaint. Although he is moved by her tears, Paris spiritedly defends himself ('What fates appoint, it bootes not us to breake it') and relates the act of judgment imposed on him. Oenone counters with an invitational speech so ardent that the Trojan is moved to laughter; she then sets forth a

[1] Not so sage and serious that Thomas Walkley could not palm off *Venus and Anchises* in 1628 as Spenser's.

[2] For evidence identifying the author as Thomas Heywood, see the introduction to J. Q. Adams's edition (Washington, 1943).

catalogue of her beauties, and again Paris jauntily explains that
since his heart is impressionable, he is at the mercy of Love;
it is Cupid who is at fault:

> What made the gods to trewant it from heaven,
> And shift them subtillie into sundrie shapes,
> But he that roves his shaftes at sixe and seven,
> Laughing at riot, revelling, and rapes?

With Oenone clinging to his green scarf, Paris breaks away and
blithely departs, but 'first hee kist her on her rose-redde lippes.'
Comedy emerges in Paris' easy defence, and Oenone's com-
plaints are aptly framed by the pastoral locale. Along with the
complaint, the invitation and the catalogue become frequent
motifs.

Cephalus and Procris by Thomas Edwards (identified simply
as a courtier) appeared in 1595, although it had been entered
in the Stationers' Register in 1593, only six months after *Venus
and Adonis*. Somewhat jerkily, Edwards interrupts his tale of
Aurora's wooing of the (briefly) loyal husband and huntsman
to comment in cryptic and almost satiric fashion on current
poets (saluting Spenser and Sidney) and poets' favourites, that
is, patrons. His language is often archaic and dialectical (fol-
lowing Spenser), and he particularly imitates Marlowe's
gnomic quality ('If wemen had no tounges, their hartes would
breake').

Michael Drayton's *Endimion and Phoebe* also appeared in
1595. Much of its charm lies in the luxuriant description of the
setting on Mt. Latmus. Here lush greenery like 'rich Tapestry,'
embroidered with curious arabesques of grapes and golden
citrons, encloses the walks; here nymphs foot it in a round and
fairies dance the 'heydegies,' and here Phoebe, disguised as a
nymph ('Begot by Pan on Isis sacred flood'), invites Endimion's
love with a catalogue of pastoral delights. Initially reluctant
since he is sworn to Diana's service, Endimion discovers on her
leaving him that Love has 'undermin'd the Fort,' and he utters
his complaint. Having fallen asleep, he is again visited by
Phoebe with her nymphs who hang garlands on the trees and
bathe him with nectar. To his confession of love, Phoebe turns
briefly reluctant; then, revealing her true nature, she carries

him to the skies. The rest of the poem takes on a neo-Platonic and mystical colouring.

Among contributors to the genre, George Chapman figures largely, first with his distinctive but difficult *Ovids Banquet of Sence* published in 1595. Hailed by Sir John Davies in a prefatory sonnet as a second Ovid whose knowledge of love is 'misticall and deepe,' Chapman provides no narrative beyond the simple fact of Ovid's appearing in a garden with Corynna where each of his senses is feasted. Yet the poem is Chapman's testament to the ravishing appeal of beauty: each pleasure Ovid experiences is grounded in sense, but by a (sometimes dazzling) poetical alchemy, the material disappears into the immaterial. Sense dissolves into intellection. The style is often abstruse, the arguments spun out in metaphysical fashion (scantily helped by his glosses); still the effect of the poem is strangely exhilarating.

Enticed by the heat of a summer's day ('Whose ardor curld the foreheads of the trees'), Corynna has come to bathe in a fountain softly banked with 'Enameld Pansies,' Solemne Violets,' 'White and red Jessamines.' In the fountain is set a curious statue of Niobe, which from afar appears like a heavy, weeping woman, but at close hand neither 'weeping, heavy, nor a woman.' Her fourteen children with their breasts gored by arrows are grouped around her; behind her are the figures of Phoebe and Apollo 'two sterne Plannets,' hewn in purple glass to reflect the colour of blood on the 'pale bosoms' of her children.[1]

[1] Recently J. F. Kermode has argued in a provocative article ('The Banquet of Sense,' *Bulletin of the John Rylands Library* XLIV [Sept. 1961], 68–99) that Chapman is being ironical and the poem is a 'Circean fall into bestiality.' Although it is difficult here to do more than take note of his argument, it seems to me he errs, largely through a too-conventional interpretation of the figures in the poem. He explains, for example, the significance of Niobe as pointing up the danger of presumption, but Chapman stresses that 'more neerely viewed,' the statue does not even appear to be the figure of a woman. Thus Ovid's nearer view becomes a symbol of what 'searching wits' apprehend rather than what the 'profane multitude' sees from afar. Kermode views Ovid and Corynna as stereotypes: the one 'a master of lascivious arts'; the other a 'libertine.' And he interprets Chapman's image in st. 68 ('O Beautie, how attractive is thy powre? . . . Raigning in Greece, Troy swum to thee in Art') as illustrative of 'disastrous beauty' since the fall of Troy was regarded as 'archetypal' and since Shakespeare had termed Helen a 'strumpet' in the *Rape of Lucrece*. Aware of the period's fondness for multiple (and disparate) significances, *we* may also think of Marlowe's immortalizing Helen.

13

The tears of Niobe, 'toomb'd in her selfe,' pour on to this 'Romaine Phœbe' Corynna as she bathes. She then takes her lute and sings. Ovid is enraptured by the notes which dance in his ear, inspiring him to such love that his flesh fades 'and into spyrit turns.' He draws nearer, apprehending her sweet odours, and since those who are formed with gentle and noble tempers are quickened by perfumes and sounds, he again is enraptured:

> Odors feede love, and love cleare heaven discovers,
> Lovers weare sweets; then sweetest mindes, be lovers.
>
> (st. 36, 8–9)

Fearful of coming nearer, he prays for courage to Juno, goddess of nuptial rights. Emboldened, he gazes and becomes ecstatic. The poet, speaking for himself, asserts that 'Unlesse th'enricher [the beloved] be as rich in fayth,' beauty is nature's witchcraft

>   tempting men to buy
> With endles showes, what endlessly will fade,
> Yet promise chapmen all eternitie:

When affection is mutual, beauty 'Seene in another' is heaven alone.[1]

> For sacred beautie is the fruite of sight,
> The curtesie that speakes before the tongue,
> The feast of soules, the glory of the light,
> Envy of age, and everlasting young,
> Pitties Commander, Cupids richest throne,
> Musick intransed, never duely sung,
> The summe and court of all proportion:
> And that I may dull speeches best afforde,
> All Rethoricks flowers, in lesse then in a worde.
>
> (st. 52)

In contrast to worldlings who hold 'nothing wisdome is, that getteth nought,'

[1] Cf. *Hero and Leander* II, 29–32:

> (Sweet are the kisses, the imbracements sweet,
> When like desires and affections meet,
> For from the earth to heaven is Cupid rais'd,
> Where fancie is in equall ballance pais'd.)

Despite his own different tone, Chapman was clearly stirred by Marlowe. Mercury, discovering 'The way to new Elisium' (I, 409–11) is probably, despite Chapman's reference to Virgil in the gloss, the immediate catalyst for stt. 51–62.

Beautie enchasing love, love gracing beautie,
To such as constant simpathies enfold,
To perfect riches dooth a sounder duetie
Then all endevours, for by all consent
All wealth and wisdome rests in true Content.

(st. 53, 5–9)

The sight of this 'beauty-clad naked Lady' prompts Ovid to exalt the senses:

The sense is given us to excite the minde,
And that can never be by sence exited
But first the sence must her contentment finde,
We therefore must procure the sence delighted,
That so the soule may use her facultie;   (st. 63, 1–5)

Corynna, glimpsing him in her mirror, blushes furiously ('Shame from a Bowre of Roses did unshrowde/And spread her crimson wings upon her face'),[1] but he defends himself so deftly that he persuades her to yield a kiss. Permitted then to touch her side, Ovid suddenly declares *against* the senses and wishes that heaven had given the soul a tongue, a language, a dialect to sing its high conceits. Then addressing Corynna as a bounteous mistress who feeds the mind (in contrast to those who surfeit on flesh), he promises to write the art of love for her since it is in her sphere that love has his health and life. Commenting on the lack of patronage in 'these dog-dayes,' he adds:

To mee (deere Soveraigne) thou are Patronesse,
And I, with that thy graces have infused,
Will make all fat and foggy braines confesse,
Riches may from a poore verse be deduced:
And that Golds love shall leave them groveling heere,
When thy perfections shall to heaven be Mused,
Deckt in bright verse, where Angels shall appeare,
  The praise of vertue, love, and beauty singing,
  Honor to Noblesse, shame to Avarice bringing.

(st. 115)

The ideas Chapman expresses here—that love is stimulated by beauty, that love must be mutual ('Enamourd like good selfe-love with her owne'), that the contentment resulting from 'beautie joyned with love' provides

---

[1] Cf. his translation of Musaeus, ll. 87–91.

> armes more proofe gainst any griefe we prove,
> Then all their vertue-scorning miserie
> Or judgments graven in Stoick gravitie,

—are part and parcel of the Renaissance attempt to reconcile the best of two possible worlds.[1]

Chapman's translation of Musaeus' epyllion, 'the incomparable Love-Poem of the world' in his estimation, was published in 1616, but it seems likely from the subject and from the use of couplets that he had translated it before completing *Hero and Leander* (1598). When Elizabethan exuberance is taken into account, Chapman's translation is fairly close, and there are typical felicities: Leander telling Hero to guard her torch,

> (Which I beholding, to that starry Powre
> May plough the darke Seas, as the Ship of Love.)

When he glimpses it,

> But Love his blood set on as bright a Fire:
> Together burn'd the Torch, and his Desire.

The tension implicit in *Ovids Banquet of Sence*—that sensible beauty (like love) is the *promise* of eternity—informs the continuation of *Hero and Leander*, but as Chapman had learned from Musaeus, Love does not compel Fate (l. 451). Chapman's digressions, which prolong the poem for four sestiads,[2] may partly be accounted for by his reluctance to bring about the tragic ending:

> because I grieve so to display,
> I use digressions thus t'encrease the day.

John Marston's brief contribution to the genre, *The Metamorphosis of Pigmalions Image* (1598), precedes a group of satires introduced by verses in which the author mockingly praises the 'Salaminian [Venerean] titillations' of his 'precedent Poem.' The tone Marston generally adopts often makes critics

---

[1] Cf. Wind, pp. 52–56, and 70–71 where he comments, 'The Stoic assumption that pleasure must be deficient in virtue, and virtue deficient in pleasure, never gained much credence among Renaissance Neoplatonists.'

[2] For the most appreciative comment on Chapman's continuation, see C. S. Lewis, *English Literature in the Sixteenth Century* (Oxford, 1954), pp. 514–16.

uneasy, and that of *Pigmalions Image* is no exception: is it an erotic epyllion or is it a 'dissembling shift' as he claimed? It is probably both[1] and is probably to be explained by Marston's hope that if he intensified the ironic tone set by Marlowe, he might freshly appeal to the young men in the Inns of Court. (He had been admitted to the Middle Temple in 1592.) From beginning to end the tone is mocking: he concludes his address 'To his Mistres' and 'none other Saint' with these lines:

> Be gracious then, and daine to show in mee,
> The mighty power of thy Deitie.
> And as thou read'st, (Faire) take compassion,
> Force me not envie my Pigmalion.
> > Then when thy kindnes grants me such sweet blisse,
> > I'le gladly write thy metamorphosis.   (A5)

Upon Pigmalion's examining his ivory statue so ardently that he wonders she does not blush, Marston adds:

> O that my Mistres were an Image too,
> That I might blameles her perfections view.

And as Pigmalion continues in his catalogue, Marston records:

> But when the faire proportion of her thigh
> Began appeare: O Ovid would he cry,
> Did ere Corinna . . .

Pigmalions Image apparently circulated in manuscript,[2] and, it would seem, unsuccessfully. On the one hand, Marston's scoffing tone had removed the bloom from the genre; on the other, he had left himself open to charges by the satirists of writing 'lewd rimes.' Hence he utilized the ploy of its satiric intention. His own bent was strongly towards the new mood of satire, and he had a precedent of sorts in that Lodge had included a satire in his volume and Edwards had introduced touches of satire in his poem. In 1600 John Weever, in turn, was to transform a typical epyllion (*Faunus and Melliflora*) into an account of the origin of satire.

If both the easy cynicism and the hard verse of Marston's

---

[1] A. Davenport in his introduction to *The Poems* (Liverpool, 1961) tends towards this view.

[2] Marston includes an attack on Hall on E3–E7, probably motivated, as J. B. Leishman points out, by Hall's attack on lascivious poetry in *Virgidemiae*, published in 1597 (*The Three Parnassus Plays*, London, 1949, pp. 88–89).

poem derive from Marlowe, the latter can also claim to have
inspired one of the most sparkling examples in the genre—
Salmacis and Hermaphroditus, first published in 1602 and
attributed in the 1640 edition to Francis Beaumont. Like
Marlowe, the poet takes obvious delight in his material, main-
taining, since his Muse is 'sportive,' an effervescent quality
throughout. Like Marlowe, he lets his narrative speed rapidly
along within firmly articulated couplets, and like Marlowe, he
too laces the sensuous passages with wit.

Phineas Fletcher's poem *Venus and Anchises*, probably writ-
ten sometime between 1605 and 1615, is like so much of that
author's work in direct lineal descent from Spenser; yet even
in the lush eroticism, passages suggest a Chapmanesque over-
tone (e.g. II, 4–6). James Shirley, who was born in 1596, one
year after the outburst of epyllia, modelled his *Narcissus* largely
on *Venus and Adonis*. Entered in the Stationers' Register on
4 January 1618, *Narcissus* exists only in the 1646 edition of
Shirley's *Poems* where the phrase *Haec olim* on the title page is
intended to suggest the youthful quality of the work or possibly,
as Dyce suggested, that it had been published previously.

It was young poets then, intoxicated with the rimes of 'sweet-
lipt Ovid,' who popularized the erotic epyllion. Utilizing some
well-known myth for the core of their narrative, they stressed
originality not of subject matter but of treatment. As we have
seen, two elements became standard: the 'complaint' of the
unhappy lover (whether male or female), and the 'invita-
tion' (whether by male or female), including a catalogue of
present charms or future delights. And as Ovid had done before
them, they interpreted the past in terms of the present, bring-
ing the pagan mythical world to England, mingling nymphs and
dryads with elves and fairies. Some critics have looked askance
at this wholesale naturalizing of myth in Elizabethan terms
(Hero's painted fan; Adonis' bonnet; Mercury, caduceus in
hand, wearing a 'thicke Bever' to protect him from the glitter-
ing sungod). But after acknowledging the period's indifference
to anachronism, we have also to recognize that a good deal of
it is calculated humour: Oenone who makes do with 'leavie
branches' for a kirtle; the injured Cupid who flies to the 'seld-
prevented Destinies' and finds them busy at a Parliament, each
one sitting on a 'wooll-packe'; Jove who is delayed by a 'busie

rout' of serving-men and promoters from entering Astraea's palace, a palace far beyond the reach of any mortal eye, where the 'dewe of justice' seldom dropped, and when it did, the drops were *very* small.

Equally deliberate is the use of a common store of rhetorical devices and motifs. The wide influence of *Hero and Leander* and *Venus and Adonis* and of Spenser in general has not infrequently brought forth charges of plagiarism directed (most frequently) at minor poets. But these charges are often unjust. Poets were trying to 'vary' their matter, to put their own stamp on what was common property. Thus the Ovidian line 'inopem me copia fecit' is endlessly elaborated (e.g. *Ovids Banquet of Sence*, stt. 101–02; *Venus and Anchises* II, 7–8; VI, 6); thus the Narcissus motif, repeatedly used, gains a new relevance when Salmacis must close her eyes while wooing to prevent Hermaphroditus' self-enamourment.

'Imitation' of the actual phrasing of one poet by another is somewhat more complex; the practice of finding 'congruent epithetons' explains it in part; the general intoxication of the sixteenth century with words and the newly achieved skill of the 1590's explains more. When a poet expressed well what had often been thought, his statement came to have the force, as Shakespeare indicates in *As You Like It*, of an axiom or a saw. Such a process can be illustrated with an example from Marlowe:

> . . . darke night is Cupids day   *Hero and Leander* I, 191
> . . . this Cupids Night (oft seene in day)
>   *Ovids Banquet of Sence* 40.6
> Some saide, the night for Lovers was the day
>   *Faunus and Melliflora* 215
> . . . Night is loves holly-day   *Venus and Anchises* II, 3.8

On the other hand, that poets unconsciously or half-consciously recalled appealing words, phrases, or lines can be shown (witness the scholars' lists of borrowings); but it can also be shown that they deliberately used them for their associative effect. For example, Lodge has the line

> That art so yong, so lovely, fresh and faire;

Marlowe has the well-known couplet

But you are faire (aye me) so wondrous faire,
So yoong, so gentle, and so debonaire

which Marston recalls deliberately when mocking his own epyllion:

Doe not I flatter, call her wondrous faire?
Virtuous, divine, most debonaire?

By turns playful, voluptuous, or delicately garbed with serious thought, the Elizabethan Ovid underwent a change. About 1632, for example, Drayton's 'Dearely-loved friend' Henry Reynolds published his *Mythomystes* or 'Short Survay' of the 'Nature and Value of True Poesy and Depth of the Ancients above our Moderne Poets.' To this he annexed the *Tale of Narcissus*, 'paraphrastically Englisht' in ottava rima, and to this he added not an 'allegorized' but a 'mythologized' interpretation. In it he sets forth a fourfold meaning: the 'Geographick sense,' the 'Physick sence,' the 'Morral sense,' and lastly the 'Divine sense' (of Pythagoras) that Narcissus prefigures one who 'flyes the light and purity of Intellectuall Beauty' and loses 'his propper, native, and celestiall vertue, and ability.' Ovid's medieval trappings are back.

For the texts old spelling is retained throughout, although I have modernized i/j and u/v; obvious misprints have been corrected and light changes of punctuation made silently; emendations (I hope properly credited) are recorded in the textual notes. The copy-text in each case is that of the earliest edition, and I am grateful to the following libraries for their kind permission to make use of their copies for this edition: the Bodleian for its (unique) copy of Chapman's translation of Musaeus; the British Museum for Chapman's completion of *Hero and Leander*; the Folger Shakespeare Library for Beaumont's *Salmacis and Hermaphroditus* and its (unique) copies of Marlowe's *Hero and Leander* and Heywood's *Oenone and Paris*; the Harvard Library for Drayton's *Endimion and Phœbe*; the Henry E. Huntington for Lodge's *Scillaes Metamorphosis*, Chapman's *Ovids Banquet of Sence*, Marston's *Pigmalions Image*, Fletcher's *Brittain's Ida*, and its (unique) copy of Weever's *Faunus and Melliflora;* Peterborough Cathedral for its (unique) copy of Edwards's *Cephalus and Procris*; and the Yale University Library for Shirley's *Narcissus*.

SCILLAES METAMORPHOSIS:

Enterlaced with the unfortunate love of Glaucus

Thomas Lodge

(1589)

1

Walking alone (all onely full of griefe)
Within a thicket nere to Isis floud,
Weeping my wants, and wailing scant reliefe,
Wringing mine armes (as one with sorrowe wood);
   The piteous streames relenting at my mone
   Withdrew their tides, and staid to heare me grone.

2

From foorth the channell, with a sorrowing crie
The Sea-god Glaucus (with his hallowed heares
Wet in the teares of his sad mothers dye)
With piteous lookes before my face appeares;
   For whome the Nimphes a mossie coate did frame.
   Embroadered with his Sillas heavenly name.

3

And as I sat under a Willow tree,
The lovelie honour of faire Thetis bower
Reposd his head upon my faintfull knee:
And when my teares had ceast their stormie shower
   He dried my cheekes, and then bespake him so,
   As when he waild I straight forgot my woe:

4

Infortunate, why wandreth thy content
From forth his scope as wearied of it selfe?
Thy bookes have schoold thee from this fond repent,
And thou canst talke by proofe of wavering pelfe:
 Unto the world such is inconstancie,
 As sapp to tree, as apple to the eye.

5

Marke, how the morne in roseat colour shines,
And straight with cloudes the Sunnie tract is clad;
Then see how pomp through waxe and waine declines,
From high to lowe, from better to the bad:
 Take moist from Sea, take colour from his kinde,
 Before the world devoid of change thou finde.

6

With secret eye looke on the earth a while,
Regard the changes Nature forceth there;
Behold the heavens, whose course all sence beguile;
Respect thy selfe, and thou shalt find it cleere,
 That infantlike thou art become a youth,
 And youth forespent a wretched age ensu'th.

7

In searching then the schoolemens cunning noates,
Of heaven, of earth, of flowers, of springing trees,
Of hearbs, of mettall, and of Thetis floates,
Of lawes and nurture kept among the Bees:
 Conclude and knowe times change by course of fate,
 Then mourne no more, but moane my haples state.

8

Here gan he pause and shake his heavie head,
And fould his armes, and then unfould them straight;
Faine would he speake, but tongue was charm'd by dread,
Whil'st I that sawe what woes did him awaight,
 Comparing his mishaps and moane with mine,
 Gan smile for joy and drie his drooping eyne.

9

But (loe) a wonder; from the channels glide
A sweet melodious noyse of musicke rose,
That made the streame to dance a pleasant tide,
The weedes and sallowes neere the bancke that groes
    Gan sing, as when the calmest windes accorde
    To greete with balmie breath the fleeting forde.

10

Upon the silver bosome of the streame
First gan faire Themis shake her amber locks,
Whom all the Nimphs that waight on Neptunes realme
Attended from the hollowe of the rocks.
    In briefe, while these rare parragons assemble,
    The watrie world to touch their teates doo tremble.

11

Footing it featlie on the grassie ground,
These Damsels circling with their brightsome faires
The love-sicke God and I, about us wound
Like starres that Ariadnes crowne repaires:
    Who once hath seene or pride of morne, or day,
    Would deeme all pompe within their cheekes did play.

12

Nais faire Nimph with Bacchus ivorie touch,
Gan tune a passion with such sweete reports,
And everie word, noate, sigh, and pause was such,
And everie Cadence fed with such consorts,
    As were the Delian Harper bent to heare,
    Her statelie straines might tempt his curious eare.

13

Of love (God wot) the lovelie Nimph complained:
But so of love as forced Love to love her;
And even in love such furious love remained,
As searching out his powrefull shaft to prove her,
    He found his quiver emptied of the best,
    And felt the arrowe sticking in his breast.

14

Under a Popler Themis did repose her,
And from a brier a sweetfull branch did plucke:
When midst the brier ere she could scarce suppose her
A Nightingale gan sing: but woe the lucke;
   The branch so neere her breast, while she did quicke her
   To turne her head, on sodaine gan to pricke her.

15

Whil'st smiling Clore midst her envious blushes,
Gan blame her feare and pretilie said thus;
Worse prickes than these are found among these bushes,
And yet such prickes are scarcelie feard of us.
   Nay soft (said Chelis), prickes doo make birds sing,
   But prickes in Ladies bosomes often sting.

16

Thus jest they on the Nightingales report,
And on the prickle of the Eglantine,
On Nais song, and all the whole consort
In publique this sweete sentence did assigne;
   That while some smile; some sigh through change of time;
   Some smart, some sport amidst their youthlie prime.

17

Such wreathes as bound the Thebans ivorie brow;
Such gay trickt garlands pleit these jollie Dames;
The flowres themselves when as the Nimphes gan vowe,
Gan vaile their crestes in honour of their names:
   And smilde their sweete and woed with so much glee,
   As if they said, sweet Nimph, come gather mee.

18

But pencive Glaucus, passionate with painings,
Amidst their revell thus began his ruth;
Nimphes, flie these Groves late blasted with my plainings,
For cruell Silla nill regard my truth:
   And leave us two consorted in our gronings,
   To register with teares our bitter monings.

19

The flouds doo faile their course to see our crosse,
The fields forsake their greene to heare our griefe,
The rockes will weepe whole springs to marke our losse,
The hills relent to store our scant reliefe,
    The aire repines, the pencive birds are heavie,
    The trees to see us paind no more are leavie.

20

Ay me, the Shepheards let their flockes want feeding,
And flockes to see their palie face are sorie,
The Nimphes to spie the flockes and shepheards needing
Prepare their teares to heare our tragicke storie:
    Whilst we surprisde with griefe cannot disclose them,
    With sighing wish the world for to suppose them.

21

He that hath seene the sweete Arcadian boy
Wiping the purple from his forced wound,
His pretie teares betokening his annoy,
His sighes, his cries, his falling on the ground,
    The Ecchoes ringing from the rockes his fall,
    The trees with teares reporting of his thrall:

22

And Venus starting at her love-mates crie,
Forcing hir birds to hast her chariot on;
And full of griefe at last with piteous eie
Seene where all pale with death he lay alone,
    Whose beautie quaild, as wont the Lillies droop
    When wastfull winter windes doo make them stoop:

23

Her daintie hand addrest to dawe her deere,
Her roseall lip alied to his pale cheeke,
Her sighes, and then her lookes and heavie cheere,
Her bitter threates, and then her passions meeke;
    How on his senseles corpes she lay a crying,
    As if the boy were then but new a dying.

24

He that hath vewd Angelica the faire
Bestraught with fancie nere the Caspian springs:
Renting the tresses of her golden haire,
How on her harpe with pitious notes she sings
   Of Rolands ruth, of Medors false depart,
   Sighing each rest from center of her heart.

25

How now she writes upon a beechen bow
Her Medors name, and bedlam like againe
Calls all the heaven to witnes of his vow,
And straight againe begins a mournefull straine,
   And how in thought of her true faith forsooken
   He fled her bowres, and how his league was broken.

26

Aye me who markes her harpe hang up againe
Upon the willowes watered with her teares,
And how she rues to read her Rolands paine,
When but the shadowe of his name appeares;
   Would make more plainings from his eyes to flee
   Than teares distill from amber weeping tree.

27

He that hath knowne the passionate mishappes
That nere Olimpus faire Lucina felt
When as her Latium love her fancie trappes,
How with suspect her inward soule dooth melt:
   Or markt the Morne her Cephalus complaining,
   May then recount the course of all our paining.

28

But tender Nimphes, to you belongs no teene;
Then favor me in flying from this bower
Whereas but care and thought of crosses been,
Leave me that loose my selfe through fancies power,
   Through fancies power which had I leave to loose it,
   No fancie then should see me for to choose it.

29

When you are fled, the Heaven shall lowre for sorrowe,
The day orecast shalbe betime with sable,
The aire from Sea such streaming showres shall borrow
As earth to beare the brunt shall not be able,
  And shippes shall safely saile whereas beforne
  The ploughman watcht the reaping of his corne.

30

Goe you in peace to Neptunes watrie sound,
No more may Glaucus play him with so prettie;
But shun resort where solace nill be found,
And plaine my Scillaes pride and want of pittie:
  Alas sweet Nimphs, my Godhead's all in vaine,
  For why this brest includes immortall paine.

31

Scilla hath eyes, but too sweete eyes hath Scilla;
Scilla hath hands, faire hands but coy in touching;
Scilla in wit surpasseth grave Sibilla,
Scilla hath words, but words well storde with grutching;
  Scilla a Saint in looke, no Saint in scorning:
  Looke Saint-like Scilla, least I die with mourning.

32

Alas why talke I? Sea-god, cease to mourne her,
For in her nay my joyes are ever ceasing:
Cease life or love, then shall I never blame her;
But neither love nor life may finde decreasing.
  A mortall wound is my immortall being,
  Which passeth thought, or eyes advised seeing.

33

Herewith his faltring tongue by sighs oppressed
Forsooke his office, and his bloud resorted
To feede the heart that wholly was distressed,
Whilst pale (like Pallas flowre) my knee supported
  His feeble head and arme, so full of anguish,
  That they which sawe his sorrowes gan to languish.

29.2 betime] bedtime

34

Themis the coyest of this beauteous traine
On hillie toppes the wonderous Moly found,
Which dipt in balmie deaw she gan to straine,
And brought her present to recure his wound:
   Clore she gathered Amaranthus flower,
   And Nais Ajax blossom in that stowre.

35

Some chafe his temples with their lovelie hands,
Some sprinkle water on his pale wan cheekes,
Some weepe, some wake, some curse affections bandes;
To see so young, so faire, become so weake:
   But not their pitious hearbs, or springs have working,
   To ease that heart where wanton love is lurking.

36

Naithles, though loath to shewe his holy kindnes,
On everie one he spent a looke for favour,
And prayed their pardon, vouching Cupids blindnes,
(Oh fancies fond that naught but sorrowes savour);
   To see a lovely God leave Sea Nimphes so:
   Who cannot doome upon his deadly woe?

37

Themis that knewe that waters long restrained
Breake foorth with greater billowes than the brookes
That swetely float through meades with flowres distained,
With cheerefull laies did raise his heavie lookes;
   And bad him speake and tell what him agreev'd:
   For griefes disclos'd (said she) are soone releev'd.

38

And as she wisht, so all the rest did woe him;
By whose incessant suites at last invited,
He thus discovered that which did undoo him,
And orderlie his hideous harmes recited,
   When first with fingers wagge he gan to still them,
   And thus with drierie tearmes of love did fill them.

38.5 with] which

39

Ah Nimphes (quoth he), had I by reason learnt
That secret art which birdes have gaind by sence,
By due foresight misfortune to prevent;
Or could my wit controule mine eyes offence:
    You then should smile and I should tell such stories,
    As woods, and waves should triumph in our glories.

40

But Nereus daughters, Sea-borne Saints attend,
Lake-breeding Geese when from the Easterne clime
They list unto the westerne waters wend
To choose their place of rest by course of time,
    Approaching Taurus haughtie topped hill
    They charme their cackle by this wondrous skill.

41

The climing mountaine neighbouring ayre welnie,
Hath harbored in his rockes and desart haunts
Whole airies of Eagles, prest to flie
That gazing on the Sonne their birth right vaunts,
    Which birds of Jove with deadlie fewde pursue
    The wandering Geese, when so they presse in vewe.

42

These fearefull flitting troopes by nature tought,
Passing these dangerous places of pursuit:
When all the desart vales they through have sought,
With pibbles stop their beakes to make them mute,
    And by this meanes their dangerous deathes prevent
    And gaine their wished waters of frequent.

43

But I fond God, (I God complaine thy follie)
Let birds by sense exceede my reason farre:
Whilom than I who was more strong and jollie
Who more contemnd affections wanton warre?
    Who lesse than I lov'd lustfull Cupids arrowes?
    Who now with curse & plagues poore Glaucus harrowes.

42.6 frequent, resort

44

How have I leapt to heare the Tritons play
A harsh retreat unto the swelling flouds?
How have I kept the Dolphins at a bay,
When as I ment to charme their wanton moods?
　　How have the angrie windes growne calme for love,
　　When as these fingers did my harpe strings move?

45

Was any Nimph, you Nimphes, was ever any
That tangled not her fingers in my tresse?
Some well I wot and of that some full many
Wisht or my faire, or their desire were lesse:
　　Even Ariadne, gazing from the skie
　　Became enamorde of poore Glaucus eye.

46

Amidst this pride of youth and beauties treasure
It was my chaunce, you floods can tell my chancing,
Fleeting along Sicillian bounds for pleasure,
To spie a Nimph of such a radiant glancing,
　　As when I lookt, a beame of subtill firing
　　From eye to heart incenst a deepe desiring.

47

Ah had the vaile of reason clad mine eye,
This foe of freedome had not burnt my heart:
But birds are blest, and most accurst am I
Who must report her glories to my smart,
　　The Nimph I sawe and lov'de her, all to cruell
　　Scilla, faire Scilla, my fond fancies juell.

48

Her haire not trust, but scatterd on her brow,
Surpassing Hiblas honnie for the view,
Or softned golden wires; I know not how
Love with a radiant beautie did pursue
　　My too judiciall eyes, in darting fire
　　That kindled straight in me my fond desire.

49

Within these snares first was my heart intrapped,
Till through those golden shrowdes mine eies did see
An yvorie shadowed front, wherein was wrapped
Those pretie bowres where Graces couched be:
    Next which her cheekes appeerd like crimson silk,
    Or ruddie rose bespred on whitest milk.

50

Twixt which the nose in lovely tenor bends,
(Too traitrous pretie for a Lovers view:)
Next which her lips like violets commends
By true proportion that which dooth insue;
    Which when they smile, present unto the eies
    The Oceans pride and yvorie paradice.

51

Her pollisht necke of milke white snowes doth shine,
As when the Moone in Winter night beholdes them:
Her breast of alablaster cleere and fine,
Whereon two rising apples faire unfolds them,
    Like Cinthias face when in her full she shineth,
    And blushing to her Love-mates bower declineth.

52

From whence in length her armes doo sweetly spred
Like two rare branchie saples in the Spring,
Yeelding five lovely sprigs from everie head,
Proportioned alike in everie thing;
    Which featly sprout in length like springborne frends,
    Whose pretie tops with five sweet roses ends.

53

But why alas should I that Marble hide
That doth adorne the one and other flanke,
From whence a mount of quickned snow doth glide;
Or els the vale that bounds this milkwhite banke,
    Where Venus and her sisters hide the fount,
    Whose lovely Nectar dooth all sweetes surmount.

54

Confounded with descriptions, I must leave them;
Lovers must thinke, and Poets must report them:
For silly wits may never well conceave them,
Unlesse a speciall grace from heaven consort them.
    Aies me, these faires attending Scilla won me:
    But now (sweet Nimphes) attend what hath undon me.

55

The lovely breast where all this beautie rested,
Shrowded within a world of deepe disdaine:
For where I thought my fancie should be feasted
With kinde affect, alas (unto my paine)
    When first I woode, the wanton straight was flying,
    And gave repulse before we talkt of trying.

56

How oft have I (too often have I done so)
In silent night when everie eye was sleeping,
Drawne neere her cave, in hope her love were won so,
Forcing the neighboring waters through my weeping
    To wake the windes, who did afflict her dwelling
    Whilst I with teares my passion was a telling.

57

When midst the Caspian seas the wanton plaid,
I drew whole wreaths of corrall from the rockes:
And in her lap my heavenly presents laid:
But she unkind rewarded me with mockes,
    Such are the fruites that spring from Ladies coying,
    Who smile at teares, and are intrapt with toying.

58

Tongue might grow wearie to report my wooings,
And heart might burst to thinke of her deniall:
May none be blamde but heaven for all these dooings,
That yeeld no helpes in midst of all my triall.
    Heart, tongue, thought, pen nil serve me to repent me,
    Disdaine her selfe should strive for to lament me:

59

Wretched Love let me die, end my love by my death;
Dead alas still I live, flie my life, fade my love.
Out alas love abides, still I joy vitall breath:
Death in love, love is death, woe is me that doo prove.
  Paine and woe, care & griefe every day about me hovers:
  Then but death what can quel al the plages of haples lovers?

60

Aies me my moanings are like water drops
That neede an age to pearce her marble heart,
I sow'd true zeale, yet fruiteles were my crops:
I plighted faith, yet falsehoode wrought my smart:
  I praisd her lookes, her lookes dispised Glaucus,
  Was ever amorous Sea-god scorned thus?

61

A hundereth swelling tides my mother spent
Upon these lockes, and all hir Nimphes were prest,
To pleit them faire when to her bowre I went:
He that hath seene the wandring Phoebus crest,
  Toucht with the Christall of Eurotas spring,
  The pride of these my bushie locks might sing.

62

But short discourse beseemes my bad successe,
Eache office of a lover I performed:
So fervently my passions did her presse,
So sweete my laies, my speech so well reformed,
  That (cruell) when she sawe naught would begile me,
  With angrie lookes the Nimph did thus exile me:

63

Packe hence, thou fondling, to the westerne Seas,
Within some calmy river shrowd thy head:
For never shall my faire thy love appease,
Since fancie from this bosome late is fled:
  And if thou love me, shewe it in departing:
  For why thy presence dooth procure my smarting.

64

This said with angrie lookes, away she hasted
As fast as flie the flouds before the winds:
When I (poore soule) with wretched sorrowes wasted,
Exclaimde on love, which wit and reason blinds:
    And banisht from hir bowre with wofull poasting
    I bent my selfe to seeke a forreine coasting.

65

At last in wandring through the greater Seas
It was my chance to passe the noted streights:
And wearied sore in seeking after ease,
Amidst the creekes, and watrie coole receits,
    I spied from farre by helpe of sonnie beames
    A fruitefull Ile begirt with Ocean streames.

66

Westward I fleeted, and with heedfull eie
Beheld the chalkie cliffes that tempt the aire,
Till at the last it was my chance to spie
A pleasant entrance to the flouds repaire;
    Through which I prest, and wondring there beheld
    On either side a sweete and fruitfull field.

67

Isis (the Ladie of that lovely streame)
Made holiday in view of my resort;
And all the Nimphes of that her watrie realme
Gan trip for joy, to make me mickle sport:
    But I (poore soule) with no such joyes contented,
    Forsooke their bowers, and secretly lamented.

68

All solitarie rome I heere about,
Now on the shoare, now in the streame I weepe,
Fire burnes within, and gastly feare without,
No rest, no ease, no hope of any sleepe:
    Poore banisht God, heere have I still remained,
    Since time my Scilla hath my sutes disdained.

69

And heere consort I now with haplesse men,
Yeelding them comfort, (though my wound be cureless)
Songs of remorse I warble now and then,
Wherein I curse fond Love and Fortune durelesse,
    Wan hope my weale, my trust but bad adventure,
    Circumference is care, my heart the center.

70

Whilest thus he spake, fierce Ate charmde his tongue,
His senses faild, his armes were folded straight,
And now he sighes, and then his heart is stung;
Againe he speakes gainst fancies fond deceit,
    And teares his tresses with his fingers faire,
    And rents his roabs, halfe mad with deepe dispaire.

71

The piteous Nimphes that viewd his heavie plight,
And heard the sequell of his bad successe,
Did loose the springs of their remorsefull sight,
And wept so sore to see his scant redresse:
    That of their teares there grew a pretie brooke,
    Whose Christall cleares the clowdes of pencive looke.

72

Alas woes me, how oft have I bewept
So faire, so yong, so lovely, and so kinde,
And whilst the God upon my bosome slept,
Behelde the scarres of his afflicted minde,
    Imprinted in his yvorie brow by care,
    That fruitlesse fancie left unto his share.

73

My wandring lines, bewitch not so my sences:
But gentle Muse direct their course aright,
Delayes in tragicke tales procure offences:
Yeeld me such feeling words, that whilst I wright,
    My working lines may fill mine eyes with languish,
    And they to note my mones may melt with anguish.

74

The wofull Glaucus thus with woes attainted,
The pencive Nimphes agreevd to see his plight,
The flouds and fields with his laments acquainted,
My selfe amazd to see this heavie sight;
　　On sodaine Thetis with her traine approched,
　　And gravely thus her amorous sonne reproched:

75

My sonne (said she), immortall have I made thee,
Amidst my watrie realmes who may compare
Or match thy might? Why then should care invade thee,
That art so yong, so lovely, fresh and faire.
　　Alas fond God, it merits great reproving
　　In States of worth, to doate on foolish loving.

76

Come wend with me, and midst thy Fathers bowre
Let us disport and frolicke for a while
In spite of Love: although he powte and lowre,
Good exercise will idle lusts beguile:
　　Let wanton Scilla coy her where she will,
　　Live thou my sonne, by reasons levell still.

77

Thus said the Goddesse: and although her words
Gave signes of counsaile, pompe and majestie:
Yet nathelesse her piteous eye affoords
Some pretie witnesse to the standers by,
　　That in her thoughts (for all her outward show)
　　She mournd to see her Sonne amated so.

78

But (welladay) her words have little force;
The hapless lover worne with working woe,
Upon the ground lay pale as any corse,
And were not teares which from his eyes did flowe,
　　And sighes that witnesse he enjoyd his breath,
　　They might have thought him Citizen of death.

79

Which spectacle of care made Thetis bow,
And call on Glaucus, and command her Sonne
To yeelde her right: and hir advice allow,
But (woe) the man whome fancie had undone
 Nill marke her rules: nor words, nor weeping teares
 Can fasten counsaile in the lovers eares.

80

The Queene of Sea, with all hir Nimphes assured
That no perswasion might releeve his care:
Kneeling adowne, their faltring tongues enured
To tempt faire Venus by their vowed praier:
 The course whereof as I could beare in minde
 With sorrowing sobbes they uttered in this kinde:

81

Borne of the Sea, thou Paphian Queene of love,
Mistris of sweete conspiring harmonie:
Lady of Cipris, for whose sweete behove
The Shepeheards praise the youth of Thessalie:
 Daughter of Jove and Sister to the Sonne,
 Assist poore Glaucus late by love undone.

82

So maist thou baine thee in th'Arcadian brookes,
And play with Vulcans rivall when thou list,
And calme his jealous anger by thy lookes,
And knit thy temples with a roseat twist
 If thou thy selfe and thine almightie Sonne,
 Assist poore Glaucus late by love undone.

83

May earth still praise thee for her kinde increase:
And beasts adore thee for their fruitfull wombes,
And fowles with noates thy praises never cease,
And Bees admire thee for their honnie combes:
 So thou thy selfe and thine almightie Sonne,
 Assist poore Glaucus late by love undone.

84

No sooner from her reverent lips were past
Those latter lines; but mounting in the East,
Faire Venus in her ivorie coatch did hast,
And toward those pencive dames, her course addrest;
 Her doves so plied their waving wings with flight,
 That straight the sacred Goddesse came in sight.

85

Upon her head she bare that gorgeous Crowne,
Wherein the poore Amyntas is a starre;
Her lovely lockes her bosome hang adowne,
(Those netts that first insnar'd the God of warre:)
 Delicious lovely shine her prettie eies,
 And one her cheekes carnatioon cloudes arise,

86

The stately roab she ware upon her back
Was lillie white, wherein with cullored silke,
Her Nimphes had blaz'd the yong Adonis wrack,
And Lædas rape by Swan as white as milke,
 And on her lap her lovely Sonne was plaste,
 Whose beautie all his mothers pompe defaste.

87

A wreath of roses hem'd his Temples in,
His tresse was curlde and cleere as beaten gold;
Haught were his lookes, and lovely was his skin,
Each part as pure as Heavens eternall mold,
 And on his eies a milkewhite wreath was spred,
 Which longst his backe, with prettie pleits did shed.

88

Two daintie wings of partie coulored plumes
Adorne his shoulders dallying with the winde;
His left hand weelds a Torch, that ever fumes:
And in his right, his bowe that fancies bind,
 And on his back his Quiver hangs well stored
 With sundrie shaftes, that sundrie hearts have gored.

89

The Deities ariv'd in place desired;
Faire Venus her to Thetis first bespake,
Princesse of Sea (quoth she), as you required
From Ceston with my Sonne my course I take:
   Frollick faire Goddesse, Nimphs forsake your plaining,
   My Sonne hath power and favour yet remaining.

90

With that the reverend powres each other kissed,
And Cupid smil'd upon the Nimphes for pleasure:
So naught but Glaucus solace there was missed,
Which to effect the Nimphes withouten measure
   Intreate the God, who at the last drewe nie
   The place, where Glaucus full of care did lie,

91

And from his bowe a furious dart hee sent
Into that wound which he had made before:
That like Achilles sworde became the teint
To cure the wound that it had carv'd before:
   And sodeinly the Sea-god started up:
   Revivde, relievd, and free from Fancies cup.

92

No more of love, no more of hate he spoke,
No more he forst the sighes from out his breast:
His sodaine joye his pleasing smiles provoke,
And all aloft he shakes his bushie creast,
   Greeting the Gods and Goddesses beside,
   And everie Nimph upon that happie tide.

93

Cupid and he together hand in hand
Approach the place of this renowned traine:
Ladies (said he), releast from amorous band,
Receive my prisoner to your grace againe.
   Glaucus gave thankes, when Thetis glad with blisse
   Embrast his neck, and his kind cheekes did kisse

89.4 with] which

94

To see the Nimphes in flockes about him play,
How Nais kempt his head, and washt his browes:
How Thetis checkt him with his welladay,
How Clore told him of his amorous vowes,
   How Venus praised him for his faithfull love,
   Within my heart a sodein joy did move.

95

Whilst in this glee this holy troope delight,
Along the streame a farre faire Scilla floated,
And coilie vaunst hir creast in open sight:
Whose beauties all the tides with wonder noated,
   Fore whom Palemon and the Tritons danced
   Whilst she hir limmes upon the tide advanced.

96

Whose swift approach made all the Godheads wonder:
Glaucus gan smile to see his lovelie foe,
Rage almost rent poore Thetis heart asonder:
Was never happie troope confused so
   As were these deities and daintie dames,
   When they beheld the cause of Glaucus blames.

97

Venus commends the carriage of her eye,
Nais upbraides the dimple in her chinne,
Cupid desires to touch the wantons thie,
Clore she sweares that everie eie dooth sinne
   That likes a Nimph that so contemneth love,
   As no attempts her lawles heart may move.

98

Thetis impatient of her wrong sustained,
With envious teares her roseat cheekes afflicted;
And thus of Scillas former pride complained;
Cupid (said she), see her that hath inflicted
   The deadlie wound that harmde my lovelie sonne,
   From whome the offspring of my care begonne.

99

Oh if there dwell within thy brest, my boy
Or grace, or pittie, or remorse (said she),
Now bend thy bowe, abate yon wantons joy,
And let these Nimphes thy rightfull justice see.
    The God soone won, gan shoote, and cleft her heart
    With such a shaft as causd her endles smart.

100

The tender Nimph attainted unawares,
Fares like the Libian Lionesse that flies
The Hunters Launce that wounds her in his snares;
Now gins shee love, and straight on Glaucus cries;
    Whilst on the shore the goddesses rejoyce,
    And all the Nimphes afflict the ayre with noyse.

101

To shoare she flitts, and swift as Affrick wind
Her footing glides upon the yeelding grasse,
And wounded by affect recure to finde
She sodainely with sighes approcht the place
    Where Glaucus sat, and wearie with her harmes
    Gan claspe the Sea-god in her amorous armes.

102

Glaucus my love (quoth she), looke on thy lover,
Smile gentle Glaucus on the Nimph that likes thee;
But starke as stone sat he, and list not prove her:
(Ah silly Nimph the selfesame God that strikes thee
    With fancies darte, and hath thy freedom slaine)
    Wounds Glaucus with the arrowe of disdaine.

103

Oh kisse no more kind Nimph, he likes no kindnes,
Love sleepes in him, to flame within thy brest;
Cleer'd are his eies, where thine are clad with blindnes;
Free'd be his thoughts, where thine must taste unrest:
    Yet nill she leave, for never love will leave her,
    But fruiteles hopes and fatall happes deceave her.

104

Lord how her lippes doo dwell upon his cheekes;
And how she lookes for babies in his eies:
And how she sighes, and sweares shee loves and leekes,
And how she vowes, and he her vowes envies:
 Trust me the envious Nimphes in looking on,
 Were forst with teares for to assist her mone.

· 105

How oft with blushes would she plead for grace,
How oft with whisperings would she tempt his eares:
How oft with Christall did she wet his face:
How oft she wipte them with her Amber heares:
 So oft me thought, I oft in heart desired
 To see the end whereto disdaine aspired.

106

Palemon with the Tritons roare for griefe,
To see the Mistris of their joyes amated:
But Glaucus scornes the Nimph, that waites reliefe:
And more she loves, the more the Sea-god hated,
 Such change, such chance, such sutes, such storms beleeve me
 Poore silly wretch did hartely agreeve me.

107

As when the fatall bird of Augurie
Seeing a stormie dismall cloude arise
Within the South, foretells with piteous crie
The weeping tempest, that on sudden hies:
 So she poore soule, in view of his disdaine
 Began to descant on her future paine.

108

And fixing eye upon the fatall ground,
Whole hoasts of flouds drew deaw from out her eyes;
And when through inward griefe the lasse did sound,
The softned grasse like billowes did arise
 To woe her brests, and wed her limmes so daintie,
 Whom wretched love had made so weake and faintie.

109

(Ayes me), me thinks I see her Thetis fingers
Renting her locks as she were woe begon her;
And now her lippes upon his lipping lingers:
Oh lingring paine, where love nill list to mone her:
    Rue me that writes, for why her ruth deserves it:
    Hope needs must faile, where sorrow scarce preserves it.

110

To make long tale were tedious to the wofull,
Wofull that read what wofull shee approoved:
In briefe her heart with deepe dispaire was full,
As since she might not win her sweete beloved.
    With hideous cries like winde borne backe she fled
    Unto the Sea, and to ward Sicillia sped.

111

Sweete Zephirus upon that fatall howre
In haples tide midst watrie world was walking;
Whose milder sighes, alas, had little power
To whisper peace amongst the Godheads talking:
    Who all in one conclude for to pursue,
    The haples Nimph, to see what would ensue.

112

Venus her selfe and her faire Sonne gan hie
Within their ivorie Coach drawne forth by doves
After this haples Nimph, their power to trie:
The Nimphes in hope to see their vowed loves,
    Gan cut the watrie boosom of the tide,
    As in Caÿster Phoebus birds doe glide.

113

Thetis in pompe upon a Tritons back
Did poast her straight, attended by her traine;
But Glaucus free from love by lovers wrack,
Seeing me pencive where I did remaine,
    Upon a Dolphin horst me (as he was)
    Thus on the Ocean hand in hand we passe.

110.3 was full] was so full

114

Our talke midway was nought but still of wonder,
Of change, of chaunce, of sorrow, and her ending;
I wept for want: he said, time bringes men under,
And secret want can finde but small befrending.
    And as he said, in that before I tried it,
    I blamde my wit forewarnd, yet never spied it.

115

What neede I talke the order of my way,
Discourse was steeresman while my barke did saile,
My ship conceit, and fancie was my bay:
(If these faile me, then faint my Muse and faile,)
    Hast brought us where the haples Nimph sojourned,
    Beating the weeping waves that for her mourned.

116

He that hath seene the Northren blastes dispoile
The pompe of Prime, and with a whistling breath
Blast and dispearse the beauties of the soile;
May thinke upon her paines more worse than death.
    Alas poore Lasse, the Ecchoes in the rockes
    Of Sicilie, her piteous plaining mockes.

117

Eccho her selfe, when Scilla cried out O love!
With piteous voice from out her hollow den,
Returnd these words, these words of sorrow, (*no love*)
No love (quoth she), then fie on traiterous men,
    Then fie on hope: *then fie on hope* (quoth Eccho)
    To everie word the Nimph did answere so.

118

For every sigh, the Rockes returnes a sigh;
For everie teare, their fountaines yeelds a drop;
Till we at last the place approached nigh,
And heard the Nimph that fed on sorrowes sop
    Make woods, and waves, and rockes, and hills admire
    The wonderous force of her untam'd desire.

119

Glaucus (quoth she) is faire: whilst Eccho sings
Glaucus is faire: but yet he hateth Scilla
The wretch reportes: and then her armes she wrings
Whilst Eccho tells her this, *he hateth Scilla,*
   No hope (quoth she): *no hope* (quoth Eccho) then.
   Then *fie on men:* when she said, fie on men.

120

Furie and Rage, Wan-hope, Dispaire, and Woe
From Ditis den by Ate sent, drewe nie:
Furie was red, with rage his eyes did gloe,
Whole flakes of fire from foorth his mouth did flie,
   His hands and armes ibath'd in blood of those
   Whome fortune, sinne, or fate made Countries foes.

121

Rage, wan and pale upon a Tiger sat,
Knawing upon the bones of mangled men;
Naught can he view, but he repinde thereat:
His lockes were Snakes bred foorth in Stigian den,
   Next whom, Dispaire that deepe disdained elf
   Delightlesse livde, still stabbing of her self.

122

Woe all in blacke, within her hands did beare
The fatall torches of a Funerall,
Her Cheekes were wet, dispearsed was hir heare,
Her voice was shrill (yet loathsome therewith all):
   Wan-hope (poore soule) on broken Ancker sitts,
   Wringing his armes as robbed of his witts.

123

These five at once the sorrowing Nimph assaile,
And captive lead her bound into the rocks.
Where howling still she strives for to prevaile,
With no availe yet strives she: for hir locks
   Are chang'd with wonder into hideous sands,
   And hard as flint become her snow-white hands.

124

The waters howle with fatall tunes about her,
The aire dooth scoule when as she turnes within them,
The winds and waves with puffes and billowes skout her;
Waves storme, aire scoules, both wind & waves begin them
  To make the place this mournful Nimph doth weepe in,
  A haples haunt whereas no Nimph may keepe in.

125

The Sea-man wandring by that famous Isle,
Shuns all with feare, dispairing Scillaes bowre;
Nimphes, Sea-gods, Syrens when they list to smile
Forsake the haunt of Scilla in that stowre:
  Ah Nimphes thought I, if everie coy one felt
  The like misshappes, their flintie hearts would melt.

126

Thetis rejoyst to see her foe deprest,
Glaucus was glad, since Scilla was enthrald;
The Nimphs gan smile, to boast their Glaucus rest:
Venus and Cupid in their throanes enstald,
  At Thetis beck to Neptunes bowre repaire,
  Whereas they feast amidst his pallace faire.

127

Of pure immortall Nectar is their drinke,
And sweete Ambrosia daintie doo repast them,
The Tritons sing, Palemon smiles to thinke
Upon the chance, and all the Nimphs doo hast them
  To trick up mossie garlands where they woon,
  For lovely Venus and her conquering Sonne.

128

From foorth the fountaines of his mothers store,
Glaucus let flie a daintie Christall baine
That washt the Nimphs with labour tir'd before:
Cupid hee trips among this lovely traine,
  Alonely I apart did write this storie
  With many a sigh and heart full sad and sorie.

129

Glaucus when all the Goddesses tooke rest,
Mounted upon a Dolphin full of glee:
Conveide me friendly from this honored feast,
And by the way, such Sonnets song to me,
    That all the Dolphins neighbouring of his glide
    Daunst with delight, his reverend course beside.

130

At last he left me, where at first he found me,
Willing me let the world and ladies knowe
Of Scillas pride, and then by oath he bound me
To write no more, of that whence shame dooth grow:
    Or tie my pen to Pennie-knaves delight,
    But live with fame, and so for fame to wright.

L'ENVOY

Ladies he left me, trust me I missay not,
But so he left me as he wild me tell you:
That Nimphs must yeeld, when faithfull lovers straie not,
Least through contempt, almightie love compell you
    With Scilla in the rockes to make your biding
    A cursed plague, for womens proud back-sliding.

HERO AND LEANDER
Christopher Marlowe
(1598)

THE ARGUMENT OF THE FIRST SESTYAD*

Heros description and her Loves,
The Phane of Venus; where he moves
His worthie Love-suite, and attaines;
Whose blisse the wrath of Fates restraines,
For Cupids grace to Mercurie,
Which tale the Author doth implie.

On Hellespont guiltie of True-loves blood,
In view and opposit two citties stood,
Seaborderers, disjoin'd by Neptunes might:
The one Abydos, the other Sestos hight.
At Sestos, Hero dwelt; Hero the faire,   5
Whom young Apollo courted for her haire,
And offred as a dower his burning throne,
Where she should sit for men to gaze upon.
The outside of her garments were of lawne,
The lining, purple silke, with guilt starres drawne,   10
Her wide sleeves greene, and bordered with a grove,
Where Venus in her naked glory strove,
To please the carelesse and disdainfull eies
Of proud Adonis that before her lies.
Her kirtle blew, whereon was many a staine,   15
Made with the blood of wretched Lovers slaine.

---

* The addition of the arguments and the division into sestiads were made by
Chapman in the second edition (1598²).

3 Seaborderers] Seaborders *1598¹*; *1598²*

Upon her head she ware a myrtle wreath,
From whence her vaile reacht to the ground beneath.
Her vaile was artificiall flowers and leaves,
Whose workmanship both man and beast deceaves.   20
Many would praise the sweet smell as she past,
When t'was the odour which her breath foorth cast,
And there for honie bees have sought in vaine,
And beat from thence, have lighted there againe.
About her necke hung chaines of peble stone,   25
Which lightned by her necke, like Diamonds shone.
She ware no gloves, for neither sunne nor wind
Would burne or parch her hands, but to her mind,
Or warme or coole them, for they tooke delite
To play upon those hands, they were so white.   30
Buskins of shels all silvered used she,
And brancht with blushing corall to the knee;
Where sparrowes pearcht, of hollow pearle and gold,
Such as the world would woonder to behold:
Those with sweet water oft her handmaid fils,   35
Which as shee went would cherupe through the bils.
Some say, for her the fairest Cupid pyn'd,
And looking in her face, was strooken blind.
But this is true, so like was one the other,
As he imagyn'd Hero was his mother.   40
And oftentimes into her bosome flew,
About her naked necke his bare armes threw,
And laid his childish head upon her brest,
And with still panting rockt, there tooke his rest.
So lovely faire was Hero, Venus Nun,   45
As nature wept, thinking she was undone;
Because she tooke more from her then she left,
And of such wondrous beautie her bereft:
Therefore in signe her treasure suffred wracke,
Since Heroes time, hath halfe the world beene blacke.   50
Amorous Leander, beautifull and yoong,
(Whose tragedie divine Musæus soong)
Dwelt at Abidus: since him dwelt there none,
For whom succeeding times make greater mone.
His dangling tresses that were never shorne,   55

44 rockt] rocke *1598*[2]

Had they beene cut, and unto Colchos borne,
Would have allu'rd the vent'rous youth of Greece
To hazard more, than for the golden Fleece.
Faire Cinthia wisht his armes might be her spheare,
Greefe makes her pale, because she mooves not there.   60
His bodie was as straight as Circes wand,
Jove might have sipt out Nectar from his hand.
Even as delicious meat is to the tast,
So was his necke in touching, and surpast
The white of Pelops shoulder. I could tell ye,   65
How smooth his brest was, & how white his bellie,
And whose immortall fingars did imprint
That heavenly path, with many a curious dint,
That runs along his backe, but my rude pen
Can hardly blazon foorth the loves of men,   70
Much lesse of powerfull gods: let it suffise,
That my slacke muse sings of Leanders eies,
Those orient cheekes and lippes, exceeding his
That leapt into the water for a kis
Of his owne shadow, and despising many,   75
Died ere he could enjoy the love of any.
Had wilde Hippolitus Leander seene,
Enamoured of his beautie had he beene,
His presence made the rudest paisant melt,
That in the vast uplandish countrie dwelt,   80
The barbarous Thratian soldier moov'd with nought,
Was moov'd with him, and for his favour sought.
Some swore he was a maid in mans attire,
For in his lookes were all that men desire,
A pleasant smiling cheeke, a speaking eye,   85
A brow for love to banquet roiallye,
And such as knew he was a man would say,
Leander, thou art made for amorous play:
Why art thou not in love, and lov'd of all?
Though thou be faire, yet be not thine owne thrall.   90
    The men of wealthie Sestos, everie yeare,
(For his sake whom their goddesse held so deare,
Rose-cheekt Adonis) kept a solemne feast:
Thither resorted many a wandring guest,
To meet their loves; such as had none at all,   95

Came lovers home, from this great festivall.
For everie street like to a Firmament
Glistered with breathing stars, who where they went,
Frighted the melancholie earth, which deem'd
Eternall heaven to burne, for so it seem'd,   100
As if another Phaeton had got
The guidance of the sunnes rich chariot.
But far above the loveliest, Hero shin'd,
And stole away th'inchaunted gazers mind,
For like Sea-nimphs inveigling harmony,   105
So was her beautie to the standers by.
Nor that night-wandring pale and watrie starre
(When yawning dragons draw her thirling carre
From Latmus mount up to the glomie skie,
Where crown'd with blazing light and majestie,   110
She proudly sits) more over-rules the flood,
Than she the hearts of those that neere her stood.
Even as, when gawdie Nymphs pursue the chace,
Wretched Ixions shaggie footed race,
Incenst with savage heat, gallop amaine   115
From steepe Pine-bearing mountains to the plaine:
So ran the people foorth to gaze upon her,
And all that view'd her, were enamour'd on her.
And as in furie of a dreadfull fight,
Their fellowes being slaine or put to flight,   120
Poore soldiers stand with fear of death dead strooken,
So at her presence all surpris'd and tooken,
Await the sentence of her scornefull eies:
He whom she favours lives, the other dies.
There might you see one sigh, another rage,   125
And some (their violent passions to asswage)
Compile sharpe satyrs, but alas too late,
For faithfull love will never turne to hate.
And many seeing great princes were denied,
Pyn'd as they went, and thinking on her died.   130
On this feast day, O cursed day and hower,
Went Hero thorow Sestos, from her tower
To Venus temple, were unhappilye,
As after chaunc'd, they did each other spye.
So faire a church as this, had Venus none,   135

The wals were of discoloured Jasper stone,
Wherein was Proteus carvd, and o'rehead,
A livelie vine of greene sea agget spread;
Where by one hand, light headed Bacchus hoong,
And with the other, wine from grapes out wroong.   140
Of Christall shining faire, the pavement was,
The towne of Sestos cal'd it Venus glasse.
There might you see the gods in sundrie shapes,
Committing headdie ryots, incest, rapes:
For know, that underneath this radiant floure,   145
Was Danaes statue in a brazen tower,
Jove slylie stealing from his sisters bed,
To dallie with Idalian Ganimed,
And for his love Europa, bellowing loud,
And tumbling with the Rainbow in a cloud: 150
Blood-quaffing Mars, heaving the yron net,
Which limping Vulcan and his Cyclops set:
Love kindling fire, to burne such townes as Troy,
Sylvanus weeping for the lovely boy
That now is turn'd into a Cypres tree,   155
Under whose shade the Wood-gods love to bee.
And in the midst a silver altar stood;
There Hero sacrificing turtles blood,
Vaild to the ground, vailing her eie-lids close,
And modestly they opened as she rose: 160
Thence flew Loves arrow with the golden head,
And thus Leander was enamoured.
Stone still he stood, and evermore he gazed,
Till with the fire that from his count'nance blazed,
Relenting Heroes gentle heart was strooke,   165
Such force and vertue hath an amorous looke.
    It lies not in our power to love, or hate,
For will in us is over-rul'd by fate.
When two are stript long ere the course begin,
We wish that one should loose, the other win.   170
And one especiallie doe we affect,
Of two gold Ingots like in each respect:
The reason no man knowes, let it suffise,

137 o'rehead] over head *1598*[2]
159 Vaild] Taild *1598*[2]

What we behold is censur'd by our eies.
Where both deliberat, the love is slight, 175
Who ever lov'd, that lov'd not at first sight?
    He kneel'd, but unto her devoutly praid;
Chast Hero to her selfe thus softly said:
Were I the saint hee worships, I would heare him,
And as shee spake those words, came somewhat nere him. 180
He started up, she blusht as one asham'd;
Wherewith Leander much more was inflam'd.
He toucht her hand, in touching it she trembled,
Love deepely grounded, hardly is dissembled.
These lovers parled by the touch of hands, 185
True love is mute, and oft amazed stands.
Thus while dum signs their yeelding harts entangled,
The aire with sparkes of living fire was spangled,
And night[a] deepe drencht in mystie Acheron,
Heav'd up her head, and halfe the world upon, 190
Breath'd darkenesse forth (darke night is Cupids day).
And now begins Leander to display
Loves holy fire, with words, with sighs and teares,
Which like sweet musicke entred Heroes eares,
And yet at everie word shee turn'd aside, 195
And alwaies cut him off as he replide.
At last, like to a bold sharpe Sophister,
With chearefull hope thus he accosted her:
    Faire creature, let me speake without offence,
I would my rude words had the influence, 200
To lead thy thoughts, as thy faire lookes doe mine,
Then shouldst thou bee his prisoner who is thine.
Be not unkind and faire, mishapen stuffe
Are of behaviour boisterous and ruffe.
O shun me not, but heare me ere you goe, 205
God knowes I cannot force love, as you doe.
My words shall be as spotlesse as my youth,
Full of simplicitie and naked truth.
This sacrifice (whose sweet perfume descending,
From Venus altar to your footsteps bending) 210
Doth testifie that you exceed her farre,
To whom you offer, and whose Nunne you are.

[a] A periphrasis of night.

Why should you worship her? her you surpasse,
As much as sparkling Diamonds flaring glasse.
A Diamond set in lead his worth retaines,   215
A heavenly Nimph, belov'd of humane swaines,
Receives no blemish, but oft-times more grace,
Which makes me hope, although I am but base,
Base in respect of thee, divine and pure,
Dutifull service may thy love procure,   220
And I in dutie will excell all other,
As thou in beautie doest exceed Loves mother.
Nor heaven, nor thou, were made to gaze upon,
As heaven preserves all things, so save thou one.
A stately builded ship, well rig'd and tall,   225
The Ocean maketh more majesticall:
Why vowest thou then to live in Sestos here,
Who on Loves seas more glorious wouldst appeare?
Like untun'd golden strings all women are,
Which long time lie untoucht, will harshly jarre.   230
Vessels of Brasse oft handled, brightly shine,
What difference betwixt the richest mine
And basest mold, but use? for both not us'de,
Are of like worth. Then treasure is abus'de,
When misers keepe it; being put to lone,   235
In time it will returne us two for one.
Rich robes themselves and others do adorne,
Neither themselves nor others, if not worne.
Who builds a pallace and rams up the gate,
Shall see it ruinous and desolate.   240
Ah simple Hero, learne thy selfe to cherish,
Lone women like to emptie houses perish.
Lesse sinnes the poore rich man that starves himselfe,
In heaping up a masse of drossie pelfe,
Than such as you: his golden earth remains,   245
Which after his disceasse, some other gains.
But this faire jem, sweet in the losse alone,
When you fleet hence, can be bequeath'd to none.
Or if it could, downe from th'enameld skie
All heaven would come to claime this legacie,   250

233 mold, earth   242 Lone] Love *1598*[2]
243 sinnes] since *1598*[2]

54

And with intestine broiles the world destroy,
And quite confound natures sweet harmony.
Well therefore by the gods decreed it is,
We humane creatures should enjoy that blisse.
One is no number, mayds are nothing then,   255
Without the sweet societie of men.
Wilt thou live single still? one shalt thou bee,
Though never-singling Hymen couple thee.
Wild savages, that drinke of running springs,
Thinke water farre excels all earthly things: 260
But they that dayly tast neat wine, despise it.
Virginitie, albeit some highly prise it,
Compar'd with marriage, had you tried them both,
Differs as much, as wine and water doth.
Base boullion for the stampes sake we allow,   265
Even so for mens impression do we you:
By which alone, our reverend fathers say,
Women receave perfection everie way.
This idoll which you terme Virginitie,
Is neither essence, subject to the eie,   270
No, nor to any one exterior sence,
Nor hath it any place of residence,
Nor is't of earth or mold celestiall,
Or capable of any forme at all.
Of that which hath no being, doe not boast,   275
Things that are not at all, are never lost.
Men foolishly doe call it vertuous,
What vertue is it, that is borne with us?
Much lesse can honour bee ascrib'd thereto;
Honour is purchac'd by the deedes wee do.   280
Beleeve me Hero, honour is not wone,
Untill some honourable deed be done.
Seeke you for chastitie, immortall fame,
And know that some have wrong'd Dianas name?
Whose name is it, if she be false or not,   285
So she be faire, but some vile toongs will blot?
But you are faire (aye me) so wondrous faire,
So yoong, so gentle, and so debonaire,
As Greece will thinke, if thus you live alone,
Some one or other keepes you as his owne.   290

Then Hero hate me not, nor from me flie,
To follow swiftly blasting infamie.
Perhaps, thy sacred Priesthood makes thee loath;
Tell me, to whom mad'st thou that heedlesse oath?
   To Venus, answered shee, and as shee spake, 295
Foorth from those two tralucent cesternes brake
A streame of liquid pearle, which downe her face
Made milk-white paths, whereon the gods might trace
To Joves high court. Hee thus replide: The rites
In which Loves beauteous Empresse most delites, 300
Are banquets, Dorick musicke, midnight-revell,
Plaies, maskes, and all that stern age counteth evill.
Thee as a holy Idiot doth she scorne,
For thou in vowing chastitie hast sworne
To rob her name and honour, and thereby 305
Commit'st a sinne far worse than perjurie,
Even sacrilege against her Deitie,
Through regular and formall puritie.
To expiat which sinne, kisse and shake hands,
Such sacrifice as this Venus demands. 310
   Thereat she smild, and did denie him so,
As put thereby, yet might he hope for mo.
Which makes him quickly re-enforce his speech,
And her in humble manner thus beseech:
   Though neither gods nor men may thee deserve, 315
Yet for her sake whom you have vow'd to serve,
Abandon fruitlesse cold Virginitie,
The gentle queene of Loves sole enemie.
Then shall you most resemble Venus Nun,
When Venus sweet rites are perform'd and done. 320
Flint-brested Pallas joies in single life,
But Pallas and your mistresse are at strife.
Love Hero then, and be not tirannous,
But heale the heart, that thou hast wounded thus,
Nor staine thy youthfull years with avarice, 325
Faire fooles delight, to be accounted nice.
The richest corne dies, if it be not reapt,
Beautie alone is lost, too warily kept.
These arguments he us'de, and many more,
Wherewith she yeelded, that was woon before. 330

56

Heroes lookes yeelded, but her words made warre,
Women are woon when they begin to jarre.
Thus having swallow'd Cupids golden hooke,
The more she striv'd, the deeper was she strooke.
Yet evilly faining anger, strove she still,   335
And would be thought to graunt against her will.
So having paus'd a while, at last shee said:
Who taught thee Rhethoricke to deceive a maid?
Aye me, such words as these should I abhor,
And yet I like them for the Orator.   340
    With that Leander stoopt, to have imbrac'd her,
But from his spreading armes away she cast her,
And thus bespake him: Gentle youth, forbeare
To touch the sacred garments which I weare.
Upon a rocke, and underneath a hill,   345
Far from the towne (where all is whist and still,
Save that the sea playing on yellow sand,
Sends foorth a ratling murmure to the land,
Whose sound allures the golden Morpheus,
In silence of the night to visite us.)   350
My turret stands, and there God knowes I play
With Venus swannes and sparrowes all the day;
A dwarfish beldame beares me companie,
That hops about the chamber where I lie,
And spends the night (that might be better spent)   355
In vaine discourse, and apish merriment.
Come thither; As she spake this, her toong tript,
For unawares (Come thither) from her slipt,
And sodainly her former colour chang'd,
And here and there her eies through anger rang'd.   360
And like a planet, mooving severall waies,
At one selfe instant, she poore soule assaies,
Loving, not to love at all, and everie part
Strove to resist the motions of her hart.
And hands so pure, so innocent, nay such,   365
As might have made heaven stoope to have a touch,
Did she uphold to Venus, and againe
Vow'd spotlesse chastitie, but all in vaine.
Cupid beats downe her praiers with his wings,
Her vowes above the emptie aire he flings: 370

All deepe enrag'd, his sinowie bow he bent,
And shot a shaft that burning from him went,
Wherewith she strooken, look'd so dolefully,
As made Love sigh, to see his tirannie.
And as she wept, her teares to pearle he turn'd,   375
And wound them on his arme, and for her mourn'd.
Then towards the pallace of the destinies,
Laden with languishment and griefe he flies,
And to those sterne nymphs humblie made request,
Both might enjoy ech other, and be blest.   380
But with a ghastly dreadfull countenaunce,
Threatning a thousand deaths at everie glaunce,
They answered Love, nor would vouchsafe so much
As one poore word, their hate to him was such.
Harken a while, and I will tell you why: 385
Heavens winged herrald, Jove-borne Mercury,
The selfe-same day that he asleepe had layd
Inchaunted Argus, spied a countrie mayd,
Whose carelesse haire, in stead of pearle t'adorne it,
Glist'red with deaw, as one that seem'd to skorne it: 390
Her breath as fragrant as the morning rose,
Her mind pure, and her toong untaught to glose.
Yet prowd she was, (for loftie pride that dwels
In tow'red courts, is oft in sheapheards cels.)
And too too well the faire vermilion knew,   395
And silver tincture of her cheekes, that drew
The love of everie swaine: On her, this god
Enamoured was, and with his snakie rod,
Did charme her nimble feet, and made her stay,
The while upon a hillocke downe he lay,   400
And sweetly on his pipe began to play,
And with smooth speech, her fancie to assay,
Till in his twining armes he lockt her fast,
And then he woo'd with kisses, and at last,
As sheap-heards do, her on the ground hee layd,   405
And tumbling in the grasse, he often strayd
Beyond the bounds of shame, in being bold
To eie those parts, which no eie should behold.
And like an insolent commaunding lover,
Boasting his parentage, would needs discover   410

The way to new Elisium: but she,
Whose only dower was her chastitie,
Having striv'ne in vaine, was now about to crie,
And crave the helpe of sheap-heards that were nie.
Herewith he stayd his furie, and began   415
To give her leaue to rise: away she ran,
After went Mercurie, who us'd such cunning,
As she to heare his tale, left off her running.
Maids are not woon by brutish force and might,
But speeches full of pleasure and delight.   420
And knowing Hermes courted her, was glad
That she such lovelinesse and beautie had
As could provoke his liking, yet was mute,
And neither would denie, nor graunt his sute.
Still vowd he love, she wanting no excuse   425
To feed him with delaies, as women use:
Or thirsting after immortalitie,
(All women are ambitious naturallie,)
Impos'd upon her lover such a taske,
As he ought not performe, nor yet she aske.   430
A draught of flowing Nectar, she requested,
Wherewith the king of Gods and men is feasted.
He readie to accomplish what she wil'd,
Stole some from Hebe (Hebe Joves cup fil'd,)
And gave it to his simple rustike love,   435
Which being knowne (as what is hid from Jove?)
He inly storm'd, and waxt more furious
Than for the fire filcht by Prometheus,
And thrusts him down from heaven: he wandring here,
In mournfull tearmes, with sad and heavie cheare   440
Complaind to Cupid. Cupid for his sake,
To be reveng'd on Jove did undertake,
And those on whom heaven, earth, and hell relies,
I mean the Adamantine Destinies,
He wounds with love, and forst them equallie   445
To dote upon deceitfull Mercurie.
They offred him the deadly fatall knife,
That sheares the slender threads of humane life,
At his faire feathered feet, the engins layd,

420 pleasure] pleasures *1598*[2]

Which th'earth from ougly Chaos den up-wayd: 450
These he regarded not, but did intreat,
That Jove, usurper of his fathers seat,
Might presently be banisht into hell,
And aged Saturne in Olympus dwell.
They granted what he crav'd, and once againe,   455
Saturne and Ops, began their golden raigne.
Murder, rape, warre, lust and trecherie,
Were with Jove clos'd in Stigian Emperie.
But long this blessed time continued not:
As soone as he his wished purpose got,   460
He recklesse of his promise, did despise
The love of th'everlasting Destinies.
They seeing it, both Love and him abhor'd,
And Jupiter unto his place restor'd.
And but that Learning, in despight of Fate,   465
Will mount aloft, and enter heaven gate,
And to the seat of Jove it selfe advaunce,
Hermes had slept in hell with ignoraunce.
Yet as a punishment they added this,
That he and Povertie should alwaies kis.   470
And to this day is everie scholler poore,
Grosse gold, from them runs headlong to the boore.
Likewise the angrie sisters thus deluded,
To venge themselves on Hermes, have concluded
That Midas brood shall sit in Honors chaire,   475
To which the Muses sonnes are only heire:
And fruitfull wits that in aspiring are,
Shall discontent, run into regions farre;
And few great lords in vertuous deeds shall joy,
But be surpris'd with every garish toy;   480
And still inrich the loftie servile clowne,
Who with incroching guile keepes learning downe.
Then muse not, Cupids sute no better sped,
Seeing in their loves the Fates were injured.

The end of the first Sestyad

458 Emperie] *1598²*; Emprie *1598¹*

THE ARGUMENT OF THE SECOND SESTYAD

Hero of love takes deeper sence,
And doth her love more recompence.
Their first nights meeting, where sweet kisses
Are th'only crownes of both their blisses.
He swims t'Abydus, and returnes;
Cold Neptune with his beautie burnes,
Whose suite he shuns, and doth aspire
Heros faire towre, and his desire.

By this, sad Hero, with love unacquainted,
Viewing Leanders face, fell downe and fainted.
He kist her, and breath'd life into her lips,
Wherewith as one displeas'd, away she trips.
Yet as she went, full often look'd behind,　　　　　　5
And many poore excuses did she find,
To linger by the way, and once she stayd,
And would have turn'd againe, but was afrayd,
In offring parlie, to be counted light.
So on she goes, and in her idle flight,　　　　　　　10
Her painted fanne of curled plumes let fall,
Thinking to traine Leander therewithall.
He being a novice, knew not what she meant,
But stayd, and after her a letter sent.
Which joyfull Hero answerd in such sort,　　　　　　15
As he had hope to scale the beauteous fort,
Wherein the liberall graces lock'd their wealth,
And therefore to her tower he got by stealth.
Wide open stood the doore, hee need not clime,
And she her selfe before the pointed time,　　　　　　20
Had spread the boord, with roses strowed the roome,
And oft look't out, and mus'd he did not come.
At last he came: O who can tell the greeting
These greedie lovers had at their first meeting.
He askt, she gave, and nothing was denied,　　　　　　25
Both to each other quickly were affied.
Looke how their hands, so were their hearts united,
And what he did, she willingly requited.
(Sweet are the kisses, the imbracements sweet,

When like desires and affections meet,   30
For from the earth to heaven is Cupid rais'd,
Where fancie is in equall ballance pais'd.)
Yet she this rashnesse sodainly repented,
And turn'd aside, and to her selfe lamented,
As if her name and honour had beene wrong'd,   35
By being possest of him for whom she long'd:
I, and shee wisht, albeit not from her hart,
That he would leave her turret and depart.
The mirthfull God of amorous pleasure smil'd,
To see how he this captive Nymph beguil'd.   40
For hitherto hee did but fan the fire,
And kept it downe that it might mount the hier.
Now waxt she jealous, least his love abated,
Fearing her owne thoughts made her to be hated.
Therefore unto him hastily she goes,   45
And like light Salmacis, her body throes
Upon his bosome, where with yeelding eyes,
She offers up her selfe a sacrifice,
To slake his anger, if he were displeas'd.
O what god would not therewith be appeas'd?   50
Like Æsops cocke, this jewell he enjoyed,
And as a brother with his sister toyed,
Supposing nothing else was to be done,
Now he her favour and good will had wone.
But know you not that creatures wanting sence,   55
By nature have a mutuall appetence,
And wanting organs to advaunce a step,
Mov'd by Loves force, unto ech other lep?
Much more in subjects having intellect,
Some hidden influence breeds like effect.   60
Albeit Leander rude in love, and raw,
Long dallying with Hero, nothing saw
That might delight him more, yet he suspected
Some amorous rites or other were neglected.
Therefore unto his bodie hirs he clung,   65
She, fearing on the rushes to be flung,
Striv'd with redoubled strength: the more she strived,
The more a gentle pleasing heat revived,
Which taught him all that elder lovers know,

62

And now the same gan so to scorch and glow,　　　　70
As in plaine termes (yet cunningly) he crav'd it:
Love alwaies makes those eloquent that have it.
Shee, with a kind of graunting, put him by it,
And ever as he thought himselfe most nigh it,
Like to the tree of Tantalus she fled,　　　　75
And seeming lavish, sav'de her maydenhead.
Ne're king more sought to keepe his diademe,
Than Hero this inestimable gemme.
Above our life we love a stedfast friend,
Yet when a token of great worth we send,　　　　80
We often kisse it, often looke thereon,
And stay the messenger that would be gon:
No marvell then, though Hero would not yeeld
So soone to part from that she deerely held.
Jewels being lost are found againe, this never,　　　　85
T'is lost but once, and once lost, lost for ever.
　　Now had the morne espy'de her lovers steeds,
Whereat she starts, puts on her purple weeds,
And red for anger that he stayd so long,
All headlong throwes her selfe the clouds among,　　　　90
And now Leander fearing to be mist,
Imbrast her sodainly, tooke leave, and kist:
Long was he taking leave, and loath to go,
And kist againe, as lovers use to do.
Sad Hero wroong him by the hand, and wept,　　　　95
Saying, let your vowes and promises be kept.
Then standing at the doore, she turnd about,
As loath to see Leander going out.
And now the sunne that through th'orizon peepes,
As pittying these lovers, downeward creepes,　　　　100
So that in silence of the cloudie night,
Though it was morning, did he take his flight.
But what the secret trustie night conceal'd
Leanders amorous habit soone reveal'd:
With Cupids myrtle was his bonet crownd,　　　　105
About his armes the purple riband wound,
Wherewith she wreath'd her largely spreading heare,
Nor could the youth abstaine, but he must weare
The sacred ring wherewith she was endow'd,

When first religious chastitie she vow'd: 110
Which made his love through Sestos to bee knowne,
And thence unto Abydus sooner blowne,
Than he could saile, for incorporeal Fame,
Whose waight consists in nothing but her name,
Is swifter than the wind, whose tardie plumes,   115
Are reeking water, and dull earthlie fumes.
Home when he came, he seem'd not to be there,
But like exiled aire thrust from his sphere,
Set in a forren place, and straight from thence,
Alcides like, by mightie violence,   120
He would have chac'd away the swelling maine,
That him from her unjustly did detaine.
Like as the sunne in a Dyameter,
Fires and inflames objects remooved farre,
And heateth kindly, shining lat'rally;   125
So beautie, sweetly quickens when t'is ny,
But being separated and remooved,
Burnes where it cherisht, murders where it loved.
Therefore even as an Index to a booke,
So to his mind was yoong Leanders looke.   130
O none but gods have power their love to hide,
Affection by the count'nance is descride.
The light of hidden fire it selfe discovers,
And love that is conceal'd, betraies poore lovers.
His secret flame apparantly was seene,   135
Leanders Father knew where hee had beene,
And for the same mildly rebuk't his sonne,
Thinking to quench the sparckles new begonne.
But love resisted once, growes passionate,
And nothing more than counsaile, lovers hate.   140
For as a hote prowd horse highly disdaines
To have his head control'd, but breakes the raines,
Spits foorth the ringled bit, and with his hoves
Checkes the submissive ground: so hee that loves,
The more he is restrain'd, the woorse he fares: 145
What is it now, but mad Leander dares?
O Hero, Hero, thus he cry'de full oft,
And then he got him to a rocke aloft,
Where having spy'de her tower, long star'd he on't,

And pray'd the narrow toyling Hellespont 150
To part in twaine, that hee might come and go,
But still the rising billowes answered no.
With that hee stript him to the yv'rie skin,
And crying, Love I come, leapt lively in.
Whereat the saphir visag'd god grew prowd, 155
And made his capring Triton sound alowd,
Imagining, that Ganimed displeas'd,
Had left the heavens, therefore on him hee seaz'd.
Leander striv'd, the waves about him wound,
And puld him to the bottome, where the ground 160
Was strewd with pearle, and in low corrall groves,
Sweet singing Meremaids, sported with their loves
On heapes of heavie gold, and tooke great pleasure
To spurne in carelesse sort the shipwracke treasure.
For here the stately azure pallace stood, 165
Where kingly Neptune and his traine abode:
The lustie god imbrast him, cald him love,
And swore he never should returne to Jove.
But when he knew it was not Ganimed,
For under water he was almost dead, 170
He heav'd him up, and looking on his face,
Beat downe the bold waves with his triple mace,
Which mounted up, intending to have kist him,
And fell in drops like teares, because they mist him.
Leander being up, began to swim, 175
And looking backe, saw Neptune follow him.
Whereat agast, the poore soule gan to crie,
O let mee visite Hero ere I die.
The god put Helles bracelet on his arme,
And swore the sea should never doe him harme. 180
He clapt his plumpe cheekes, with his tresses playd,
And smiling wantonly, his love bewrayd.
He watcht his armes, and as they opend wide,
At every stroke, betwixt them would he slide,
And steale a kisse, and then run out and daunce, 185
And as he turnd, cast many a lustfull glaunce,
And threw him gawdie toies to please his eie,
And dive into the water, and there prie
Upon his brest, his thighs, and everie lim,

And up againe, and close beside him swim, 190
And talke of love: Leander made replie,
You are deceav'd, I am no woman I.
Thereat smilde Neptune, and then told a tale,
How that a sheapheard sitting in a vale,
Playd with a boy so faire and kind, 195
As for his love both earth and heaven pyn'd;
That of the cooling river durst not drinke,
Least water-nymphs should pull him from the brinke.
And when hee sported in the fragrant lawnes,
Gote-footed Satyrs and up-staring Fawnes 200
Would steale him thence. Ere halfe this tale was done:
Aye me, Leander cryde, th'enamoured sunne,
That now should shine on Thetis glassie bower,
Descends upon my radiant Heroes tower.
O that these tardie armes of mine were wings, 205
And as he spake, upon the waves he springs.
Neptune was angrie that hee gave no eare,
And in his heart revenging malice bare:
He flung at him his mace, but as it went,
He cald it in, for love made him repent. 210
The mace returning backe, his owne hand hit,
As meaning to be veng'd for darting it.
When this fresh bleeding wound Leander viewd,
His colour went and came, as if he rewd
The greefe which Neptune felt. In gentle brests, 215
Relenting thoughts, remorse and pittie rests.
And who have hard hearts, and obdurat minds,
But vicious, harebraind, and illit'rat hinds?
The god seeing him with pittie to be moved,
Thereon concluded that he was beloved. 220
(Love is too full of faith, too credulous,
With follie and false hope deluding us.)
Wherefore Leanders fancie to surprize,
To the rich Ocean for gifts he flies.
'Tis wisedome to give much, a gift prevailes, 225
When deepe perswading Oratorie failes.
By this Leander being nere the land,

200 up-staring Fawnes: cf. 'up looke,/(Like rurall Faunes),' *Cephalus and Procris*, l. 508

66

Cast downe his wearie feet, and felt the sand.
Breathlesse albeit he were, he rested not,
Till to the solitarie tower he got, 230
And knockt and cald, at which celestiall noise
The longing heart of Hero much more joies
Then nymphs & sheapheards, when the timbrell rings,
Or crooked Dolphin when the sailer sings;
She stayd not for her robes, but straight arose, 235
And drunke with gladnesse, to the dore she goes.
Where seeing a naked man, she scriecht for feare,
Such sights as this, to tender maids are rare,
And ran into the darke her selfe to hide.
Rich jewels in the darke are soonest spide. 240
Unto her was he led, or rather drawne,
By those white limmes, which sparckled through the lawne.
The neerer that he came, the more she fled,
And seeking refuge, slipt into her bed.
Whereon Leander sitting, thus began, 245
Through numming cold, all feeble, faint and wan:
    If not for love, yet love, for pittie sake,
Me in thy bed and maiden bosome take,
At least vouchsafe these armes some little roome,
Who hoping to imbrace thee, cherely swome. 250
This head was beat with manie a churlish billow,
And therefore let it rest upon thy pillow.
Herewith afrighted Hero shrunke away,
And in her luke-warme place Leander lay,
Whose lively heat like fire from heaven fet, 255
Would animate grosse clay, and higher set
The drooping thoughts of base declining soules,
Then drerie Mars carowsing Nectar boules.
His hands he cast upon her like a snare,
She overcome with shame and sallow feare, 260
Like chast Diana, when Acteon spyde her,
Being sodainly betraide, dyv'd downe to hide her.
And as her silver body downeward went,
With both her hands she made the bed a tent,
And in her owne mind thought her selfe secure, 265
O'recast with dim and darksome coverture.
   246 Through] Though *1598*[2]

And now she lets him whisper in her eare,
Flatter, intreat, promise, protest and sweare,
Yet ever as he greedily assayd
To touch those dainties, she the Harpey playd,   270
And every lim did as a soldier stout,
Defend the fort, and keep the foe-man out.
For though the rising yv'rie mount he scal'd,
Which is with azure circling lines empal'd,
Much like a globe, (a globe may I tearme this,   275
By which love sailes to regions full of blis,)
Yet there with Sysiphus he toyld in vaine,
Till gentle parlie did the truce obtaine.
Wherein Leander on her quivering brest,
Breathlesse spoke some thing, and sigh'd out the rest;   280
Which so prevail'd, as he with small ado,
Inclos'd her in his armes and kist her to.
And everie kisse to her was as a charme,
And to Leander as a fresh alarme,
So that the truce was broke, and she alas,   285
(Poore sillie maiden) at his mercie was.
Love is not ful of pittie (as men say)
But deaffe and cruell, where he meanes to pray.
Even as a bird, which in our hands we wring,
Foorth plungeth, and oft flutters with her wing,   290
She trembling strove, this strife of hers (like that
Which made the world) another world begat,
Of unknowne joy. Treason was in her thought,
And cunningly to yeeld her selfe she sought.
Seeming not woon, yet woon she was at length,   295
In such warres women use but halfe their strength.
Leander now like Theban Hercules,
Entred the orchard of th'Esperides.
Whose fruit none rightly can describe, but hee
That puls or shakes it from the golden tree: 300
And now she wisht this night were never done,
And sigh'd to thinke upon th'approching sunne,
For much it greev'd her that the bright day-light,
Should know the pleasure of this blessed night.
And then like Mars and Ericine displayd,   305

291–300 follow 278 in the editions of 1598; corrected by Singer (1821).

Both in each others armes chaind as they layd.
Againe she knew not how to frame her looke,
Or speake to him who in a moment tooke,
That which so long so charily she kept,
And faine by stealth away she would have crept,   310
And to some corner secretly have gone,
Leaving Leander in the bed alone.
But as her naked feet were whipping out,
He on the suddaine cling'd her so about,
That Meremaid-like unto the floore she slid,   315
One halfe appear'd, the other halfe was hid.
Thus neere the bed she blushing stood upright,
And from her countenance behold ye might,
A kind of twilight breake, which through the heare,
As from an orient cloud, glymse here and there.   320
And round about the chamber this false morne,
Brought foorth the day before the day was borne.
So Heroes ruddie cheeke, Hero betrayd,
And her all naked to his sight displayd.
Whence his admiring eyes more pleasure tooke,   325
Than Dis, on heapes of gold fixing his looke.
By this Apollos golden harpe began,
To sound foorth musicke to the Ocean,
Which watchfull Hesperus no sooner heard,
But he the day bright-bearing Car prepar'd.   330
And ran before, as Harbenger of light,
And with his flaring beames mockt ougly night,
Till she o'recome with anguish, shame, and rage,
Dang'd downe to hell her loathsome carriage.

316 One] And *1598*²   334 Dang'd] Hurld *1598*²

Desunt nonnulla

69

THE DIVINE POEM OF MUSÆUS: HERO AND LEANDER

Translated by George Chapman

(1616)

Goddesse, relate the witnesse-bearing-light
Of Loves, that would not beare a humane sight,
The Sea-man that transported Marriages
Shipt in the Night, his bosome plowing th'seas:
The Love joyes that in gloomy clouds did flye   5
The cleere beames of th'immortall mornings eye.
Abydus and faire Sestus, where I heare
The Night-hid Nuptials of young Hero were.
Leanders swimming to her, and a Light,
A Light that was administresse of sight   10
To cloudy Venus, and did serve t'addresse
Night-wedding Heroes Nuptiall Offices;[a]
A Light that tooke the very forme of Love:
Which had bene Justice in æthereall Jove,
When the Nocturnal duty had bene done,   15
T'advance amongst the Consort of the Sunne,
And call the Starre, that Nuptiall Loves did guide,
And to the Bridegroome gave, and grac't the Bride.[b]
Because it was Companion[c] to the Death

---

[a] γαμοστόλος signifies one, *qui Nuptias apparat vel instruit.*
[b] νυμφοστόλον ἄστρον ἐρώτων; νυμφοστόλος, *est qui sponsam sponso adducit seu consiliat.*
[c] συνέριθος, *socius in aliquo opere.*

17 And call [*sc.* it] the Starre . . .

Of Loves, whose kinde cares cost their dearest breath:[d] 20
And that Fame-freighted ship[e] from Shipwracke kept,
That such sweet Nuptials broght, they never slept.
Till Aire was with a Bitter floud inflate,
That bore their firme Loves as infixte a hate.[f]
But (Goddesse) forth; and Both, one yssue sing: 25
The Light extinct, Leander perishing.
 Two townes there were that with one Sea were wald;
Built neere, and Opposite: this, Sestus cald;
Abydus that: Then Love his Bow bent hy,
And at both Citties, let one Arrow fly. 30
That Two (a Virgin and a Youth) inflam'd:
The Youth was sweetly grac't Leander nam'd;
The Virgin, Hero. Sestus, she renownes,
Abydus he, in Birth: of both which Townes
Both were the Beuty-circled starres; and Both, 35
Grac't with like lookes, as with one Love and Troth.
 If that way lye thy course, seeke for my sake,
A Tower, that Sestian Hero once did make
Her Watch-Tower: and a Torch stood holding there,
By which, Leander his Sea-course did stere. 40
Seeke likewise, of Abydus ancient Towres,
The Roaring Sea lamenting to these houres
Leanders Love, and Death. But saie, howe came
Hee (at Abydus borne) to feele the flame
Of Heroes Love at Sestus? and to binde 45
In Chaines of equall fire, bright Heroes minde?
 The Gracefull Hero, borne of gentle blood,
Was Venus Priest; and since she understood

---

[d] ἐρωμανέων ὀδυνάων. Ἐρωμανής signifies, *Perdite amans;* and therefore I enlarge the Verball Translation.

[e] ἀγγελίην τ'ἐφύλαξεν ἀκοιμήτων &c. Ἀγγελία, besides what is translated in the Latine; *res est nuntiata; Item mandatum a Nuntio perlatum; Item Fama,* and therefore I translate it, Fame-freighted ship, because Leander calles himselfe ὁλκὸς ἔρωτος, which is translated *Navis amoris,* though ὁλκός properly signifies *sulcus,* or *Tractus navis, vel serpentis, vel ætherea sagittæ,* &c.

[f] ἐχθρὸν ἀήτην. Ἔχθος, ἔχθρα and ἐχθρός, are of one signification; or have their deduction one; and seeme to be deduc't ἀπὸ τοῦ ἔχεσθαι, I. *hærere. Ut sit odium quod animo infixum hæret.* For *odium* is by Cicero defin'de, *ira inveterata.* I have therefore translated it according to this deduction, because it expresses better: and taking the winde for the fate of the winde, which conceiv'd and appointed before, makes it as inveterate or infixt.

No Nuptiall Language: from her Parents she
Dwelt in a Towre, that over-lookt the Sea. 50
For shamefastnesse and chastity, she raign'd
Another Goddesse. Nor was ever traind
In Womens companies; nor learn'd to tred
A gracefull Dance, to which such yeares are bred.
The envious spights of Women she did fly, 55
(Women for Beauty their owne sex envy.)
All her Devotion was to Venus done,
And to his heavenly Mother her great Sonne
Would reconcile, with Sacrifices ever;
And ever trembled at his flaming Quiver. 60
Yet scap't not so his fiery shafts, her Brest:
For now, the popular Venerean Feast,
Which to Adonis, and great Cyprias State,
The Sestians yearely us'de to celebrate,
Was Come: and to that holy day came all, 65
That in the bordering Isles, the Sea did wall.
To it in Flockes they flew; from Cyprus these,
Environ'd with the rough Carpathian Seas:
These from Hæmonia; nor remain'd a Man
Of all the Townes, in th'Isles Cytherean: 70
Not one was left, that us'de to dance upon
The toppes of odorifferous Libanon:
Not one of Phrygia, not one of All
The Neighbors, seated neere the Festivall:
Nor one of opposite Abydus Shore: 75
None of all these, that Virgins favours wore
Were absent: All such, fill the flowing way,
When Fame proclaimes a solemne holy day.
Not bent so much to offer Holy Flames,
As to the Beauties of assembled Dames. 80
 The Virgin Hero enter'd th'oly place,
And gracefull beames cast round about her face,
Like to the bright Orbe of the rising Moone.
The Top-spheres of her snowy cheekes puts on
A glowing rednesse, like the two hu'd Rose, 85
Her odorous Bud beginning to disclose.
You would have saide, in all her Lineaments

69 Hæmonia, Thessaly

A Meddow full of Roses she presents.
All over her she blush't;^g which (putting on
Her white Robe, reaching to her Ankles) shone,   90
(While she in passing, did her feete dispose)
As she had wholly bene a mooving Rose.
Graces, in Numbers, from her parts did flow:
The Ancients therefore (since they did not know
Heroes unbounded Beauties) falsely fain'd   95
Onely three Graces; for when Hero strain'd
Into a smile her Priestly Modestie,
A hundred Graces grew from either eye.
A fit one, sure the Cyprian Goddesse found
To be her Ministresse; and so highly crown'd   100
With worth, her Grace was, past all other Dames,
That, of a Priest made to the Queene of Flames,
A New Queene of them she in all eyes shin'de:
And did so undermine each tender minde
Of all the yong-men: that there was not One   105
But wish't faire Hero wer his wife, or None.
Nor could she stirre about the wel-built Phane, •
This way, or that; but every way shee wan
A following minde in all Men: which their eyes
Lighted with all their inmost Faculties   110
Cleerely confirm'd: And One (admiring) said:
All Sparta I have travail'd, and survai'd
The Citty Lacedemon; where we heare

^g χροιὴν γὰρ μελέων ἐρυθαίνετο. *Colore enim membrorum rubebat.* A most
excellent Hyperbole, being to be understood, she blusht al over her. Or, then
followes another elegancie, as strange & hard to conceive. The mere verball
translation of the Latine, being in the sence either imperfect, or utterly in-
elegant, which I must yet leave to your judgement, for your owne satisfaction.
The words are

——————————— νισσομένης δὲ
καὶ ῥόδα λευκοχίτωνος ὑπὸ σφυρὰ λάμπετο κούρης

——————————— *Euntis vero*
Etiam Rosæ candidam (indutæ) tunicam sub talis
splendebant puellæ.

To understand which, that her white weede was al underlin'd with Roses, &
that they shin'd out of it as shee went, is passing poore and absurd: and as
grosse to have her stuck all over with Roses. And therefore to make the sence
answerable in heighth and elegancy to the former, she seem'd (blushing all over
her White Robe, even below her Ankles, as she went) a moving Rose, as having
the blush of many Roses about her.

73

All Beauties Labors, and contentions were;
A woman yet, so wise, and delicate   115
I never saw. It may be, Venus gate
One of the yonger Graces, to supply
The place of Priest-hood to her Deity.
Even tyr'de I am with sight, yet doth not finde
A satisfaction by my sight, my Minde.   120
O could I once ascend sweete Heroes bed,
Let me be straight found in her bosome dead:
I would not wish to be in heaven a God,
Were Hero heere my wife. But, if forbod
To lay prophane hands on thy holye Priest,   125
O Venus, with another such assist
My Nuptial Longings. Thus pray'd all that spake;
The rest their wounds hid, and in Frenzies brake.
Her Beauties Fire, being so supprest, so rag'd.
But thou, Leander, more then all engag'd,   130
Wouldst not, when thou hadst view'd th'amasing Maide,
Waste with close stings, and seeke no open aide;
But, with the flaming Arrowes of her eyes
Wounded unwares, thou wouldst in sacrifice
Vent th'inflammation thy burnt blood did prove,   135
Or Live with sacred Medicine of her Love.
    But now the Love-brand in his eie-beames burn'd,
And with th'unconquer'd fire, his heart was turn'd
Into a Coale: together wrought the Flame;
The vertuous beauty of a spotlesse Dame,   140
Sharper to Men is, then the swiftest Shaft.
His Eye the way by which his Heart is caught:
And from the stroke his eye sustaines, the wounde
Open's within, and doth his Intrailes sounde.
Amaze then tooke him, Impudence, and Shame   145
Made Earthquakes in him, with their Frost and Flame:
His Heart betwixt them tost, till Reverence
Tooke all these Prisoners in him: and from thence
Her matchless beauty, with astonishment
Increast his bands: til Aguish Love, that lent   150
Shame, and Observance, Licenc'st their remove;
And wisely liking Impudence in Love:
Silent he went, and stood against the Maide,

74

And in side glances faintly he convaide
His crafty eyes about her; with dumbe showes   155
Tempting her minde to Error. And now growes
She to conceive his subtle flame and joy'd
Since he was gracefull. Then herselfe imploy'd
Her womanish cunning, turning from him quite
Her Lovely Count'nance; giving yet some Light   160
Even by her darke signes, of her kindling fire;
With up and down-lookes, whetting his desire.
He joy'd at heart to see Loves sence in her,
And no contempt of what he did prefer.
And while he wish't unseene to urge the rest,   165
The day shrunke downe her beames to lowest West
And East. The Even-starre tooke vantage of her shade;[h]
Then boldly he, his kinde approches made:
And as he saw the Russet clouds encrease,
He strain'd her Rosie hand, and held his peace,   170
But sigh'd, as Silence had his bosom broke;
When She, as silent, put on Angers cloake,
And drew her hand backe. He descerning well
Her would, and would not:[i] to her boldlier fell:
And her elaborate Robe, with much cost wrought,   175
About her waste embracing: On he brought
His Love to th'in-parts of the reverend Phane:
She, (as her Love-sparkes more and more did wane)
Went slowly on, and with a womans words
Threatning Leander, thus his boldnesse bords: 180
    Why Stranger, Are you mad? Ill-fated Man,[j]
Why hale you thus, a Virgin Sestian?
Keepe on your way: Let go, Feare to offend

---

[h] ἀνέφαινε βαθύσκιος Ἕσπερος ἀστήρ. *Apparuit umbrosa Hesperus stella. E regione*
is before, which I English, & East. Th' Even starre tooke vantage of her shade,
viz: of the Evening shade, which is the cause that Starres appeare.

[i] χαλίφρονα νεύματα κούρης *instabiles nutus puellæ*, I English, her would, and
would not. χαλίφρων, ὁ χάλις τὰς φρένας, signifying, *Cui mens laxata est & enerva*:
and of extremity therein, *Amens, demens.* Χαλιφρονέω, *sum* χαλίφρων.

[j] *Demens sum,* she calls him δύσμορε, which signifies *cui difficile fatum obtingit,*
according to which I English it; *infelix* (being the worde in the Latine) not
expressing so particularly, because the word unhappie in our Language hath
divers Understandings; as waggish or subtle, &c. And the other well expressing
an ill abodement in Hero, of his ill or hard fate: imagining straight, the strange
& sodaine alteration in her, to be fatall.

The Noblesse of my birth-rights either Friend;
It ill become's you to solicite thus   185
The Priest of Venus; hopelesse, dangerous
The bar'd-up way is to a Virgins bed.ᵏ
Thus, for the Maiden forme, she menaced.
But he well knew that when these Female mines¹
Breake out in fury, they are certaine signes   190
Of their perswasions. Womens threats once showne,
Shewes in it onely all you wish your Owne.
And therefore of the rubi-coloured Maide,
The odorous Necke he with a kisse assaid,
And stricken with the sting of Love, he prai'd: 195
Deare Venus, next to Venus you must go;
And next Minerva; trace Minerva to;
Your like, with earthly Dames no light can show:
To Joves great Daughters, I must liken you.
Blest was thy great Begetter; blest was she   200
Whose wombe did beare thee, but most blessedly
The Wombe it selfe far'd, that thy throwes did prove.
O heare my prayer: pitty the Neede of Love.
As Priest of Venus, practise Venus Rites.
Come, and instruct me in her Beds delights.   205
It fits not you, a Virgin, to vow aides
To Venus service; Venus Loves no Maides.
If Venus institutions you prefer,
And faithfull Ceremonies vow to her,
Nuptials and Beds they be. If her Love bindes,   210
Love loves sweet Laws, that soften humane mindes.
Make me your servant: Husband, if you pleas'd;
Whom Cupid with his burning shafts hath seis'd,
And hunted to you; as swift Hermes drave

ᵏ λέκτρον ἀμήχανον; παρθενικῆς going before, it is Latin'd, *Virginis ad Lectum difficile est ire*. But ἀμήχανος signifies, *nullis machinis expugnabilis*: The way unto a Virgins bedde is utterly bar'd.

¹ κυπριδίων οάρων αὐτάγγελοί εἰσιν ἀπειλαί. *Venerearum consuetudinum per se nuntiæ sunt minæ*. Exceeding elegant. Αὐτάγγελος signifying, *qui sibi nuntius est, id est, qui sine aliorum opera sua ipse nuntiat*, According to which I have English't it. Ὄαρος, *Lusus veneri*. Ἀπειλαί also, which signifies *minæ*, having a reciprocall signification in our tongue, beeing Englisht Mines: Mines, as it is privileg'd amongest us being English, signifying Mines made under the earth. I have past it with that word, being fitte for this place in that understanding.

189 *mines*] mindes

With his Gold Rod, Joves bold sonne to be slave 215
To Lydia's soveraigne virgin; but for me,
Venus insulting, forc't my feete to thee.
I was not guided by wise Mercury.
Virgin, you know, when Atalanta fled
Out of Arcadia, kinde Melanions bed, 220
(Affecting Virgine life), your Angry Queene,
Whom first she us'd with a malignant spleene
At last possest him of her compleat heart.
And you (deere Love) because I would avert
Your Goddesse anger; I would faine perswade. 225
With these Love-luring words,[m] conform'd he made
The Maid Recusant to his bloods desire;
And set her soft minde on an erring fire.
Dumbe she was strooke: and downe to earth she threw
Her Rosie eyes, hid in Vermillion hew, 230
Made red with shame. Oft with her foote she rac't
Earths upper part; and oft (as quite ungrac't)
About her shoulders gathered up her weede.
All these fore-tokens are that Men shall speede.
Of a perswaded Virgin to her Bed, 235
Promise is most given, when the least is said.
And now she tooke in, Loves sweet bitter sting:
Burn'd in a fire, that cool'd her surfetting.
Her Beauties likewise, strooke her Friend amaz'd:
For while her eyes fix't on the Pavement gaz'd, 240
Love on Leanders lookes shew'd Fury seas'd.
Never enough his greedy eyes were pleas'd
To view the faire glosse of her tender Necke.[n]
At last this sweet voice past, and out did breake
A ruddy moisture from her bashfull eyes: 245
Stranger, perhaps thy words might exercise
Motion in Flints, as well as my soft brest.
Who taught thee words, that erre from East to West

[m] ἐρωτοτόκοισι μύθοις. Ἐρωτοτόκος σάρξ, *Corpus amorem pariens, & alliciens,*
according to which I have turned it.
[n] ἀπαλόχροον αὐχένα κούρης. Ἀπαλόχροος signifies, *qui tenera & delicata est cute;*
tenerum therefore not enough expressing, I have enlarg'd the expression as in
his place.

215–216 Hercules enslaved to Omphale
220 Melanion, Hippomenes (Apollodorus iii.9.)

In their wilde liberty?° O woe is me:
To this my Native soile, who guided thee?   250
All thou hast saide is vaine; for how canst thou
(Not to be trusted: One I do not know)
Hope to excite in me, a mixed Love?
T'is cleere, that Law by no meanes will approve
Nuptials with us; for thou canst never gaine   255
My Parents graces. If thou wouldst remaine
Close on my shore, as outcast from thine owne;
Venus will be in darkest corners knowne.
Mans tongue is friend to scandall; loose acts done
In surest secret: in the open Sunne   260
And every Market place, will burne thine eares.
But say, what name sustainst thou? What soile beares
Name of thy Countrey? Mine, I cannot hide;
My farre spred name is Hero: I abide
Hous'd in an all-seene Towre, whose tops touch heaven,ᴾ 265
Built on a steepe shore, that to Sea is driven
Before the City Sestus, one sole Maide
Attending; and this irkesome life is laide
By my austere Friends wils, on one so yong;
No like-year'd Virgins nere; no youthfull throng   270
To meete in some delights, Dances, or so:
But Day and Night, the windy Sea doth throw
Wilde murmuring cuffes about our deafned eares.
This sayd: her white Robe hid her cheekes like spheres.
And then (with shame-affected, since she us'de   275
Words that desir'd youths, and her Friends accus'd)
She blam'd her selfe for them, and them for her.
Meane space, Leander felt Loves Arrow erre

° πολυπλανέων ἐπέων is turn'd, *Variorum verborum*. Πολυπλανής, signifying
multivagus, erroneus, or *errorum plenus*, intending that sort of error that is in the
Planets; of whose wandering, they are called πλάνητες ἀστέρες, *sidera errantia*.
So that Hero tax't him for so bolde a liberty in wordes, as er'd *toto cœlo*, from
what was fit, or becam the youth of one so gracefull: which made her breake into
the admyring exclamation; that one so yong and gracious, shold put on so
experiencst and licentious a boldnesse, as in that holy temple encorag'd him to
make Love to her.

ᴾ δόμος οὐρανομήκης, it is Translated *Domo altissima*; but because it is a com-
pound, and hath a grace superiour to the other, in his more neere and verball
conversion, οὐρανομήκης signifying, *Cœlum sua proceritate tangens*, I have so
render'd it.

Through all his thoughts; devising how he might
Encounter Love, that dar'd him so to fight.   280
Minde-changing Love wounds men, and cures againe:
Those Mortals, over whom he list's to raigne,
Th'All-Tamer stoopes to, in advising how
They may with some ease beare the yoke, his Bow.
So, our Leander, whom he hurt, he heal'd: 285
Who, having long his hidden fire conceal'd,
And vex't with thoughts he thirsted to impart,
His stay he quitted, with this quickest Art:
Virgin, for thy Love, I will swim a wave
That Ships denies: and though with fire it rave.   290
In way to thy Bed, all the Seas in one
I would despise: the Hellespont were none.
All Nights to swim to one sweet bedde with thee,�q
Were nothing; if when Love had landed me,
All hid in weeds, and in Veneran fome,   295
I brought (withall) bright Heroes husband home.
Not farre from hence, and just against thy Towne
Abydus stands, that my Birth cal's mine owne.
Hold but a Torch then in thy heaven-high Towre:ʳ
(Which I beholding, to that starry Powre   300
May plough the darke Seas, as the Ship of Love.)
I will not care to see Boötes move
Downe to the Sea: Nor sharpe Orion traile
His never-wet Carre; but arrive my saile
Against my Country, at thy pleasing shore.   305
But (deere) take heed, that no ungentle blo're
Thy Torch extinguish, bearing all the Light
By which my life sailes, least I lose thee quite.
Would'st thou my Name know (as thou dost my house)
It is Leander, lovely Hero's Spouse.   310
Thus this kinde couple, their close Marriage made,
And friendship ever to be held in shade,

�q ὑγρὸς ἀκοίτης translated *madidus Maritus*, when as ἀκοίτης is taken heere for
ὁμοκοίτης, signifying *unum & idem cubile habens*, which is more particular and
true.

ʳ ἠλιβάτου [σέο πύργου] φαεσφόρον [*sc.* λύχνον], &c. Ἠλίβατος signifies, Latin
altus aut profundus ut ab eius accessu aberres, intending the Tower uppon which
Hero stoode.

306 blo're, blast

(Onely by witnesse of one Nuptiall Light.)
Both vow'd; agreed that Hero every Night,
Should hold her Torch out: every Night, her Love   315
The tedious passage of the Sea should prove.
The whole Even of the watchful Nuptials spent,
Against their wils, the sterne powre of constraint
Enforc't their parting. Hero to her Towre;
Leander, (minding his returning howre)   320
Tooke of the Turret Markes, for feare he fail'd,
And to well-founded broad Abydus sail'd.
All Night Both thirsted for the secret strife
Of each yong-married lovely Man and Wife.
And all day after, No desire shot home,   325
But that the Chamber-decking Night were come.
And now, Nights sooty clowdes clap't all saile on,
Fraught all with sleepe: yet tooke Leander none,
But on th'oppos'd shore of the noise-full Seas,
The Messenger of glittering Marriages   330
Look't wishly for: Or rather long'd to see,
The witnesse of their Light to Misery,
Farre off discover'd in their Covert bed.
When Hero saw the blackest Curtaine spred
That vail'd the darke night: her bright Torch she shew'd. 335
Whose Light no sooner th'eager Lover view'd,
But Love his blood set on as bright a Fire:
Together burn'd the Torch, and his Desire.
But hearing of the Sea the horrid rore,
With which the tender ayre the mad waves tore: 340
At first he trembled: but at last he rear'd
High as the storme his spirit, and thus chear'd,
(Using these words to it) his resolute minde:
Love dreadfull is; the Sea with nought inclinde:
But Sea is Water; outward all his yre,   345
When Love lights his feare with an inward fire.
Take fire (my heart), feare nought that flits and raves:
Be Love himselfe to me, despise these waves.
Art thou to know, that Venus birth was here?
Commands the Sea, and all that greeves us there?   350
This sayd, his faire Limbes of his weede he strip't:
Which at his head with both hands bound, he shipt.

Lept from the Shore, and cast into the Sea
His lovely body: thrusting all his way
Up to the Torch, that still he thought did call: 355
He Ores, he Sterer, he the Ship, and All.
Hero advanc't upon a Towre so hye,
As soone would lose on it, the fixed'st eye.
And like her Goddesse star, with her Light shining:
The windes, that alwayes (as at her repining),   360
Would blast her pleasures, with her vaile she che'kt,
And from their envies did her Torch protect.
And this she never left, till she had brought
Leander, to the Havenfull shore he sought.
Then downe she ran, and up she lighted then   365
To her Towres top, the weariest of Men.
First, at the Gates, (without a syllable us'd)
She hug'd her panting husband, all diffus'd
With fomy drops, still stilling from his haire:
Then brought she him in to the inmost Faire   370
Of all, her Virgin Chamber; that, (at best)
Was with her beauties, ten times better drest.
His body then she clens'd: his body oyl'd
With Rosie Odors: and his bosome (soyl'd
With the unsavoury Sea) she render'd sweet.   375
Then, in the high-made bed, (even panting yet)
Her selfe she powr'd about her husbands brest,
And these words utter'd: With too much unrest,
O Husband, you have bought this little peace.
Husband, No other man hath paid th'encrease   380
Of that huge sum of paines you tooke for me.
And yet I know, it is enough for thee
To suffer for my Love, the fishy savours
The working Sea breaths. Come, lay all thy labors
On my all-thankfull bosome. All this said,   385
He straight ungirdled her; and Both parts paid
To Venus, what her gentle statutes bound.
Here Weddings were, but not a Musicall sound,
Here bed-rites offer'd, but no hymnes gave praise.
Nor Poet, sacred wedlocks worth did raise.   390
No Torches gilt the honor'd Nuptiall bed.

356 Cf. *Heroides XVIII*, 148: idem navigium, navita, vector ero!

Nor any youths much-moving dances led.
No Father, nor no reverend Mother sung
Hymen, O Hymen, blessing Loves so yong.
But when the consummating Howres had croun'd   395
The doun-right Nuptials, a calme bed was found.
Silence the Roome fixt; Darknesse deck't the Bride,
But Hymnes, and such Rites, farre were laide aside.
Night was sole Gracer of this Nuptiall house:
Cheerefull Aurora never saw the Spouse   400
In any Beds that were too broadly known,
Away he fled still, to his Region,
And breath'd insatiate of the absent Sun.
    Hero kept all this from her parents still;
Her Priestly weede was large, and would not fill: 405
A Maid by Day she was, a Wife by Night,
Which both so lov'd, they wisht it never light.
And thus (Both) hiding the strong Need of Love:
In Venus secret sphere, rejoyc't to move.
But soone their joy di'de; and that still-tost state 410
Of their stolne Nuptials, drew but little date.
For when the frosty winter kept his Justs,
Rousing together all the horrid Gusts,
That from the ever-whirling pits arise,
And those weake deepes, that drive up to the skies,   415
Against the drench't foundations, making knocke
Their curled forheads, then with many a shocke
The windes and seas met; made the stormes aloud
Beate all the rough Sea with a Pitchy cloud.
And then the blacke Barke, buffeted with gales,   420
Earth checkes so rudely, that in Two it fals,
The Seaman flying Winters faithlesse Sea.
Yet (brave Leander) all this bent at thee,
Could not compell in thee one fit of feare:
But when the cruell faithlesse Messenger   425
(The Towre) appear'd, and shew'd th'accustom'd light,
It stung thee on, secure of all the spight
The raging Sea spit. But since Winter came,
Unhappy Hero should have cool'd her flame,
And lye without Leander; no more lighting   430
Her short-liv'd Bed-starre; but strange fate exciting

As well as Love, and both their pow'rs combin'd
Enticing her; in her hand, never shin'd
The fatall Love Torch (but this one houre) more.
Night came: And now, the Sea against the shore   435
Muster'd her winds up: from whose Wintry jawes
They belch't their rude breaths out, in bitterest flawes.
In midst of which, Leander, with the Pride
Of his deere hope, to boord his matchlesse Bride:
Up, on the rough backe of the high sea, leapes: 440
And then waves thrust up waves; the watry heapes
Tumbled together: Sea and sky were mixt,
The fighting windes, the frame of earth unfixt.
Zephire and Eurus flew in eithers face;
Notus and Boreas wrastler-like imbrace,   445
And tosse each other with their bristled backes.
Inevitable were the horrid crackes
The shaken Sea gave: Ruthfull were the wrackes
Leander suffer'd, in the savage gale
Th'inexorable whirlepits did exhale.   450
Often he pray'd to Venus, borne of Seas:
Neptune their King: and Boreas, that t'would please
His Godhead, for the Nimph Attheas sake,
Not to forget the like stelth he did make
For her deare Love, touch't then, with his sad state;   455
But none would helpe him: Love compels not Fate.
Every way tost with waves, and Aires rude breath
Justling together, he was crush't to death.
No more his youthfull force his feete commands,
Unmov'd lay now his late all-moving hands.   460
His throat was turn'd free channel to the flood,
And drinke went downe that did him farre from good.
No more the false Light, for the curst winde burn'd
That of Leander ever-to-be-mourn'd,
Blew out the Love, and soule; when Hero still   465
Had watchfull eyes, and a most constant will
To guide the voyage: and the morning shin'd,
Yet not by her Light, she her Love could finde.
She stood distract with miserable woes;
And round about the Seas broad shoulders, throwes   470

453 Attheas for 'Aτθίδos . . . νύμφης, i.e., Orithyia

83

Her eye, to second the extinguisht Light:
And tried if any way her husbands sight
Erring in any part, she could descry.
When, at her Turrets foote, she saw him lye,
Mangled with Rockes, and all embru'd; she tore   475
About her brest, the curious weede she wore.
And with a shrieke, from off her Turrets height,
Cast her faire body headlong, that fell right
On her dead husband: spent with him her breath,
And each won other, in the worst of death.   480

HERO AND LEANDER
Completed by George Chapman
(1598)

THE ARGUMENT OF THE THIRD SESTYAD

Leander to the envious light
Resignes his night-sports with the night,
And swims the Hellespont againe;
Thesme the Deitie soveraigne
Of Customes and religious rites   5
Appeares, improving his delites
Since Nuptiall honors he neglected;
Which straight he vowes shall be effected.
Faire Hero left Devirginate,
Waies, and with furie wailes her state: 10
But with her love and womans wit
She argues, and approveth it.

New light gives new directions, Fortunes new
To fashion our indevours that ensue,
More harsh (at lest more hard) more grave and hie
Our subject runs, and our sterne Muse must flie.
Loves edge is taken off, and that light flame,   5
Those thoughts, joyes, longings, that before became
High unexperienst blood, and maids sharpe plights
Must now grow staid, and censure the delights,
That being enjoyd aske judgement; now we praise,
As having parted: Evenings crowne the daies.   10
    And now ye wanton loves, and yong desires,
Pied vanitie, the mint of strange Attires;
Ye lisping Flatteries, and obsequious Glances,

Relentfull Musicks, and attractive Dances,
And you detested Charmes constraining love,   15
Shun loves stolne sports by that these Lovers prove.
    By this the Soveraigne of Heavens golden fires,
And yong Leander, Lord of his desires,
Together from their lovers armes arose:
Leander into Hellespontus throwes   20
His Hero-handled bodie, whose delight
Made him disdaine each other Epethite.
And as amidst the enamourd waves he swims,
The God of gold of purpose guilt his lims,[a]
That this word guilt, including double sence,   25
The double guilt of his *Incontinence*,
Might be exprest, that had no stay t'employ
The treasure which the Love-god let him joy
In his deare Hero, with such sacred thrift,
As had beseemd so sanctified a gift: 30
But like a greedie vulgar Prodigall
Would on the stock dispend, and rudely fall
Before his time, to that unblessed blessing,
Which for lusts plague doth perish with possessing.
    Joy graven in sence, like snow in water wasts;   35
    Without preserve of vertue nothing lasts.
What man is he that with a welthie eie
Enjoyes a beautie richer than the skie,
Through whose white skin, softer then soundest sleep,
With damaske eyes, the rubie blood doth peep,   40
And runs in branches through her azure vaines,
Whose mixture and first fire, his love attaines;
Whose both hands limit both Loves deities,
And sweeten humane thoughts like Paradise;
Whose disposition silken is and kinde,   45
Directed with an earth-exempted minde;
Who thinks not heaven with such a love is given?
And who like earth would spend that dower of heaven,
With ranke desire to joy it all at first?
What simply kils our hunger, quencheth thirst,   50
Clothes but our nakednes, and makes us live;
Praise doth not any of her favours give:
    [a] He cals Phœbus the God of Gold, since the vertue of his beams creates it.

But what doth plentifully minister
Beautious apparell and delicious cheere,
So orderd that it still excites desire,   55
And still gives pleasure freenes to aspire
The palme of *Bountie*, ever moyst preserving:
To loves sweet life this is the courtly carving.
Thus *Time*, and all-states-ordering *Ceremonie*
Had banisht all offence: *Times* golden Thie   60
Upholds the flowrie bodie of the earth
In sacred harmonie, and every birth
Of men, and actions makes legitimate,
Being usde aright; *The use of time is Fate.*
   Yet did the gentle flood transfer once more   65
This prize of Love home to his fathers shore;
Where he unlades himselfe of that false welth
That makes few rich, treasures composde by stelth;
And to his sister kinde Hermione,
(Who on the shore kneeld, praying to the sea   70
For his returne) he all Loves goods did show
In Hero seasde for him, in him for Hero.
   His most kinde sister all his secrets knew,
And to her singing like a shower he flew,
Sprinkling the earth, that to their tombs tooke in   75
Streames dead for love to leave his ivorie skin,
Which yet a snowie fome did leave above,
As soule to the dead water that did love;
And from thence did the first white Roses spring,
(For love is sweet and faire in every thing)   80
And all the sweetned shore as he did goe,
Was crownd with odrous roses white as snow.
Love-blest Leander was with love so filled,
That love to all that toucht him he instilled.
And as the colours of all things we see,   85
To our sights powers communicated bee:
So to all objects that in compasse came
Of any sence he had, his sences flame
Flowd from his parts with force so virtuall,
It fir'd with sence things meere insensuall.   90
    Now (with warme baths and odours comforted)

90 meere]; (weere, T. Brooke)

When he lay downe he kindly kist his bed,
As consecrating it to Heros right,
And vowd thereafter that what ever sight
Put him in minde of Hero, or her blisse,   95
Should be her Altar to prefer a kisse.
    Then laid he forth his late inriched armes,
In whose white circle Love writ all his charmes,
And made his characters sweet Heros lims,
When on his breasts warme sea she sideling swims.   100
And as those armes (held up in circle) met,
He said: See sister Heros Carquenet,
Which she had rather weare about her neck,
Then all the jewels that doth Juno deck.
    But as he shooke with passionate desire,   105
To put in flame his other secret fire,
A musick so divine did pierce his eare,
As never yet his ravisht sence did heare:
When suddenly a light of twentie hews
Brake through the roofe, and like the Rainbow views   110
Amazd Leander; in whose beames came downe
The Goddesse *Ceremonie*, with a Crowne
Of all the stars, and heaven with her descended.
Her flaming haire to her bright feete extended,
By which hung all the bench of Deities;   115
And in a chaine, compact of eares and eies,
She led Religion; all her bodie was
Cleere and transparent as the purest glasse:
For she was all presented to the sence;
Devotion, Order, State, and Reverence   120
Her shadowes were; Societie, Memorie;
All which her sight made live, her absence die.
A rich disparent Pentackle she weares,
Drawne full of circles and strange characters:
Her face was changeable to everie eie;   125
One way lookt ill, another graciouslie;
Which while men viewd, they cheerfull were & holy:
But looking off, vicious and melancholy:
The snakie paths to each observed law
Did *Policie* in her broad bosome draw: 130
One hand a Mathematique Christall swayes,

Which gathering in one line a thousand rayes
From her bright eyes, *Confusion* burnes to death,
And all estates of men distinguisheth.
By it *Morallitie* and *Comelinesse*   135
Themselves in all their sightly figures dresse.
Her other hand a lawrell rod applies,
To beate back *Barbarisme*, and *Avarice*,
That followd, eating earth and excrement
And humane lims; and would make proud ascent   140
To seates of Gods, were *Ceremonie* slaine;
The *Howrs* and *Graces* bore her glorious traine,
And all the sweetes of our societie
Were Spherde, and treasurde in her bountious eie.
Thus she appeard, and sharply did reprove   145
Leanders bluntnes in his violent love;
Tolde him how poore was substance without rites,
Like bils unsignd, desires without delites;
Like meates unseasond; like ranke corne that growes
On Cottages, that none or reapes or sowes: 150
Not being with civill forms confirm'd and bounded,
For humane dignities and comforts founded:
But loose and secret all their glories hide,
Feare fils the chamber, darknes decks the Bride.
    She vanisht, leaving pierst Leanders hart   155
With sence of his unceremonious part,
In which with plaine neglect of Nuptiall rites,
He close and flatly fell to his delites:
And instantly he vowd to celebrate
All rites pertaining to his maried state.   160
So up he gets and to his father goes,
To whose glad eares he doth his vowes disclose:
The Nuptials are resolv'd with utmost powre,
And he at night would swim to Heros towre.
From whence he ment to Sestus forked Bay   165
To bring her covertly, where ships must stay,
Sent by his father throughly rigd and mand,
To waft her safely to Abydus Strand.
There leave we him, and with fresh wing pursue
Astonisht Hero, whose most wished view   170

167 his] (L. C. Martin): her *1598²*

I thus long have forborne, because I left her
So out of countnance, and her spirits bereft her.
To looke of one abasht is impudence,
When of sleight faults he hath too deepe a sence.
Her blushing het her chamber: she lookt out,   175
And all the ayre she purpled round about,
And after it a foule black day befell,
Which ever since a red morne doth foretell,
And still renewes our woes for Heros wo,
And foule it prov'd, because it figur'd so   180
The next nights horror, which prepare to heare;
I faile if it prophane your daintiest eare.
 Then thou most strangely-intellectuall fire,
That proper to my soule hast power t'inspire
Her burning faculties, and with the wings   185
Of thy unspheared flame visitst the springs
Of spirits immortall; Now (as swift as Time
Doth follow Motion) finde th'eternall Clime
Of his free soule, whose living subject stood
Up to the chin in the Pyerean flood,   190
And drunke to me halfe this Musean storie,
Inscribing it to deathles Memorie:
Confer with it, and make my pledge as deepe,
That neithers draught be consecrate to sleepe.
Tell it how much his late desires I tender,   195
(If yet it know not) and to light surrender
My soules darke ofspring, willing it should die
To loves, to passions, and societie.
 Sweet Hero left upon her bed alone,
Her maidenhead, her vowes, Leander gone,   200
And nothing with her but a violent crew
Of new come thoughts that yet she never knew,
Even to her selfe a stranger; was much like
Th'Iberian citie that wars hand did strike
By English force in princely Essex guide,   205
When peace assur'd her towres had fortifide;
And golden-fingred India had bestowd
Such wealth on her, that strength and Empire flowd
Into her Turrets; and her virgin waste

 183 thou] (T. Brooke); how *1598*[2]

The wealthie girdle of the Sea embraste: 210
Till our Leander that made Mars his Cupid,
For soft love-sutes, with iron thunders chid:
Swum to her Towers, dissolv'd her virgin zone;
Lead in his power, and made Confusion
Run through her streets amazd, that she supposde   215
She had not been in her owne walls inclosde,
But rapt by wonder to some forraine state,
Seeing all her issue so disconsolate:
And all her peacefull mansions possest
With wars just spoyle, and many a forraine guest   220
From every corner driving an enjoyer,
Supplying it with power of a destroyer.
So far'd fayre Hero in th'expugned fort
Of her chast bosome, and of every sort
Strange thoughts possest her, ransacking her brest   225
For that that was not there, her wonted rest.
She was a mother straight and bore with paine
Thoughts that spake straight and wisht their mother slaine;
She hates their lives, & they their own & hers:
Such strife still growes where sin the race prefers.   230
Love is a golden bubble full of dreames,
That waking breakes, and fils us with extreames.
She mus'd how she could looke upon her Sire,
And not shew that without, that was intire.
For as a glasse is an inanimate eie,   235
And outward formes imbraceth inwardlie:
So is the eye an animate glasse that showes
In-formes without us. And as Phœbus throwes
His beames abroad, though he in clowdes be closde,
Still glancing by them till he finde opposde   240
A loose and rorid vapour that is fit
T'event his searching beames, and useth it
To forme a tender twentie-coloured eie,
Cast in a circle round about the skie.
So when our firie soule, our bodies starre,   245
(That ever is in motion circulare)
Conceives a forme; in seeking to display it
Through all our clowdie parts, it doth convey it

241 rorid, dewy

Forth at the eye, as the most pregnant place,
And that reflects it round about the face.   250
And this event uncourtly Hero thought
Her inward guilt would in her lookes have wrought:
For yet the worlds stale cunning she resisted
To beare foule thoughts, yet forge what lookes she listed,
And held it for a very sillie sleight,   255
To make a perfect mettall counterfeit,
Glad to disclaime her selfe, proud of an Art,
That makes the face a Pandar to the hart.
Those be the painted Moones, whose lights prophane
Beauties true Heaven, at full still in their wane.   260
Those be the Lapwing faces that still crie,
Here tis, when that they vow is nothing nie.
Base fooles, when every moorish fowle can teach
That which men thinke the height of humane reach.
But custome that the Apoplexie is   265
Of beddred nature and lives led amis,
And takes away all feeling of offence,
Yet brazde not Heros brow with impudence;
And this she thought most hard to bring to pas,
To seeme in countnance other then she was,   270
As if she had two soules; one for the face,
One for the hart; and that they shifted place
As either list to utter, or conceale
What they conceiv'd: or as one soule did deale
With both affayres at once, keeps and ejects   275
Both at an instant contrarie effects:
Retention and ejection in her powrs
Being acts alike: for this one vice of ours,
That forms the thought, and swaies the countenance,
Rules both our motion and our utterance.   280
    These and more grave conceits toyld Heros spirits:
For though the light of her discoursive wits
Perhaps might finde some little hole to pas
Through all these worldly cinctures; yet (alas)
There was a heavenly flame incompast her;   285
Her Goddesse, in whose Phane she did prefer
Her virgin vowes; from whose impulsive sight
She knew the black shield of the darkest night

Could not defend her, nor wits subtilst art:
This was the point pierst Hero to the hart.   290
Who heavie to the death, with a deep sigh
And hand that languisht, tooke a robe was nigh,
Exceeding large, and of black Cypres made,
In which she sate, hid from the day in shade,
Even over head and face downe to her feete;   295
Her left hand made it at her bosome meete;
Her right hand leand on her hart-bowing knee,
Wrapt in unshapefull foulds twas death to see:
Her knee stay'd that, and that her falling face,
Each limme helpt other to put on disgrace.   300
No forme was seene, where forme held all her sight:
But like an Embrion that saw ne'er light:
Or like a scorched statue made a cole
With three-wingd lightning: or a wretched soule
Muffled with endles darknes, she did sit: 305
The night had never such a heavie spirit.
Yet might an imitating eye well see,
How fast her cleere teares melted on her knee
Through her black vaile, and turnd as black as it,
Mourning to be her teares: then wrought her wit   310
With her broke vow, her Goddesse wrath, her fame,
All tooles that enginous despayre could frame:
Which made her strow the floore with her torne haire,
And spread her mantle peece-meale in the aire.
Like Joves sons club, strong passion strook her downe,   315
And with a piteous shrieke inforst her swoune:
Her shrieke made with another shrieke ascend
The frighted Matron that on her did tend:
And as with her owne crie her sence was slaine,
So with the other it was calde againe.   320
She rose and to her bed made forced way,
And layd her downe even where Leander lay:
And all this while the red sea of her blood
Ebd with Leander: but now turnd the flood,
And all her fleete of sprites came swelling in   325
With childe of saile, and did hot fight begin
With those severe conceits, she too much markt,

302 ne'er] never *1598²*

93

And here Leanders beauties were imbarkt.
He came in swimming painted all with joyes,
Such as might sweeten hell: his thought destroyes   330
All her destroying thoughts: she thought she felt
His heart in hers with her contentions melt,
And chid her soule that it could so much erre,
To check the true joyes he deserv'd in her.
Her fresh heat blood cast figures in her eyes,   335
And she supposde she saw in Neptunes skyes
How her star wandred, washt in smarting brine
For her loves sake, that with immortall wine
Should be embath'd, and swim in more hearts ease,
Than there was water in the Sestian seas.   340
Then said her Cupid-prompted spirit: Shall I
Sing mones to such delightsome harmony?
Shall slick-tongde fame patch up with voyces rude,
The drunken bastard of the multitude,
(Begot when father Judgement is away,   345
And gossip-like, sayes because others say,
Takes newes as if it were too hot to eate,
And spits it slavering forth for dog-fees meate)
Make me for forging a phantastique vow,
Presume to beare what makes grave matrons bow?   350
Good vowes are never broken with good deedes,
For then good deedes were bad: vowes are but seedes,
And good deeds fruits; even those good deedes that grow
From other stocks than from th'observed vow.
That is a good deede that prevents a bad: 355
Had I not yeelded, slaine my selfe I had.
Hero Leander is, Leander Hero:
Such vertue love hath to make one of two.
If then Leander did my maydenhead git,
Leander being my selfe I still retaine it.   360
We breake chast vowes when we live loosely ever:
But bound as we are, we live loosely never.
Two constant lovers being joynd in one,
Yeelding to one another, yeeld to none.
We know not how to vow, till love unblinde us,   365
And vowes made ignorantly never binde us.
Too true it is that when t'is gone men hate

The joyes as vaine they tooke in loves estate:
But that's since they have lost the heavenly light
Should shew them way to judge of all things right.   370
When life is gone death must implant his terror,
As death is foe to life, so love to error.
Before we love how range we through this sphere,
Searching the sundrie fancies hunted here:
Now with desire of wealth transported quite   375
Beyond our free humanities delight:
Now with ambition climing falling towrs,
Whose hope to scale, our feare to fall devours:
Now rapt with pastimes, pomp, all joyes impure;
In things without us no delight is sure.   380
But love with all joyes crownd, within doth sit;
O Goddesse pitie love and pardon it.
This spake she weeping: but her Goddesse eare
Burnd with too sterne a heat, and would not heare.
Aie me, hath heavens straight fingers no more graces   385
For such as Hero, then for homeliest faces?
Yet she hopte well, and in her sweet conceit
Waying her arguments, she thought them weight:
And that the logick of Leanders beautie,
And them together would bring proofes of dutie.   390
And if her soule, that was a skilfull glance
Of Heavens great essence, found such imperance
In her loves beauties; she had confidence
Jove lov'd him too, and pardond her offence.
   Beautie in heaven and earth this grace doth win,   395
   It supples rigor, and it lessens sin.
Thus, her sharpe wit, her love, her secrecie,
Trouping together, made her wonder why
She should not leave her bed, and to the Temple?
Her health said she must live; her sex, dissemble.   400
She viewd Leanders place, and wisht he were
Turnd to his place, so his place were Leander.
Aye me (said she) that loves sweet life and sence
Should doe it harme! my love had not gone hence,
Had he been like his place. O blessed place,   405
Image of Constancie. Thus my loves grace

383 she] he *1598²*

95

Parts no where but it leaves some thing behinde
Worth observation: he renownes his kinde.
His motion is like heavens Orbiculer:
For where he once is, he is ever there.   410
This place was mine: Leander now t'is thine;
Thou being my selfe, then it is double mine:
Mine, and Leanders mine, Leanders mine.
O see what wealth it yeelds me, nay yeelds him:
For I am in it, he for me doth swim.   415
Rich, fruitfull love, that doubling selfe estates
Elixer-like contracts, though separates.
Deare place, I kisse thee, and doe welcome thee,
As from Leander ever sent to mee.

The end of the Third Sestyad

THE ARGUMENT OF THE FOURTH SESTYAD

> *Hero, in sacred habit deckt,*
> *Doth private sacrifice effect.*
> *Her Skarfs description wrought by fate,*
> *Ostents that threaten her estate.*
> *The strange, yet Phisicall events,*   5
> *Leanders counterfeit presents.*
> *In thunder Ciprides descends,*
> *Presaging both the lovers ends.*
> *Ecte the Goddesse of remorce,*
> *With vocall and articulate force*   10
> *Inspires Leucote, Venus swan,*
> *T' excuse the beautious Sestian.*
> *Venus, to wreake her rites abuses,*
> *Creates the monster Eronusis;*[a]
> *Enflaming Heros Sacrifice,*   15
> *With lightning darted from her eyes:*
> *And thereof springs the painted beast,*
> *That ever since taints every breast.*

Now from Leanders place she rose, and found
Her haire and rent robe scattred on the ground:
Which taking up, she every peece did lay

[a] Eronusis, Dissimulation.

96

Upon an Altar; where in youth of day
She usde t'exhibite private Sacrifice: 5
Those would she offer to the Deities
Of her faire Goddesse, and her powerfull son,
As relicks of her late-felt passion:
And in that holy sort she vowd to end them,
In hope her violent fancies that did rend them,   10
Would as quite fade in her loves holy fire,
As they should in the flames she ment t'inspire.
Then put she on all her religious weedes,
That deckt her in her secret sacred deedes:
A crowne of Isickles, that sunne nor fire   15
Could ever melt, and figur'd chast desire.
A golden star shinde in her naked breast,
In honour of the Queene-light of the East.
In her right hand she held a silver wand,
On whose bright top Peristera did stand,   20
Who was a Nymph, but now transformd a Dove,
And in her life was deare in Venus love:
And for her sake she ever since that time,
Chusde Doves to draw her Coach through heavens blew clime.
Her plentious haire in curled billowes swims   25
On her bright shoulder: her harmonious lims
Sustainde no more but a most subtile vaile
That hung on them, as it durst not assaile
Their different concord: for the weakest ayre
Could raise it swelling from her bewties fayre   30
Nor did it cover, but adumbrate onelie
Her most heart-piercing parts, that a blest eie
Might see (as it did shadow) fearfullie
All that the all-love-deserving Paradise:
It was as blew as the most freezing skies,   35
Neere the Seas hew, for thence her Goddesse came:
On it a skarfe she wore of wondrous frame;
In midst whereof she wrought a virgins face,
From whose each cheeke a firie blush did chace
Two crimson flames, that did two waies extend,   40
Spreading the ample skarfe to either end,
Which figur'd the division of her minde,
Whiles yet she rested bashfully inclinde,

E*   97

And stood not resolute to wed Leander.
This serv'd her white neck for a purple sphere,   45
And cast it selfe at full breadth downe her back.
There (since the first breath that begun the wrack
Of her free quiet from Leanders lips)
She wrought a Sea in one flame full of ships:
But that one ship where all her wealth did passe   50
(Like simple marchants goods) Leander was:
For in that Sea she naked figured him;
Her diving needle taught him how to swim,
And to each thred did such resemblance give,
For joy to be so like him, it did live.   55
    Things senceles live by art, and rationall die,
    By rude contempt of art and industrie.
Scarce could she work but in her strength of thought,
She feard she prickt Leander as she wrought:
And oft would shrieke so, that her Guardian frighted,   60
Would staring haste, as with some mischiefe cited.
    They double life that dead things griefs sustayne:
    They kill that feele not their friends living payne.
Sometimes she feard he sought her infamie,
And then as she was working of his eie,   65
She thought to pricke it out to quench her ill:
But as she prickt, it grew more perfect still.
    Trifling attempts no serious acts advance;
    The fire of love is blowne by dalliance.
In working his fayre neck she did so grace it,   70
She still was working her owne armes t'imbrace it:
That, and his shoulders, and his hands were seene
Above the streame, and with a pure Sea greene
She did so queintly shadow every lim,
All might be seene beneath the waves to swim.   75
    In this conceited skarfe she wrought beside
A Moone in change, and shooting stars did glide
In number after her with bloodie beames,
Which figur'd her affects in their extreames,
Pursuing Nature in her Cynthian bodie,   80
And did her thoughts running on change implie:
For maids take more delights when they prepare
And thinke of wives states, than when wives they are.

Beneath all these she wrought a Fisherman,
Drawing his nets from forth that Ocean;   85
Who drew so hard ye might discover well,
The toughned sinewes in his neck did swell:
His inward straines drave out his blood-shot eyes,
And springs of sweat did in his forehead rise:
Yet was of nought but of a Serpent sped,   90
That in his bosome flew and stung him dead.
And this by fate into her minde was sent,
Not wrought by meere instinct of her intent.
At the skarfs other end her hand did frame,
Neere the forkt point of the devided flame,   95
A countrie virgin keeping of a Vine,
Who did of hollow bulrushes combine
Snares for the stubble-loving Grashopper,
And by her lay her skrip that nourisht her.
Within a myrtle shade she sate and sung,   100
And tufts of waving reedes about her sprung:
Where lurkt two Foxes, that while she applide
Her trifling snares, their theeveries did devide:
One to the vine, another to her skrip,
That she did negligently overslip: 105
By which her fruitfull vine and holesome fare
She suffred spoyld to make a childish snare.
These omenous fancies did her soule expresse,
And every finger made a Prophetesse,
To shew what death was hid in loves disguise,   110
And make her judgement conquer destinies.
O what sweet formes fayre Ladies soules doe shrowd,
Were they made seene & forced through their blood,
If through their beauties like rich work through lawn,
They would set forth their minds with vertues drawn,   115
In letting graces from their fingers flie,
To still their yas thoughts with industrie:
That their plied wits in numbred silks might sing
Passions huge conquest, and their needels leading
Affection prisoner through their own-built citties,   120
Pinniond with stories and Arachnean ditties.
    Proceed we now with Heros sacrifice;
117 yas, i.e., eyas, youthful

She odours burnd, and from their smoke did rise
Unsavorie fumes, that ayre with plagues inspired,
And then the consecrated sticks she fired;   125
On whose pale flame an angrie spirit flew,
And beate it downe still as it upward grew.
The virgin Tapers that on th'altar stood,
When she inflam'd them, burnd as red as blood:
All sad ostents of that too neere successe,   130
That made such moving beauties motionlesse.
Then Hero wept; but her affrighted eyes
She quickly wrested from the sacrifice:
Shut them, and inwards for Leander lookt,
Searcht her soft bosome, and from thence she pluckt   135
His lovely picture: which when she had viewd,
Her beauties were with all loves joyes renewd.
The odors sweetned, and the fires burnd cleere,
Leanders forme left no ill object there.
Such was his beautie that the force of light,   140
Whose knowledge teacheth wonders infinite,
The strength of number and proportion,
Nature had plaste in it to make it knowne
Art was her daughter, and what humane wits
For studie lost, intombd in drossie spirits.   145
After this accident (which for her glorie
Hero could not but make a historie)
Th'inhabitants of Sestus, and Abydus
Did everie yeare with feasts propitious
To faire Leanders picture sacrifice,   150
And they were persons of especiall prize
That were allowd it, as an ornament
T'inrich their houses; for the continent
Of the strange vertues all approv'd it held:
For even the very looke of it repeld   155
All blastings, witchcrafts, and the strifes of nature
In those diseases that no hearbs could cure.
The woolfie sting of Avarice it would pull,
And make the rankest miser bountifull.
It kild the feare of thunder and of death;   160
The discords that conceits ingendereth
Twixt man and wife, it for the time would cease:

The flames of love it quencht, and would increase:
Held in a princes hand it would put out
The dreadfulst Comet: it would ease all doubt   165
Of threatned mischiefes: it would bring asleepe
Such as were mad: it would enforce to weepe
Most barbarous eyes: and many more effects
This picture wrought, and sprung Leandrian sects,
Of which was Hero first: For he whose forme   170
(Held in her hand) cleerd such a fatall storme,
From hell she thought his person would defend her,
Which night and Hellespont would quickly send her.
With this confirmd, she vowd to banish quite
All thought of any check to her delite: 175
And in contempt of sillie bashfulnes,
She would the faith of her desires professe:
Where her Religion should be Policie,
To follow love with zeale her pietie:
Her chamber her Cathedrall Church should be,   180
And her Leander her chiefe Deitie.
For in her love these did the gods forego;
And though her knowledge did not teach her so,
Yet did it teach her this, that what her hart
Did greatest hold in her selfe greatest part,   185
That she did make her god; and t'was lesse nought
To leave gods in profession and in thought,
Than in her love and life: for therein lies
Most of her duties, and their dignities;
And raile the brain-bald world at what it will,   190
Thats the grand Atheisme that raignes in it still.
Yet singularitie she would use no more,
For she was singular too much before:
But she would please the world with fayre pretext;
Love would not leave her conscience perplext.   195
Great men that will have lesse doe for them, still
Must beare them out, though th'acts be nere so ill.
Meannes must Pandar be to Excellence,
Pleasure attones Falshood and Conscience:
Dissembling was the worst (thought Hero then)   200
And that was best now she must live with men.

198 Excellence] Excellencie *1598*[2]

O vertuous love that taught her to doe best,
When she did worst, and when she thought it lest.
Thus would she still proceed in works divine,
And in her sacred state of priesthood shine,   205
Handling the holy rites with hands as bold,
As if therein she did Joves thunder hold;
And need not feare those menaces of error,
Which she at others threw with greatest terror.
O lovely Hero, nothing is thy sin,   210
Wayd with those foule faults other Priests are in;
That having neither faiths, nor works, nor bewties,
T'engender any scuse for slubberd duties,
With as much countnance fill their holie chayres,
And sweat denouncements gainst prophane affayres,   215
As if their lives were cut out by their places,
And they the only fathers of the Graces.
   Now as with setled minde she did repaire
Her thoughts to sacrifice her ravisht haire
And her torne robe which on the altar lay,   220
And only for Religions fire did stay;
She heard a thunder by the Cyclops beaten,
In such a volley as the world did threaten,
Given Venus as she parted th'ayrie Sphere,
Discending now to chide with Hero here: 225
When suddenly the Goddesse waggoners,
The Swans and Turtles that in coupled pheres
Through all worlds bosoms draw her influence,
Lighted in Heros window, and from thence
To her fayre shoulders flew the gentle Doves,   230
Gracefull Ædone that sweet pleasure loves,
And ruffoot Chreste with the tufted crowne,
Both which did kisse her, though their Goddes frownd.
The Swans did in the solid flood, her glasse,
Proyne their fayre plumes; of which the fairest was   235
Jove-lov'd Leucote, that pure brightnes is;
The other bountie-loving Dapsilis.
All were in heaven, now they with Hero were:
But Venus lookes brought wrath, and urged feare.
Her robe was skarlet, black her heads attire,   240
And through her naked breast shinde streames of fire,

As when the rarefied ayre is driven
In flashing streames, and opes the darkned heaven.
In her white hand a wreath of yew she bore,
And breaking th'icie wreath sweet Hero wore,   245
She forst about her browes her wreath of yew,
And sayd: Now minion to thy fate be trew,
Though not to me; indure what this portends;
Begin where lightnes will, in shame it ends.
Love makes thee cunning; thou art currant now   250
By being counterfeit: thy broken vow
Deceit with her pide garters must rejoyne,
And with her stampe thou countnances must coyne:
Coynes and pure deceits for purities,
And still a mayd wilt seeme in cosoned eies,   255
And have an antike face to laugh within,
While thy smooth lookes make men digest thy sin.
But since thy lips (lest thought forsworne) forswore,
Be never virgins vow worth trusting more.
   When Beauties dearest did her Goddesse heare   260
Breathe such rebukes gainst that she could not cleare.
Dumbe sorrow spake alowd in teares and blood
That from her griefe-burst vaines in piteous flood,
From the sweet conduits of her savor fell:
The gentle Turtles did with moanes make swell   265
Their shining gorges: the white black-eyde Swans
Did sing as wofull Epicedians,
As they would straightwaies dye: when pities Queene
The Goddesse Ecte, that had ever beene
Hid in a watrie clowde neere Heros cries,   270
Since the first instant of her broken eies,
Gave bright Leucote voyce, and made her speake,
To ease her anguish, whose swolne breast did breake
With anger at her Goddesse, that did touch
Hero so neere for that she usde so much.   275
And thrusting her white neck at Venus, sayd:
Why may not amorous Hero seeme a mayd,
Though she be none, as well as you suppresse
In modest cheekes your inward wantonnesse?
How often have wee drawne you from above,   280

264 savor]; (favor, T. Brooke)

T'exchange with mortals rites for rites in love?
Why in your preist then call you that offence
That shines in you, and is your influence?
With this the furies stopt Leucotes lips,
Enjoynd by Venus, who with Rosie whips   285
Beate the kind Bird. Fierce lightning from her eyes
Did set on fire faire Heros sacrifice,
Which was her torne robe, and inforced hayre;
And the bright flame became a mayd most faire.
For her aspect: her tresses were of wire,[b]   290
Knit like a net, where harts all set on fire
Strugled in pants and could not get releast:
Her armes were all with golden pincers drest,
And twentie fashiond knots, pullies, and brakes,
And all her bodie girdled with painted Snakes.   295
Her doune parts in a Scorpions taile combinde,
Freckled with twentie colours; pyed wings shinde
Out of her shoulders; Cloth had never die,
Nor sweeter colours never viewed eie,
In scorching Turkie, Cares, Tartarie,   300
Than shinde about this spirit notorious;
Nor was Arachnes web so glorious.
Of lightning and of shreds she was begot;
More hold in base dissemblers is there not.
Her name was Eronusis. Venus flew   305
From Heros sight, and at her Chariot drew
This wondrous creature to so steepe a height,
That all the world she might command with sleight
Of her gay wings: and then she bad her hast,
Since Hero had dissembled, and disgrast   310
Her rites so much, and every breast infect
With her deceits; she made her Architect
Of all dissimulation, and since then
Never was any trust in maides nor men.
                    O it spighted   315
Fayre Venus hart to see her most delighted,
And one she chusde for temper of her minde,
To be the only ruler of her kinde,
So soone to let her virgin race be ended;

[b] Description and creation of Dissimulation.

Not simply for the fault a whit offended,   320
But that in strife for chastnes with the Moone,
Spitefull Diana bad her shew but one,
That was her servant vowd, and liv'd a mayd,
And now she thought to answer that upbrayd,
Hero had lost her answer; who knowes not   325
Venus would seeme as farre from any spot
Of light demeanour, as the very skin
Twixt Cynthias browes? Sin is asham'd of Sin.
Up Venus flew, and scarce durst up for feare
Of Phœbes laughter, when she past her Sphere: 330
And so most ugly clowded was the light,
That day was hid in day; night came ere night,
And Venus could not through the thick ayre pierce,
Till the daies king, god of undanted verse,
Because she was so plentifull a theame   335
To such as wore his Lawrell *Anademe*,
Like to a firie bullet made descent,
And from her passage those fat vapours rent,
That being not throughly rarefide to raine,
Melted like pitch as blew as any vaine,   340
And scalding tempests made the earth to shrinke
Under their fervor, and the world did thinke
In every drop a torturing Spirit flew,
It pierst so deeply, and it burnd so blew.
 Betwixt all this and Hero, Hero held   345
Leanders picture as a Persian shield:
And she was free from feare of worst successe;
The more ill threats us, we suspect the lesse:
As we grow haples, violence subtle growes,
Dumb, deafe, & blind, & comes when no man knowes. 350

The end of the fourth Sestyad

THE ARGUMENT OF THE FIFT SESTYAD

Day doubles her accustomd date,
As loth the night, incenst by fate,
Should wrack our lovers; Heros plight,
Longs for Leander, and the night:

Which ere her thirstie wish recovers,   5
She sends for two betrothed lovers,
And marries them, that (with their crew,
Their sports and ceremonies due)
She covertly might celebrate
With secret joy her owne estate.   10
She makes a feast, at which appeares
The wilde Nymph Teras, that still beares
An Ivory Lute, tels Omenous tales,
And sings at solemne festivales.

Now was bright Hero weary of the day,
Thought an Olympiad in Leanders stay.
Sol, and the soft-foote Howrs hung on his armes,
And would not let him swim, foreseeing his harmes:
That day Aurora double grace obtainde   5
Of her love Phœbus; she his Horses rainde,
Set on his golden knee, and as she list
She puld him back; and as she puld, she kist
To have him turne to bed; he lov'd her more,
To see the love Leander Hero bore.   10
Examples profit much; ten times in one,
In persons full of note, good deedes are done.
    Day was so long, men walking fell asleepe,
The heavie humors that their eyes did steepe,
Made them feare mischiefs. The hard streets were beds   15
For covetous churles, and for ambitious heads,
That spight of Nature would their busines plie.
All thought they had the falling *Epilepsie,*
Men groveld so upon the smotherd ground,
And pittie did the hart of heaven confound.   20
The Gods, the Graces, and the Muses came
Downe to the Destinies, to stay the frame
Of the true lovers deaths, and all worlds teares:
But death before had stopt their cruell eares.
All the Celestials parted mourning then,   25
Pierst with our humane miseries more then men.
Ah, nothing doth the world with mischiefe fill,
But want of feeling one anothers ill.
    With their descent the day grew something fayre,

And cast a brighter robe upon the ayre.   30
Hero to shorten time with merriment,
For yong Alcmane, and bright Mya sent,
Two lovers that had long crav'd mariage dues
At Heros hands: but she did still refuse,
For lovely Mya was her consort vowd   35
In her maids state, and therefore not allowd
To amorous Nuptials: yet faire Hero now
Intended to dispence with her cold vow,
Since hers was broken, and to marrie her:
The rites would pleasing matter minister   40
To her conceits, and shorten tedious day.
They came; sweet Musick usherd th'odorous way,
And wanton Ayre in twentie sweet forms danst
After her fingers; Beautie and Love advanst
Their ensignes in the downles rosie faces   45
Of youths and maids, led after by the Graces.
For all these Hero made a friendly feast,
Welcomd them kindly, did much love protest,
Winning their harts with all the meanes she might,
That when her fault should chance t'abide the light,   50
Their loves might cover or extenuate it,
And high in her worst fate make pittie sit.
    She married them, and in the banquet came
Borne by the virgins: Hero striv'd to frame
Her thoughts to mirth. Aye me, but hard it is   55
To imitate a false and forced blis.
Ill may a sad minde forge a merrie face,
Nor hath constrained laughter any grace.
Then layd she wine on cares to make them sinke;
Who feares the threats of fortune, let him drinke.   60
    To these quick Nuptials entred suddenly
Admired Teras with the Ebon Thye,
A Nymph that haunted the greene Sestyan groves,
And would consort soft virgins in their loves,
At gaysome Triumphs, and on solemne dayes,   65
Singing prophetike Elegies and Layes:
And fingring of a silver Lute she tide
With black and purple skarfs by her left side.
Apollo gave it, and her skill withall,

And she was term'd his Dwarfe she was so small.   70
Yet great in vertue, for his beames enclosde
His vertues in her: never was proposde
Riddle to her, or Augurie, strange or new,
But she resolv'd it: never sleight tale flew
From her charmd lips without important sence,   75
Shewne in some grave succeeding consequence.
    This little Silvane with her songs and tales
Gave such estate to feasts and Nuptiales,
That though oft times she forewent Tragedies,
Yet for her strangenes still she pleasde their eyes,   80
And for her smalnes they admir'd her so,
They thought her perfect borne and could not grow.
    All eyes were on her: Hero did command
An Altar deckt with sacred state should stand,
At the Feasts upper end close by the Bride,   85
On which the pretie Nymph might sit espide.
Then all were silent; every one so heares,
As all their sences climbd into their eares:
And first this amorous tale that fitted well
Fayre Hero and the Nuptials she did tell: 90

The tale of Teras

    Hymen that now is god of Nuptiall rites,
And crownes with honor love and his delights,
Of Athens was a youth so sweet of face,
That many thought him of the femall race:
Such quickning brightnes did his cleere eyes dart,   95
Warme went their beames to his beholders hart.
In such pure leagues his beauties were combinde,
That there your Nuptiall contracts first were signde.
For as proportion, white and crimsine, meet
In Beauties mixture, all right cleere, and sweet;   100
The eye responsible, the golden haire,
And none is held without the other faire:
All spring together, all together fade;
Such intermixt affections should invade
Two perfect lovers: which being yet unseene,   105
Their vertues and their comforts copied beene,

In Beauties concord, subject to the eie;
And that, in Hymen, pleasde so matchleslie,
That lovers were esteemde in their full grace,
Like forme and colour mixt in Hymens face;　　　　110
And such sweete concord was thought worthie then
Of torches, musick, feasts, and greatest men:
So Hymen lookt, that even the chastest minde
He mov'd to joyne in joyes of sacred kinde:
For onely now his chins first doune consorted　　　115
His heads rich fleece, in golden curles contorted;
And as he was so lov'd, he lov'd so too,
So should best bewties, bound by Nuptialls doo.
　　Bright Eucharis, who was by all men saide
The noblest, fayrest, and the richest maide　　　　120
Of all th'Athenian damzels, Hymen lov'd
With such transmission, that his heart remov'd
From his white brest to hers, but her estate
In passing his was so interminate
For wealth and honor, that his love durst feede　　　125
On nought but sight and hearing, nor could breede
Hope of requitall, the grand prise of love;
Nor could he heare or see but he must prove
How his rare bewties musick would agree
With maids in consort: therefore robbed he　　　　130
His chin of those same few first fruits it bore,
And clad in such attire as Virgins wore,
He kept them companie, and might right well,
For he did all but Eucharis excell
In all the fayre of Beautie: yet he wanted　　　　135
Vertue to make his owne desires implanted
In his deare Eucharis; for women never
Love beautie in their sex, but envie ever.
His judgement yet (that durst not suite addresse,
Nor past due meanes presume of due successe)　　　140
Reason gat fortune in the end to speede
To his best prayers: but strange it seemd indeede,
That fortune should a chast affection blesse,
Preferment seldome graceth bashfulnesse.
Nor grast it Hymen yet; but many a dart　　　　145

142 prayers] (Dyce); prayes *1598²*

And many an amorous thought enthrald his hart,
Ere he obtaind her; and he sick became,
Forst to abstaine her sight, and then the flame
Rag'd in his bosome. O what griefe did fill him:
Sight made him sick, and want of sight did kill him.   150
The virgins wondred where Diœtia stayd,
For so did Hymen terme himselfe a mayd.
At length with sickly lookes he greeted them:
Tis strange to see gainst what an extreame streame
A lover strives; poore Hymen lookt so ill,   155
That as in merit he increased still,
By suffring much, so he in grace decreast.
Women are most wonne when men merit least:
If merit looke not well, love bids stand by,
Loves speciall lesson is to please the eye.   160
And Hymen soone recovering all he lost,
Deceiving still these maids, but himselfe most.
His love and he with many virgin dames,
Noble by birth, noble by beauties flames,
Leaving the towne with songs and hallowed lights,   165
To doe great Ceres Eleusina rites
Of zealous Sacrifice, were made a pray
To barbarous Rovers that in ambush lay,
And with rude hands enforst their shining spoyle,
Farre from the darkned Citie, tir'd with toyle.   170
And when the yellow issue of the skie
Came trouping forth, jelous of crueltie
To their bright fellowes of this under heaven,
Into a double night they saw them driven,
A horride Cave, the theeves black mansion,   175
Where wearie of the journey they had gon,
Their last nights watch, and drunke with their sweete gains,
Dull Morpheus entred, laden with silken chains,
Stronger then iron, and bound the swelling vaines
And tyred sences of these lawles Swaines.   180
But when the virgin lights thus dimly burnd;
O what a hell was heaven in! how they mournd
And wrung their hands, and wound their gentle forms
Into the shapes of sorrow! Golden storms
Fell from their eyes: As when the Sunne appeares,   185

And yet it raines, so shewd their eyes their teares.
And as when funerall dames watch a dead corse,
Weeping about it, telling with remorse
What paines he felt, how long in paine he lay,
How little food he eate, what he would say; 190
And then mixe mournfull tales of others deaths,
Smothering themselves in clowds of their owne breaths;
At length, one cheering other, call for wine,
The golden boale drinks teares out of their eine,
As they drinke wine from it; and round it goes, 195
Each helping other to relieve their woes:
So cast these virgins beauties mutuall raies,
One lights another, face the face displaies;
Lips by reflexion kist, and hands hands shooke,
Even by the whitenes each of other tooke. 200
  But Hymen now usde friendly Morpheus aide,
Slew every theefe, and rescude every maide.
And now did his enamourd passion take
Hart from his hartie deede, whose worth did make
His hope of bounteous Eucharis more strong; 205
And now came Love with Proteus, who had long
Inggl'd the little god with prayers and gifts,
Ran through all shapes, and varied all his shifts,
To win Loves stay with him, and make him love him:
And when he saw no strength of sleight could move him 210
To make him love, or stay, he nimbly turnd
Into Loves selfe, he so extreamely burnd.
And thus came Love with Proteus and his powre,
T'encounter Eucharis: first like the flowre
That Junos milke did spring, the silver Lillie, 215
He fell on Hymens hand, who straight did spie
The bounteous Godhead, and with wondrous joy
Offred it Eucharis. She wondrous coy
Drew back her hand: the subtle flowre did woo it,
And drawing it neere, mixt so you could not know it. 220
As two cleere Tapers mixe in one their light,
So did the Lillie and the hand their white:
She viewd it, and her view the forme bestowes
Amongst her spirits: for as colour flowes
From superficies of each thing we see, 225

III

Even so with colours formes emitted bee:
And where Loves forme is, love is, love is forme;
He entred at the eye, his sacred storme
Rose from the hand, loves sweetest instrument:
It stird her bloods sea so, that high it went,   230
And beate in bashfull waves gainst the white shore
Of her divided cheekes; it rag'd the more,
Because the tide went gainst the haughtie winde
Of her estate and birth: And as we finde
In fainting ebs, the flowrie Zephire hurles   235
The greene-hayrd Hellespont, broke in silver curles,
Gainst Heros towre: but in his blasts retreate,
The waves obeying him, they after beate,
Leaving the chalkie shore a great way pale,
Then moyst it freshly with another gale: 240
So ebd and flowde the blood in Eucharis face,
Coynesse and Love striv'd which had greatest grace,
Virginitie did fight on Coynesse side;
Feare of her parents frownes, and femall pride,
Lothing the lower place more than it loves   245
The high contents desert and vertue moves.
With love fought Hymens beautie and his valure,
Which scarce could so much favour yet allure
To come to strike, but fameles idle stood,
Action is firie valours soveraigne good.   250
But Love once entred, wisht no greater ayde
Then he could find within; thought thought betrayd,
The bribde, but incorrupted Garrison
Sung *Io Hymen*; there those songs begun,
And Love was growne so rich with such a gaine,   255
And wanton with the ease of his free raigne,
That he would turne into her roughest frownes
To turne them out; and thus he Hymen crownes
King of his thoughts, mans greatest Emperie:
This was his first brave step to deitie.   260
　　Home to the mourning cittie they repayre,
With newes as holesome as the morning ayre
To the sad parents of each saved maid:
But Hymen and his Eucharis had laid
This plat, to make the flame of their delight   265

Round as the Moone at full, and full as bright.
　Because the parents of chast Eucharis
Exceeding Hymens so, might crosse their blis;
And as the world rewards deserts, that law
Cannot assist with force: so when they saw　　　　270
Their daughter safe, take vantage of their owne,
Praise Hymens valour much, nothing bestowne:
Hymen must leave the virgins in a Grove
Farre off from Athens, and go first to prove
If to restore them all with fame and life,　　　　275
He should enjoy his dearest as his wife.
This told to all the maids, the most agree:
The riper sort knowing what t'is to bee
The first mouth of a newes so farre deriv'd,
And that to heare and beare newes brave folks liv'd,　　280
As being a carriage speciall hard to beare
Occurrents, these occurrents being so deare,
They did with grace protest, they were content
T'accost their friends with all their complement
For Hymens good: but to incurre their harme,　　　285
There he must pardon them. This wit went warme
To Adolesches braine, a Nymph borne hie,
Made all of voyce and fire, that upwards flie:
Her hart and all her forces neither traine
Climbd to her tongue, and thither fell her braine,　　290
Since it could goe no higher, and it must go:
All powers she had, even her tongue, did so.
In spirit and quicknes she much joy did take,
And lov'd her tongue, only for quicknes sake,
And she would hast and tell. The rest all stay,　　　295
Hymen goes one, the Nymph another way:
And what became of her Ile tell at last:
Yet take her visage now: moyst lipt, long fa'st,
Thin like an iron wedge, so sharpe and tart,
As twere of purpose made to cleave Loves hart.　　300
Well were this lovely Beautie rid of her,
And Hymen did at Athens now prefer
His welcome suite, which he with joy aspirde:
A hundred princely youths with him retirde
To fetch the Nymphs: Chariots and Musick went,　　305

And home they came: heaven with applauses rent.
The Nuptials straight proceed, whiles all the towne
Fresh in their joyes might doe them most renowne.
First gold-lockt Hymen did to Church repaire,
Like a quick offring burnd in flames of haire.   310
And after, with a virgin firmament,
The Godhead-proving Bride attended went
Before them all; she lookt in her command,
As if forme-giving Cyprias silver hand
Gripte all their beauties, and crusht out one flame,   315
She blusht to see how beautie overcame
The thoughts of all men. Next before her went
Five lovely children deckt with ornament
Of her sweet colours, bearing Torches by,
For light was held a happie Augurie   320
Of generation, whose efficient right
Is nothing else but to produce to light.
The od disparent number they did chuse,
To shew the union married loves should use,
Since in two equall parts it will not sever,   325
But the midst holds one to rejoyne it ever,
As common to both parts: men therfore deeme,
That equall number Gods doe not esteeme,
Being authors of sweet peace and unitie,
But pleasing to th'infernall Emperie,   330
Under whose ensignes Wars and Discords fight,
Since an even number you may disunite
In two parts equall, nought in middle left,
To reunite each part from other reft:
And five they hold in most especiall prise,   335
Since t'is the first od number that doth rise
From the two formost numbers unitie
That od and even are; which are two, and three,
For one no number is: but thence doth flow
The powerfull race of number. Next did go   340
A noble Matron that did spinning beare
A huswifes rock and spindle, and did weare
A Weathers skin, with all the snowy fleece,
To intimate that even the daintiest peece,

342 rock, distaff

114

And noblest borne dame should industrious bee: 345
That which does good disgraceth no degree.
   And now to Junos Temple they are come,
Where her grave Priest stood in the mariage rome.
On his right arme did hang a skarlet vaile,
And from his shoulders to the ground did traile, 350
On either side, Ribands of white and blew;
With the red vaile he hid the bashfull hew
Of the chast Bride, to shew the modest shame,
In coupling with a man should grace a dame.
Then tooke he the disparent Silks, and tide 355
The Lovers by the wasts, and side to side,
In token that thereafter they must binde
In one selfe sacred knot each others minde.
Before them on an Altar he presented
Both fire and water: which was first invented, 360
Since to ingenerate every humane creature,
And every other birth produ'st by Nature,
Moysture and heate must mixe: so man and wife
For humane race must joyne in Nuptiall life.
Then one of Junos Birds, the painted Jay, 365
He sacrifisde, and tooke the gall away.
All which he did behinde the Altar throw,
In signe no bitternes of hate should grow
Twixt maried loves, nor any least disdaine.
Nothing they spake, for twas esteemed too plaine 370
For the most silken mildnes of a maid,
To let a publique audience heare it said
She boldly tooke the man: and so respected
Was bashfulnes in Athens: it erected
To chast Agneia, which is Shamefastnesse, 375
A sacred Temple, holding her a Goddesse.
And now to Feasts, Masks, and triumphant showes,
The shining troupes returnd, even till earths throwes
Brought forth with joy the thickest part of night,
When the sweet Nuptiall song that usde to cite 380
All to their rest, was by Phemonoe sung,
First Delphian Prophetesse, whose graces sprung
Out of the Muses well: she sung before
The Bride into her chamber: at which dore

A Matron and a Torch-bearer did stand; 385
A painted box of Confits in her hand
The Matron held, and so did other some
That compast round the honourd Nuptiall rome.
The custome was that every maid did weare,
During her maidenhead, a silken Sphere 390
About her waste, above her inmost weede,
Knit with Minervas knot, and that was freede
By the faire Bridegrome on the mariage night,
With many ceremonies of delight:
And yet eternisde Hymens tender Bride, 395
To suffer it dissolv'd so sweetly cride.
The maids that heard so lov'd, and did adore her,
They wisht with all their hearts to suffer for her.
So had the Matrons, that with Confits stood
About the chamber, such affectionate blood, 400
And so true feeling of her harmeles paines,
That every one a showre of Confits raines.
For which the Brideyouths scrambling on the ground,
In noyse of that sweet haile her cryes were drownd.
And thus blest Hymen joyde his gracious Bride, 405
And for his joy was after deifide.
    The Saffron mirror by which Phœbus love,
Greene Tellus decks her, now he held above
The clowdy mountaines: and the noble maide,
Sharp-visag'd Adolesche, that was straide 410
Out of her way, in hasting with her newes,
Not till this houre th'Athenian turrets viewes,
And now brought home by guides, she heard by all
That her long kept occurrents would be stale,
And how faire Hymens honors did excell 415
For those rare newes, which she came short to tell.
To heare her deare tongue robd of such a joy
Made the well-spoken Nymph take such a toy,
That downe she sunke: when lightning from above
Shrunk her leane body, and for meere free love, 420
Turnd her into the pied-plum'd Psittacus,
That now the Parrat is surnam'd by us,
Who still with counterfeit confusion prates
    404 her] (Dyce); their *1598²*

Nought but newes common to the commonst mates.
This tolde, strange Teras toucht her Lute and sung   425
This dittie, that the Torchie evening sprung.

EPITHALAMION TERATOS

Come, come deare night, Loves Mart of kisses,
Sweet close of his ambitious line,
The fruitfull summer of his blisses,
Loves glorie doth in darknes shine.   430
O come soft rest of Cares, come night,
Come naked vertues only tire,
The reaped harvest of the light,
Bound up in sheaves of sacred fire.
   Love cals to warre,   435
   Sighs his Alarmes,
   Lips his swords are,
   The field his Armes.
Come Night and lay thy velvet hand
On glorious Dayes outfacing face;   440
And all thy crouned flames command
For Torches to our Nuptiall grace.
   Love cals to warre,
   Sighs his Alarmes,
   Lips his swords are,   445
   The field his Armes.
No neede have we of factious Day,
To cast in envie of thy peace
Her bals of Discord in thy way:
Here beauties day doth never cease,   450
Day is abstracted here,
And varied in a triple sphere.
Hero, Alcmane, Mya so outshine thee,
Ere thou come here let Thetis thrice refine thee.
   Love cals to warre,   455
   Sighs his Alarmes,
   Lips his swords are,
   The field his Armes.
The Evening starre I see:
Rise youths, the Evening starre   460

Helps Love to summon warre,
Both now imbracing bee.
Rise youths, loves right claims more then banquets, rise.
Now the bright Marygolds that deck the skies,
Phœbus celestiall flowrs, that (contrarie   465
To his flowers here) ope when he shuts his eie,
And shuts when he doth open, crowne your sports:
Now love in night, and night in love exhorts
Courtship and Dances: All your parts employ,
And suite nights rich expansure with your joy,   470
Love paints his longings in sweet virgins eyes:
Rise youths, loves right claims more then banquets, rise.
Rise virgins, let fayre Nuptiall loves enfolde
Your fruitles breasts: the maidenheads ye holde
Are not your owne alone, but parted are;   475
Part in disposing them your Parents share,
And that a third part is: so must ye save
Your loves a third, and you your thirds must have.
Love paints his longings in sweet virgins eyes:
Rise youths, loves right claims more then banquets, rise.   480

     Herewith the amorous spirit that was so kinde
To Teras haire, and combd it downe with winde,
Still as it Comet-like brake from her braine,
Would needes have Teras gone, and did refraine
To blow it downe: which staring up, dismaid   485
The timorous feast, and she no longer staid:
But bowing to the Bridegrome and the Bride,
Did like a shooting exhalation glide
Out of their sights: the turning of her back
Made them all shrieke, it lookt so ghastly black.   490
O haples Hero, that most haples clowde
Thy soone-succeeding Tragedie foreshowde.
Thus all the Nuptiall crew to joyes depart,
But much-wrongd Hero stood Hels blackest dart:
Whose wound because I grieve so to display,   495
I use digressions thus t'encrease the day.

The end of the fift Sestyad

THE ARGUMENT OF THE SIXT SESTYAD

Leucote flyes to all the windes,
And from the fates their outrage bindes,
That Hero and her love may meete,
Leander (with Loves compleate Fleete
Mand in himselfe) puts forth to Seas,   5
When straight the ruthles Destinies
With Ate stirre the windes to warre
Upon the Hellespont: Their jarre
Drownes poore Leander. Heros eyes
Wet witnesses of his surprise,   10
Her Torch blowne out, Griefe casts her downe
Upon her love, and both doth drowne,
In whose just ruth the God of Seas
Transformes them to th' Acanthides.

No longer could the day nor Destinies
Delay the night, who now did frowning rise
Into her Throne: and at her humorous brests
Visions and Dreames lay sucking: all mens rests
Fell like the mists of death upon their eyes,
Dayes too long darts so kild their faculties.
The windes yet, like the flowrs to cease began;
For bright Leucote, Venus whitest Swan,
That held sweet Hero deare, spread her fayre wings,
Like to a field of snow, and message brings   10
From Venus to the Fates, t'entreate them lay
Their charge upon the windes their rage to stay,
That the sterne battaile of the Seas might cease,
And guard Leander to his love in peace.
The Fates consent, (aye me, dissembling Fates)   15
They shewd their favours to conceale their hates,
And draw Leander on, least Seas too hie
Should stay his too obsequious destinie:
Who like a fleering slavish Parasite,
In warping profit or a traiterous sleight,   20
Hoopes round his rotten bodie with devotes,
And pricks his descant face full of false notes,
Praysing with open throte (and othes as fowle
As his false heart) the beautie of an Owle,

Kissing his skipping hand with charmed skips,   25
That cannot leave, but leapes upon his lips
Like a cock-sparrow, or a shameles queane
Sharpe at a red-lipt youth, and nought doth meane
Of all his antick shewes, but doth repayre
More tender fawnes, and takes a scattred hayre   30
From his tame subjects shoulder; whips, and cals
For every thing he lacks; creepes gainst the wals
With backward humblesse, to give needles way:
Thus his false fate did with Leander play.
   First to black Eurus flies the white Leucote,   35
Borne mongst the Negros in the Levant Sea,
On whose curld head the glowing Sun doth rise,
And shewes the soveraigne will of Destinies,
To have him cease his blasts, and downe he lies.
Next, to the fennie Notus course she holds,   40
And found him leaning with his armes in folds
Upon a rock, his white hayre full of showres,
And him she chargeth by the fatall powres,
To hold in his wet cheekes his clowdie voyce.
To Zephire then that doth in flowres rejoyce.   45
To snake-foote Boreas next she did remove,
And found him tossing of his ravisht love,
To heate his frostie bosome hid in snow,
Who with Leucotes sight did cease to blow.
Thus all were still to Heros harts desire,   50
Who with all speede did consecrate a fire
Of flaming Gummes, and comfortable Spice,
To light her Torch, which in such curious price
She held, being object to Leanders sight,
That nought but fires perfum'd must give it light.   55
She lov'd it so, she griev'd to see it burne,
Since it would waste and soone to ashes turne:
Yet if it burnd not, twere not worth her eyes,
What made it nothing, gave it all the prize.
Sweet Torch, true Glasse of our societie;   60
What man does good, but he consumes thereby?
But thou wert lov'd for good, held high, given show:
Poore vertue loth'd for good, obscur'd, held low.
Doe good, be pinde; be deedles good, disgrast:

Unles we feede on men, we let them fast. 65
Yet Hero with these thoughts her Torch did spend.
When Bees makes waxe, Nature doth not intend
It shall be made a Torch: but we that know
The proper vertue of it make it so,
And when t'is made we light it: nor did Nature 70
Propose one life to maids, but each such creature
Makes by her soule the best of her free state,
Which without love is rude, disconsolate,
And wants loves fire to make it milde and bright,
Till when, maids are but Torches wanting light. 75
Thus gainst our griefe, not cause of griefe we fight,
The right of nought is gleande, but the delight.
Up went she, but to tell how she descended,
Would God she were not dead, or my verse ended.
She was the rule of wishes, summe and end 80
For all the parts that did on love depend:
Yet cast the Torch his brightnes further forth:
But what shines neerest best, holds truest worth.
Leander did not through such tempests swim
To kisse the Torch, although it lighted him: 85
But all his powres in her desires awaked,
Her love and vertues cloth'd him richly naked.
Men kisse but fire that only shewes pursue,
Her Torch and Hero, figure shew and vertue.

Now at opposde Abydus nought was heard, 90
But bleating flocks, and many a bellowing herd,
Slaine for the Nuptials, cracks of falling woods,
Blowes of broad axes, powrings out of floods.
The guiltie Hellespont was mixt and stainde
With bloodie Torrents, that the shambles raind; 95
Not arguments of feast, but shewes that bled,
Foretelling that red night that followed.
More blood was spilt, more honors were addrest,
Then could have graced any happie feast.
Rich banquets, triumphs, every pomp employes 100
His sumptuous hand: no misers nuptiall joyes.
Ayre felt continuall thunder with the noyse,
Made in the generall mariage violence:
And no man knew the cause of this expence,

But the two haples Lords, Leanders Sire,   105
And poore Leander, poorest where the fire
Of credulous love made him most rich surmisde.
As short was he of that himselfe he prisde,
As is an emptie Gallant full of forme,
That thinks each looke an act, each drop a storme,   110
That fals from his brave breathings; most brought up
In our Metropolis, and hath his cup
Brought after him to feasts; and much Palme beares,
For his rare judgement in th'attire he weares,
Hath seene the hot Low Countries, not their heat,   115
Observes their rampires and their buildings yet.
And for your sweet discourse with mouthes is heard,
Giving instructions with his very beard.
Hath gone with an Ambassadour, and been
A great mans mate in travailing, even to Rhene,   120
And then puts all his worth in such a face,
As he saw brave men make, and strives for grace
To get his newes forth; as when you descrie
A ship with all her sayle contends to flie
Out of the narrow Thames with windes unapt,   125
Now crosseth here, then there, then this way rapt,
And then hath one point reacht; then alters all,
And to another crooked reach doth fall
Of halfe a burdbolts shoote; keeping more coyle,
Then if she danst upon the Oceans toyle: 130
So serious is his trifling companie,
In all his swelling ship of vacantrie.
And so short of himselfe in his high thought,
Was our Leander in his fortunes brought,
And in his fort of love that he thought won,   135
But otherwise he skornes comparison.
      O sweet Leander, thy large worth I hide
In a short grave; ill favourd stormes must chide
Thy sacred favour; I in floods of inck,
Must drowne thy graces, which white papers drink,   140
Even as thy beauties did the foule black Seas:
I must describe the hell of thy disease,
That heaven did merit: yet I needes must see
Our painted fooles and cockhorse Pessantrie

Still still usurp, with long lives, loves, and lust,   145
The seates of vertue, cutting short as dust
Her deare bought issue; ill to worse converts,
And tramples in the blood of all deserts.
   Night close and silent now goes fast before
The Captaines and their souldiers to the shore,   150
On whom attended the appointed Fleete
At Sestus Bay, that should Leander meete,
Who fainde he in another ship would passe:
Which must not be, for no one meane there was
To get his love home, but the course he tooke.   155
Forth did his beautie for his beautie looke,
And saw her through her Torch, as you beholde
Sometimes within the Sunne a face of golde,
Form'd in strong thoughts, by that traditions force,
That saies a God sits there and guides his course.   160
His sister was with him, to whom he shewd
His guide by Sea: and sayd: Oft have you viewd
In one heaven many starres, but never yet
In one starre many heavens till now were met.
See lovely sister, see, now Hero shines   165
No heaven but her appeares: each star repines,
And all are clad in clowdes, as if they mournd,
To be by influence of Earth out-burnd.
Yet doth she shine, and teacheth vertues traine,
Still to be constant in Hels blackest raigne,   170
Though even the gods themselves do so entreat them
As they did hate, and Earth as she would eate them.
   Off went his silken robe, and in he leapt;
Whom the kinde waves so licorously cleapt,
Thickning for haste one in another so,   175
To kisse his skin, that he might almost go
To Heros Towre, had that kind minuit lasted.
But now the cruell fates with Ate hasted
To all the windes, and made them battaile fight
Upon the Hellespont, for eithers right   180
Pretended to the windie monarchie.
And forth they brake, the Seas mixt with the skie,
And tost distrest Leander, being in hell,
As high as heaven; Blisse not in height doth dwell.

The Destinies sate dancing on the waves,   185
To see the glorious windes with mutuall braves
Consume each other: O true glasse to see,
How ruinous ambitious Statists bee
To their owne glories! Poore Leander cried
For help to Sea-borne Venus; she denied: 190
To Boreas, that for his Atthæas sake,
He would some pittie on his Hero take,
And for his owne loves sake, on his desires:
But Glorie never blowes cold Pitties fires.
Then calde he Neptune, who through all the noise 195
Knew with affright his wrackt Leanders voice:
And up he rose; for haste his forehead hit
Gainst heavens hard Christall; his proud waves he smit
With his forkt scepter, that could not obay,
Much greater powers then Neptunes gave them sway. 200
They lov'd Leander so, in groanes they brake
When they came neere him; and such space did take
Twixt one another, loth to issue on,
That in their shallow furrowes earth was shone,
And the poore lover tooke a little breath: 205
But the curst Fates sate spinning of his death
On every wave, and with the servile windes
Tumbled them on him: And now Hero findes
By that she felt her deare Leanders state:
She wept and prayed for him to every fate, 210
And every winde that whipt her with her haire
About the face, she kist and spake it faire,
Kneeld to it, gave it drinke out of her eyes
To quench his thirst: but still their cruelties
Even her poore Torch envied, and rudely beate 215
The bating flame from that deare foode it eate:
Deare, for it nourisht her Leanders life,
Which with her robe she rescude from their strife:
But silke too soft was, such hard hearts to breake,
And she deare soule, even as her silke, faint, weake 220
Could not preserve it: out, O out it went.
Leander still cald Neptune, that now rent
His brackish curles, and tore his wrinckled face

191 Atthæas, i.e., Orithyia; cf. Chapman's Musaeus, l. 453

Where teares in billowes did each other chace,
And (burst with ruth) he hurld his marble Mace   225
At the sterne Fates: it wounded Lachesis
That drew Leanders thread, and could not misse
The thread it selfe, as it her hand did hit,
But smote it full and quite did sunder it.
The more kinde Neptune rag'd, the more he raste   230
His loves lives fort, and kild as he embraste.
Anger doth still his owne mishap encrease;
If any comfort live, it is in peace.
O theevish Fates, to let Blood, Flesh, and Sence
Build two fayre Temples for their Excellence,   235
To rob it with a poysoned influence.
Though soules gifts starve, the bodies are held dear
In ugliest things; Sence-sport preserves a Beare.
But here nought serves our turnes; O heaven & earth,
How most most wretched is our humane birth?   240
And now did all the tyrannous crew depart,
Knowing there was a storme in Heros hart,
Greater then they could make, & skornd their smart.
She bowd her selfe so low out of her Towre,
That wonder twas she fell not ere her howre,   245
With searching the lamenting waves for him;
Like a poore Snayle, her gentle supple lim
Hung on her Turrets top so most downe right,
As she would dive beneath the darknes quite,
To finde her Jewell; Jewell, her Leander,   250
A name of all earths Jewels pleasde not her,
Like his deare name: Leander, still my choice,
Come nought but my Leander; O my voice
Turne to Leander: hence-forth be all sounds,
Accents, and phrases that shew all griefes wounds,   255
Analisde in Leander. O black change!
Trumpets doe you with thunder of your clange,
Drive out this changes horror, my voyce faints:
Where all joy was, now shrieke out all complaints.
Thus cryed she, for her mixed soule could tell   260
Her love was dead: And when the morning fell
Prostrate upon the weeping earth for woe,
Blushes that bled out of her cheekes did show

Leander brought by Neptune, brusde and torne
With Citties ruines he to Rocks had worne,   265
To filthie usering Rocks that would have blood,
Though they could get of him no other good.
She saw him, and the sight was much much more,
Then might have serv'd to kill her; should her store
Of giant sorrowes speake? Burst, dye, bleede,   270
And leave poore plaints to us that shall succeede.
She fell on her loves bosome, hugg'd it fast,
And with Leanders name she breath'd her last.
    Neptune for pittie in his armes did take them,
Flung them into the ayre, and did awake them.   275
Like two sweet birds surnam'd th' *Acanthides*,
Which we call Thistle-warps, that neere no Seas
Dare ever come, but still in couples flie,
And feede on Thistle tops, to testifie
The hardnes of their first life in their last: 280
The first in thornes of love, and sorrowes past,
And so most beautifull their colours show,
As none (so little) like them: her sad brow
A sable velvet feather covers quite,
Even like the forehead cloths that in the night,   285
Or when they sorrow, Ladies use to weare:
Their wings blew, red and yellow mixt appeare,
Colours, that as we construe colours paint
Their states to life; the yellow shewes their saint,
The devill Venus, left them; blew their truth,   290
The red and black ensignes of death and ruth.
And this true honor from their love-deaths sprung,
They were the first that ever Poet sung.

OENONE AND PARIS

Thomas Heywood

(1594)

1

When Sun-bright Phebus in his fierie carre,
Ended his passage through the vernall signes,
And all the trees that on the mountaines are,
Aspyring Cedars, and the loftie pines,
   And verdaunt flowers mantled all in greene
   Newlye received their liveries from their Queene,

2

The Phrigian Paris earelie in a morning,
Rose from th'imbracements of his new-stolne bryde:
Him selfe in silkes, his steede with studdes adorning,
With speedie course fast to the groves he plyde,
   Pursuing game as farre as Ida mountaine.
   There hee alight's, and sitts him by a fountaine.

3

Fastening his Palferey to a beechen spring,
He softly paced to a pleasant bower.
There had the Silvanes planted many a thing,
Flora bedecked it with eche smelling flower,
   The Primrose, Cow-slippe, and the Daffadillie,
   The Pinke, the Daysie, Violet, and Lillie.

4

Whether he muzed on his beauteous rape,
Or of Oenone selfe (sweet soule) forsaken,

Whether hee thanked Neptune for his escape,
Or sea-borne Venus for his prize so taken,
   Whether hee came to view the wanton Fawnes,
   Or see the Satyres tripping through the Lawnes,

5

There sate hee still, still musing as hee sate.
Leaning his elbowe on a mosse-growne stumpe,
His comely temples shadowed with his hatte,
Like frowning Juno in an angrie dumpe.
   A scarfe of greene about his necke hee wore,
   Wherein a huntesmans horne hee hanging bore.

6

In his right hand a bore-speare well hee weildes.
Plated with golde, but pointed with sharpe steele,
Thus armed doeth Dictynna trace the feildes
With all her trayne attending at her heele.
   Plantes were his seate, the leaves hee made his pillow,
   Hee sees a nymph, whose chaplet was of willow.

7

Lowlye shee sate her in the pleasaunt coole,
Her face al swoolne with still distilling teares:
Who breathing out a passion (sayth), Ah foole,
Thy sighes surchardge the fewnesse of thy yeares.
   They fill thy favour full of wrinkled furrowes,
   Ingratefull Trojan, cause of all my sorrowes.

8

A source of teares (præamble to a passion)
Hath stopt the passage of her further mone:
Yet lookes shee up, after a mournefull fashion,
As Phillis looked for Demophoon.
   And nowe shee sawe him, for shee is almost by him.
   (Close were hee hid, if lovers could not spye him.)

9

When whistlye pacing with a modest gate,
Softly shee trippeth on the bearing flowers,
And gently came, and towcht him where hee sate,
Shadowed from Tytan in the leavy bowers.
    As once the goddesse Citherea came,
    To finde Adonis following of his game.

10

Pausing a while (for passions made her pause),
Shee thus beganne, (that hardly found beginning)
And art thou come to prosequute the cause?
Of well or woe, my loosing or my winning?
    Say gentle Trojan, wordes that may delight me,
    And for thy former lust I will acquite thee.

11

Loe howe Aurora with her blushing face,
Bewrayes her lust with Cephalus her lover,
Thy Crimson rose the Lilly doeth out-chase,
Thy favour doeth thy fatall faultes discover.
    That guile-full Curtisan, whome thou hast taken,
    Mak's poore Oenone utterly forsaken.

12

Fowle fall that forreine hecfar of the Greekes,
Who (yet a youngling) was brave Theseus rape.
Nought else save lust, and breach of love shee seekes.
Ah, couldest thou not her suttle snares escape?
    If thou doest love thy life, thy selfe, thy syre,
    Master these raging flames of thy desire.

13

Band bee that barke that brought from Lacedemon
That snowt-fayre Princesse with her tempting face,
Could neither chaungeling Proteus, nor Palemon?
Seas soveraigne Neptune, with the three-forkt mace?
    Why would not some fayre sea-god make a motion
    To drench that painted Idoll in the Ocean?

13.4 the] (sugg. Adams); thy

14

Where was chast Thetis in that stormie stower?
Or frostie Triton with shrill sounding trumpet?
Oh wherefore did you not display your power
Pursuing dire revenge upon that strumpet?
    Had shee bene steeped in the surging billowes,
    I had not gyrt my temples with these willowes.

15

Whole worldes of warriours will besiege your citie,
King Menelaus will not loose his Juell,
Then fayre-fac'd Phrygian, if thou harborest pitie,
Returne her backe, (the Greekes are fierce and cruell).
    Returne her backe, thy right thou mayst enjoy,
    With neither wracke, nor fatall ende to Troy.

16

Else wilt thou proove that burning fire-brand,
Whereof the fayre Cassandra prophecied,
With her all Phrigia did thy rape withstand,
But mothers dreame right hast thou verifyed
    If these things fall out as they may perhappes.
    Love me, and so prevent all after-clappes.

17

Th'unbridled rage of your too blinde affection,
Will cause ten hundred thousand mourning widowes,
Then cleave sweete Paris, to thy first election,
Kisse, and imbrace me in these verdaunt meddowes.
    If these (as earst they did) can not content thee,
    Yet voutch thou safe at leasure to frequent me.

18

Since first thou tolde me of thy fatall vision,
Of Juno, Pallas, and fayre Citherea,
Of my inferiours have I borne derision,
Of blacke-browde Phillis, and browne Galatæa.
    These countrey girles do frollicke with their lovers,
    But as for me, my face, my fate discovers.
    17.4 these] those

130

19

On yonder banke of Croceate Jillyflowres,
Where last I see thee with thy hooke in hand,
I deem'd the witnessing of higher powers,
In greater stead then now (I see) would stand.
    Even there (yea, there) misdoubting what befell,
    My speechlesse tongue could hardly bidde farewell.

20

Then did thy eies with pearled teares reveale,
The shallow love which thou didst alwayes beare me.
Thy flattering tongue thy falshood did conceale.
Behold thy visage: blushing can not cleare thee.
    Then didst thou promise to returne againe
    Ere Cinthia thrise had fild her emptie waine.

21

Lo thrise the Sunne hath compast all the signes,
Thrise have these groves beene mantled as you see them,
And blustring Boreas with his chill colde windes
Hath thrise disrobde them sithen you did flee them.
    Dailie sithe thy dissembling speech did faile mee,
    By these still streaming fountaines I bewaile me.

22

Ere Phebus yokes his fierie foming steedes,
Ascending up into his Ivorie chaire,
Eche morne, I seate me by yon stinking weedes,
Faire smelling flowers agree not with my care.
    My care, which none but thou did first procure,
    Which none (save poore Oenone) could endure.

23

Now ease my heart with that sweete tongue of thine,
And wring my lillie fingers in thy fists,
That hand (faire hand) more soft and smooth then mine,

19.1 Cf. 'the yellow Gillofer or Wall floure,' Rembert Dodoens (tr. H. Lyte),
A New Herball, 1578. Emended to *roseate* in Adams
20.4 thy] (sugg. Adams); my

And yet my limber armes have azured wristes.
　Once did Apollo more delight to have me,
　Then did the Nimphes of Ida ever crave thee.

24

Let that well sounding organ of thy thought
Adde heavenlie harmonie unto my hearing,
May it but seeme remors-full, as it ought,
Well will I keepe my gold-like lockes from tearing,
　And chaunge my chaplett into lawrell baies,
　Which hath bene worne, & withered many daies.

25

But now sad sorrow hath her language choked,
His lowring looke foretolde he was remorslesse.
Her great impatience hath this storme provoked.
(How should she otherwise?) her teares were forceless.
　In this dull extasie, a while I leave her,
　And turne to him that did of Joye bereave her.

26

Not meanelie mooved at her first approche,
In flowting tearmes he thought to reprehend her,
Disdaining anie Nimph should now incroche,
Or to his highnesse anie sutes surrender.
　But when hee knewe she was his quondam wife,
　The white and redde were in his face at strife.

27

Nowe doeth his hearts interpreter beginne
To pleade excuse, (for love can finde excuses.)
The blushing morne bewrayes her nightly sinne:
His crimson colour tells his late abuses.
　But setting shame and blushing both aside,
　Thus he beginnes to parlie with his bride:

28

Oenone fayrer then the dames of Troy,
Staine to the Nimphes of fountaines, flowres, and trees,
A blot to those that woone in Castalye,
Fayre Cinthiaes overmatch, in bewty, (more then these)
  When Arte to nature had thy face resigned,
  The Rose, and Lilly, shee in the same combined.

29

Grace to these hilles, and dales, & lovely brookes,
Disgrace to walled cities, traffique townes,
Fame to the swift foote huntresses in these nookes,
Shame to the girles yclad in gorgeous gownes.
  Flower of the forest, primrose of the parke,
  Lilly of these lawnes, Apolloes chiefest marke.

30

Soothly it greeves mee at thy wofull teares,
Which would they were in mee to remedie,
Thy ruthfull words still sounding in my eares,
Argue thy love, thy losse, thy great extremitie.
  Which then they would, but now they wil not move me,
  For then I could, but now I can not love thee.

31

Thy just complaint might urge a just remorse,
Had not the winged Lad bewitcht my sences,
My former love was of sufficient force.
But second to loves-selfe a sute commences.
  The second sute must beare away the pryse,
  Second excludes the first, and so it dyes.

32

T'was love that made me surfet with thy beauty,
And loves fayre Queene was authour of our pleasure.
The waiward wag did make us know our duty,
And I have loved thee in a modest measure,
  Hymen the god and authour of our marrying,
  All these, not I, were cause of thy miscarrying.

32.3 waiward wag] (sugg. Adams); blinded waiward wag

33

So have the fates amongest them selves decreed.
What fates appoint, it bootes not us to breake it.
The Senate of the gods of this agreed,
Why seek'st thou then with bitter woes to wreake it?
　　Persist fayre Nimph, attentively to heare me,
　　And thou shalt see how well as I can cleare me.

34

Within this valley, as thy selfe doest knowe,
A place there is begirt with mighty oakes,
Where elders, elmes, and espine trees doe growe,
Whose ore-grown trunks withstand the hardest stroks,
　　A nooke, where neither simple ewe doeth feede,
　　Nor horned ramme plucks up the springing weede.

35

Even in the hollow compasse of this angle,
Unseene of Titans narrowe searching shine,
Least wanton follie should my minde intangle,
That place I chused out to chaunt a ryme.
　　But rymes, nor odes, that place it was not for them,
　　Sad Morpheus charmes did cause me to abhorre them.

36

Drowsilie leaning on my shepheardes crooke,
A sudden earthquake made the mountaines quiver,
My feare appeared in my ghastlie look,
Head, heart, legges, limmes, my Jointures all did shiver.
　　Deepelie admiring at this sudden motion,
　　I gave my selfe precisely to devotion.

37

When loe, the messenger of mightie Jove
Did with his snakie wand appeare before me,
With Juno, Pallas, and the Queene of love,
Who with their gestures gentlie did adore me.
　　Starting abacke, their presence did affright me,
　　Not knowing that which sithens did delight me.

38

And now th'immortall oratour began
To chere me up that had so sadlie drooped:
Thou borne of Hecuba, take courage man.
With that, to helpe me up, he meeklie stooped.
   I feared no more, (for who is afraid of fairenesse
   Or wanton ladies appearing in their barenesse?)

39

This golden ball, that Jove threwe downe (quoth he)
From the tribunall of his stately throne,
Give to the fayrest goddesse of these three.
Which said, he vanished leaving us alone.
   Well hoping this would happen to my glorie,
   I read the posie, *Detur pulchriori.*

40

Viewing the first, I tooke the heavenly ball,
And rashly, almost laide it in her hand,
Supposing her the fayrest of them all,
But second sight the same did countermaund.
   And as the second should have borne the prise,
   Looking askance, the third bad otherwise.

41

Fayre was the first, the second was as fayre,
The third no whit inferiour to the twaine,
All would be victors, (and they worthie are)
But one alone the victorie must gaine.
   That such should winne, I joyed much beleeve me.
   That such shuld lose, this was the thing did grieve me.

42

Againe, the first exactly I did view,
The second too: one of these twaine must have it.
Looking a-squint, as I doe nowe at you,
The third, her beawtie from them both did crave it.
   In this quandarie, musing made me mute,
   Till Juno first began to breake her sute.

43

She promised kingdomes, riches, and renowne.
Pallas, what ever arte and nature taught her.
The Mother, a Monarchie, to weare a Crowne.
Vertue, witte, wisedome freely gives the daughter.
   I heard them both, and nowe I sit and muse,
   Whether it is better, wisedome or wealth to chuse.

44

But then bespake the beawteous Queene of love,
Gracing her fayre cheekes with a lovely smile.
Shepheard (quoth she), hearken to thy behoove:
Let neither giftes, nor gold, thy minde beguile,
   Arte asketh study, Crownes a care to keepe them,
   Both full of toyle, and travell, if thou seeke them.

45

My selfe will give thee what thou most desirest,
The fayrest Ladie all the whole earth affoordeth,
Give me the ball, who ever thou requirest,
Chuse whom & where thou wilt, loves Queene accordeth.
   This said, with prize and victorie she departed,
   Merry, and blithe, the rest but sory-hearted.

46

Pardon (fayre Nimph), if ought I have offended,
I do, what all the gods conspire together.
Not I, but Cupid, is to be condemned,
Roving, that shoots his darts, he knoweth not whether.
   Who, happely greeved at my first election,
   Wounded my heart with contrary affection.

47

(Sweete) stint thy teares, that like a pearled shoure
Drops from the heavens, in a summers day,
Yeelding sweete moisture unto every flower,
Even such were thine, at my depart away.
   Thy wofull words, with sighs, abruptly broken,
   Thy love and loyaltie did well betoken.

48

Likewise my sighes like exhalations,
Burst from th'interiour cavernes of my hart,
My ruthfull tongue made bitter exclamations,
Sounding throughout these groves in every part.
    Looke as the lowring clowdes deface the skies,
    So was my face obscured with mine eyes.

49

As for the promise past, which I did make thee,
Resting us by this silver-streaming fount,
When last to Joves safe guide I did betake me,
Pacing along this pleasant shadie mount,
    To take my speedy journey into Troy,
    When entercourse of griefe bereft our joy.

50

Farre swifter then the winged Pegasus,
Shearing the ayre with brave Bellerephon,
Our pine-tree barke brought us to Tenedos,
Coasting from thence to stately Ilion.
    There knew I, what I had not knowne beforne,
    Which made me promise such a short returne.

51

The noble offspring whence I am descended,
Sonne to King Priamus, and Queene Hecuba,
Brother to Hector, for his woorth commended,
Throughout the regions of Asia.
    My grandsire was the great Laomedon,
    That built the clowd-hye towres of Ilion.

52

I knew not this, when like a lowly swayne,
I kept my goates within these neighbour bounds,
Treading the measures in this grassy plaine,
Viewing the Fayries hoppe their merrie round.
    I knewe not this when first of all I knewe thee,
    Which had I knowne, I had disdain'd to view thee.

49.3 me] (sugg. Adams); thee

53

Oh at that worde, a sudden trembling,
And uncothe feare possessed every member,
Replye she would once more without dissembling,
But sighes and sorrowes did her language hinder.
   As doe the windy stormes drive haile and rayne,
   So sighs drive teares from forth her troubled brayne.

54

Like to a gosling in a puttockes clawes,
Or silly dove, on whome the hauke hath seazed,
Or to a young lambe in a Lyons pawes,
Whose wrathfull furor can not be appeazed,
   Even so lyes poore Oenone on the playne,
   That living, dyed: yet dead, reviv'th againe.

55

And now at length this fit shee doeth recover,
And riseth up as wakened from a slumber,
Cleare shines the sunne when all the storme is over.
Salt teares, (as earst) doe not her minde accumber.
   Yet sighes, (a preface to ensuing talke.)
   She thus goeth on him in his speech to balke:

56

This stately pine, wherein thou has ingraven
My name and thine, Lo where it springeth by thee,
These broad-spread beeches, (harbor for the Raven)
Where under thou hast vowed never to deny me,
   Beare in their barkes thy solemne protestations,
   Which (nowe I finde) were meere dissimulations.

57

And loe, one poplar planted in this Arber,
In whose rough rhyne these verses thou hast carved:
When Paris thoughtes a second love doe harber,
Sythe fayre Oenone hath so well deserved,
   Never shall mylchie goate in Ida go,
   Nor silver swanne swimme in the streames of Po.

58

Xanthus swift waves shall runne against the head,
And clyme the toppes of hye ascending mountaines.
Runne backewarde Xanthus ? I am ill bestead,
Sweete Naiades haunt yee no more these fountaines.
   And snow-white swannes, come helpe me with your breath,
   That I with you may sing against my death.

59

Flint-hearted Phrygian, thou hast broke thy vowe,
Blush, and beholde a Nimph for love that rages,
And thou fayre Poplare still increase and growe,
To be an historie to after-ages.
   Witnesse this holly-oke, whereon thou leanest,
   Thou hast dissembled, (tell me what thou meanest ?)

60

Ah (Paris) when like to a simple groome,
Among the gote-heardes thou these groves frequented,
Seeing the skipping Satyres in the broome,
With bagpypes shrill, and oken quills contented,
   Then didst thou yeeld Oenone pricke and prayes,
   Which now is buryed in eternall dayes.

61

Oft hast thou seene me in the meades below,
Lively to leade the Nymphes about the trees,
And on these bankes, where Aesacus doth flow,
Dauncing to teach Dianaes Votaryes,
   When Faunus, father of the rurall gods,
   Swore that I did surpasse them all by odds.

62

Oft hast thou seene me, with thy selfe unseene
Of any Nymph, save of my selfe alone.
Whole after-noones to parlye in this greene,
But all these pleasures and delightes are gone.
   Oft have thy lippes joynd with these lippes of mine,
   Sending out sugred sighes to Paphos shrine.

63

Oft hast thou found me by this pleasant Myrtle,
(Greene myrtle) dedicate to loves fayre Queene,
Whose leavie branches stead me for a kirtle,
Whose spreading toppe hath oft our shadow beene,
    When thou sat chaunting out thy love-sick charmes,
    Holding me deftly in thy limber armes.

64

You plants of Phebus, hunny-smelling bayes,
Witnesse with me of thy deceite and flatterie,
Whose compasse kept us from the sunnes hotte rayes,
When my poore heart by thee sustein'd a batterie.
    Ah leave the court, full fraught with fortunes showres,
    And live in love among these leavie bowres.

65

The Dawlian byrd with thousand notes at least,
Reserves them till the grisping of the even,
A prickle is prepared for her breast,
To celebrate this night, an happie steeven.
    The whistling blackebirds, and the pleasant thrushes,
    With mirthfull Mavis flocke about the bushes.

66

The Satyres, and goat-footed Aegipines,
Will with their rurall musicke come and meete thee,
With boxen pypes, and countrey Tamburines,
Faunus and olde Sylvanus, they will greete thee.
    Then leave not them, which seem thus to admire thee,
    And leave not her, that doeth so sore desire thee.

67

The faire Napæe, beawtie of these bankes,
As once they daunced at thy wedding day,
So will they now, and yeelde thee thousand thankes,
Footing it finely to intreat thy stay.

65.2 grisping, twilight   66.1 Aegipines, Pans   67.1 Napæe,
nymphs of hill and grove

The fountaine Nymphes, that haunt these pleasant springs,
One sort will trip it, while another sings.

68

The nimble Fayries taking hand in hand,
Will skippe lyke rather lambkins in the downes,
The tender grasse unbended still shall stand,
Coole Zephyrus still flaring up their gownes,
    And every shepheardes swayne will tune his ode,
    And more then these, to welcome thy abode.

69

Woonder of Troy, Natures exactest cunning,
Glorie of shepheardes, Idaes chiefe Decorum,
Directorie of my chusing and my shunning,
More then a man, save in that *fœx Amorum*.
    That trothlesse Tindaris thy faith defaceth,
    That lust, thy love; that fault, thy fame disgraceth.

70

Then sojourne here where lovely Cupid raigneth,
Within the precinct of this countrey soyle,
Whose fruitfull fallowes, Mavors never staineth,
With bloodie massacres in any broyle:
    Here Cinthia lives, that loves the painefull farmour,
    Not brave Bellona, glistring in her armour.

71

Fayre, wage no warre, nor give no warriours wages,
If thou catch blowes, I shall nor breathe, nor blowe,
My life is pawned, if thou lackest gages,
My heart is scortched, if thy anger glowe.
    For every curtlax glauncing on thy creast,
    Craseth the tender heart within my breast.

72

The lust of Læda summons thee to fight,
I, and be sure, the Greekes will be revenged,

68.2 Cf. 'rather Lambes,' Spenser, *S.C.*, Feb., 83

I wish no warres, but Hellen, haplesse wight,
Causeth their rankes and battailes to be renged.
  I feare thy stroakes from fierce Achilles glave
  Will bring thy poore Oenone to her grave.

73

To bruise thy corslet, bursteth me with care,
To pierce thy steele, doeth penetrate my soule.
Wounded by foes, Oenone worse will fare,
For of my teares thou canst not take the towle.
  But if thou needes wilt warre, then warre with me:
  A meeker battaile, trust me can not be.

74

I am thy foe, doe what thou canst to force me,
Tilt fayre, (but fayrely) least thy stroakes rebound,
Sit fast, and close, or else I will unhorse thee,
Yet fall the first, to save thee from the ground.
  If I be foundred, t'is but a meere chaunce,
  I force not to be foyled with thy launce.

75

Thy armes, for armour: sute, for swords may stead thee:
My selfe unarmed, lighter will I strippe.
Thou hast the oddes, and yet I dare to lead thee;
Ayme where thou wilt, first stroke shall be at lippe.
  The next encounter can doe little harme,
  Well can I winde mee in thy twining arme.

76

And if I lye the undermost of all,
It's not the vantage that can make me feare:
Thou canst not hurt mee with a backewarde fall,
Poore women-kinde are bredde, and borne to beare.
  If to this warre thou canst thy liking frame,
  Bee what thou wilt, and I will be the same.

77

Be Phaoes Boateman, I will be thy barke,
Bathe in this fountaine here a while to sport thee,
Thy milke-white skinne, the pebbles shall not marke,
Twixt them and thee Ile lye me, least they hurt thee.
   Oh be my sternesman, I will be thy barge,
   It's not thy weight that can me overcharge.

78

Be thou Pigmalion, I his yvorie worke,
Though woman-like, a colde and sencelesse stone,
Suffer me in thy naked bedde to lurke,
Clippe, kisse, colle, love me like Pigmalion.
   Thou need'st not pray (as he did) for my life,
   Of such a picture I can make thy wife.

79

At this, the Trojan ganne to chase a laughter,
He would, and yet no longer could forbeare it,
And seemed joyfull, Cupid had so caught her,
Like wanton gyrles beloved, and love to heare it.
   This fell unkindnesse did so fowlie fret her,
   That speake she would, but weeping would not let her.

80

Toyes stoppe his tongue: but teares her talking hinders:
Mirth maketh him: but mourning makes her mute:
Loves burning coales are turned into cynders,
Which cold conceite she lysteth not to bruit.
   Yet like to Tytan peeping through a clowde,
   She breakes her mind, that earst her woe did shrowd:

81

Thinke not the sonne of great Laomedon,
Or brave Cysseus broode may be ashamed
To tearme me daughter; (though nowe woe begon)
My curious beawty is not to be blamed,
   My hand a scepter well may seeme to holde,
   My temples may support a crowne of golde.

82

My hayres, disheveled Arachnes twynes,
Are likest to Apolloes golden wyers,
My cheekes engrained with vermillion lynes,
My quaint conceites have kindled quenchlesse fyers,
  My chrystall lampes, whilome thy whole delight,
  Shine like two bright carbuncles in the night.

83

As when bright Tytan in his purple hew,
Leades foorth his lemman to his daily race,
And with a lovely kisse takes his adew,
Such are the splendant colours of my face,
  To which fayre Cinthia in loves despite
  Hath entermixt some of her silver white.

84

Like Amphetrite, floating on the waves,
Strippes up her sleeves to bare her naked wrists:
And drowning it within the streame, she raves
For Corrall branches, to adorne her fists,
  Her Ivorie hande, inferiour unto mine,
  My Corrall-colloured lippes like Rubies shine.

85

My breath, like Zephirus delightfull steame,
That softlie murmureth among the trees,
To rocke the Love-God in a wanton dreame,
His curled pate laide on his Psiches knees:
  My selfe as faire as Cupid or his Love,
  Unworthie, Paris should me thus reproove.

86

My voice, like Venus when she smiling came,
Drawne in her chariot, by her Silver Dooves,
To call the God of Battaile by his name,
When Vulcans wierie Nette, bewraied their looves:
  Disdainfull Paris, doest thou then abhorre mee?
  What reason hast thou that I am not for thee?

87

Are Jybes the guerdon for my great good will?
Are scoffes and flowtes the love I merited?
Hath hurtfull Helen scooled thee so ill
That love for lust must thus be disinherited?
   For ever, maie her whoorish trickes be scand
   That breakes the knot of sacred Hymens band.

88

Ah, litle doest thou know Affections force,
Thou hadst not dealt thus falslie hadst thou knowne it.
Weare my corryvall but a sencelesse Corse
That bred seditious seede, and heare hath sowne it:
   Still had I lived unloathed of my Lover,
   That now forlorne, am forst my face to cover.

89

Dost thou disdaine me, for thou art so fayre?
Why, collours fade, and Beautie it will perish.
Would thou reject mee wert not Priams Heire?
My fayre, thy face: my wealth, thy want might cherish,
   Mine is for ay, thy beautie is but lent:
   What greater wealth I pray thee, then Content?

90

Is not my byrth equivalent with thine?
I am a Nimph, thou but a mortall creature.
Am I not tricked up in velvets fine?
Nature, not Arte, hath portraiturde my feature.
   Unto Eternitie thou maist mee summon,
   Of thee lesse prised then a gadding woman.

91

Forethinke thee not that heare thou didst frequent mee,
Passing the Spring-tide of thy blooming Age:
Of mee (base Nimph) thou needst not to repent thee,
I am thy peere in Honors equipage.
   But looving Manhood, more then Phœbus Deitie,
   Thus am I plagued for my great Impietie.

89.3 not] (Adams); thou

145

92

Weigh with thy selfe howe dearely I have loved thee,
Receiving him that offers to reject mee,
Had not thy tempting teares with pitty mooved me,
Nought else had force to make me to affect thee,
   Which had I scand them in a right construction,
   My coy disdaine had bred thy fowle destruction.

93

But finding thee, loe, I have lost my selfe,
To keepe thee dry, my dotage hath me drowned,
Like him that busily to save his pelfe,
Both looseth welth, and is him selfe confounded.
   Seeking to save thy life, by graunting love,
   I susteine sorrowe never to remoove.

94

When shaggy Satyres in these mountaines sought me,
And Faunes showte till echoing hilles resoundes,
First, fearefull least some sudden furie caught me,
The rest, to heale their ever curelesse woundes,
   I hidde me close, and never come among them.
   Thou art the onely cause that thus I wrong them.

95

Thou and thy rape have done me double wrong,
But were she here, howe sore would I assault her?
For Acidalia suffers her too long,
Thoe I have offered incense at her alter.
   All were I wearyed with Paris guile,
   Yet have I sent sweete sighes to Cyprus Ile.

96

A thousand sithes I kept her yeerely heastes
At Cithara, and Paphos loving temple,
Of long I haunted not Dianaes feastes,
But lover-like was foolish, sottish, simple.
   Witnesse thou Priapus, with whose fayre flowers,
   I deckt her altars and decayed bowers.

96.1 sithes, times

146

97

Never hereafter will I yeelde her honner,
Her shrined vestures ever bee defaced,
Never hereafter will I looke upon her,
Her painted picture will I see disgraced.
    Her selfe, her sonne, her favorites, and her friendes,
    For this injustice can not make amendes.

98

She gave my love, whome I have loved so well,
To one that beares her vertue in her browes,
And for a ball, my sollace did she sell,
Ah breake her promise, credite, faith, and vowes?
    So shall the Queene of beawtie live defamed,
    Till of her toyish trickes shee be ashamed.

99

Yet once again fayre Trojan, let me heare thee
Speake graciously, (thy colour grace portendeth.)
If I have wooed thee, shall another weare thee?
I once had woonne thee too: this onely rendeth,
    And teares my heart, halfe melted into teares,
    The breach whereof within my face appeares.

100

When this was said, no more she had to say,
Yet thousand thoughts are in her minde concurring:
Shee feares his farewell, least he would not stay,
Which when she thinks, she stands, no member sturring.
    But now, the Trojans turne began to speake,
    Who, sumwhat sadly, with her thus did breake:

101

Fayre Nimph, thy passions unto mee are painfull,
My eares do glow to heere thy sad Discourses.
I am not surlie, proude, fell, and disdainfull:
Thou seest my trickling teares are turnd to sources.
    Nor am I as I woonted, blithe and jollye,
    My future fortunes summons mee to follye.

101.6 My] (sugg. Adams); Thy

102

Cupid, the cause that first of all I loved thee,
Is the occasion, that I needes must leave thee:
The same besiegde my hart, and hath remooved mee,
The selfe same heart, that whilome did receave thee,
  Not hard and stonie, or (as thou tearmst it) flinted,
  But wax-like, easie to be soone imprinted.

103

The Potters claye receaveth any fashion,
The melting Snow takes any deepe Impression,
A tender heart is pearced with a passion,
A grievous crime is pardoned by confession:
  My heart in Cupids handes, to steare and stay;
  More soft then wax, then Snow, then Potters clay.

104

If he drawe backe his force, his might, his strength,
Which bindes mee bondslave, to a second Ladie,
Gaining free-will and libertie at length,
Soone shalt thou see, I will doo all that maie bee:
  For with his fierie darte, so sore he stingeth,
  That from one Spunge, both fire and water wringeth.

105

Th'attractive Adamant can drawe no Iron,
If the pure Diamond be placed neere it:
The love that doth my heart and thought inviron
Admits thy Plea and sute, and faine would heare it:
  But that faire Diamond, to whome I am affected,
  Withstands thy sute, and makes thee bee rejected.

106

The purenes of her white and red Complection,
As Jeat the strawe, perforce doth drawe my sences:
She is the Loade-starre of my whole direction,
Thus love with lust unequallie dispenses.
  A Lovers thought, it evermore aspireth:
  For more he surfetteth, he more desireth.

107

She is no Bawde, no base and filthie woman,
But one whome heaven and earth have both admired:
She is not whoorish, toyish, foolish, common,
But whom heavens king, & loves queene have conspired
   To grace mee with: yea, and so much the rather,
   For Venus is her Planet, Jove her father.

108

But leaving her, returne wee to our selves,
Whose heart-sicke woundes are hardly to bee healed.
Where Cupid mindes to enter, there he delves,
And digging deepe, the bargaine must be sealed,
   But plowing slender furrowes in our hartes,
   Easie resistance is against his dartes.

109

What made the gods to trewant it from heaven,
And shift them subtillie into sundrie shapes,
But he that roves his shaftes at sixe and seven,
Laughing at riot, revelling, and rapes?
   His force made Jove with Danaës to jest,
   Beguiling faire Alcmena and the rest.

110

His scapes with fayre Europa shew loves might,
When like a milke-white bull, with silver hornes,
His curled front, up-heaved, fayre to sight,
Venting, he browzeth on the budding thornes,
   And beast like bellowing through the fruitful meads,
   He followeth fast, whither his fayre hecfer leades.

111

Love made him falsifie his nuptiall oath
To Juno; love is in no lawe contained.
Well might she make the King of heaven wroath,
And yet his crankes will never be refrained.
   So cunningly Calisto he beguil'd,
   A mayde was thought to get a mayde with childe.

112

A many moe might quickelie bee recited,
For her, a snake: for this, a feathered swanne:
And he that always foyled where he fighted,
Hath bene even captivated as a man.
    The wanton wagge he spareth not one nor other,
    For he hath dared to dart them at his mother.

113

The Imperious boy made Hercules to stoope,
That tamed tyrants, and did master monsters,
And pent him up within a slender coope.
Ah lordly love, the minde of man misconsters,
    He makes Alcides put apart his glave,
    And to his tentes t'followe him like a slave.

114

For his victorious clubbe, he holdes a rocke,
Bound by his mistresse to a daylie taske,
And for his Lions spoyles, a womans frocke,
Spinning as much as Iole would aske.
    Who would have deemed, that he which conquered all,
    Should thus by love come to so foule a fall?

115

The lawes of love are full of pure divinitie;
Beawtie, it is attractive and devine,
This caused Cinthia, that had vowde virginitie,
Her horned compasse to the earth decline,
    To give long sleeping Latmian swayne a kisse,
    His fayrenesse did deserve no lesse then this.

116

Thy selfe no lesse o'er-heated with this flame:
Well I remember thou diddest often tell mee
That Phebus hath requested even the same

113.6 t'followe him] to followe him   114.4 Iole for Omphale
116.1 o'er-heated] over-heated

Which I obtained. Phebus did excell mee.
  It was Cupid, carelesse of thy love and life,
  That stung thee deepely to be Paris wife.

117

On him therefore, and on his foule abuses,
That rudely ruleth, let barely him bee blamed,
And make mee witlesse for my late excuses,
Let unkinde Paris never more bee named.
  If on the ragged rockes a shippe be splitted,
  The sternesman, not the Carake, should be twitted.

118

Loe Sol unbrideleth his sweating steedes,
And watereth them within the Westerne deepe,
And Tytan, tearing of his smoaking weedes,
His fierie charryot in the waves doeth steepe.
  The nightingale beginnes to tune her layes:
  Good night fayre nymph, now I must go my wayes.

119

Oh take mee too (quoth she), goe not alone,
With this shee pluckt him by the skarfe, and stayde him,
And held him till her holde was almost gone.
When strength avayled not, with tongue she prayed him.
  Hee breaketh holde, and from her armes hee skippes,
  Yet first hee kist her on her rose-redde lippes.

120

With this sad extasie shee was accloyed,
For this kinde kisse (I gesse) did almost kill her.
Shee sownded, either greeved, or over-joyed.
Accursed kisse, that sought so soone to spill her.
  Thus lay shee, blood and breath of strength bereft her,
  Which when the Trojan see, he straightwaies left her.

121

And mounting bravely on his stiffe neckt steede
Galloppes with switch and spurre, and tilting launce.
Horse echoing hoofe againe her woe did breede,
Whose hollowe sound doeth wake her from her traunce.
  Rising as from a sleepe to looke about her,
  Thus she laments, for that hee went without her.

122

Bending her eyes downe to the grasse-greene plaine,
Her chalke-white fist upon a flower she seazes,
(Powring foorth silver droppes,) sayth once againe:
Where is that hearbe that cureth all diseases?
  Ah those his amorous cheekes, with pretty dimples,
  Hath wrought a wound not to bee cur'd by simples.

123

If hearbes could cure the heart that Cupid woundeth,
There is no slippe, no bud, no flowre that springeth,
But I can shewe his force whereon he groundeth
His name and nature: Cupid when he stingeth,
  And shootes his shaftes to rankle in my heart,
  There is no helpe by Aesculapius arte.

124

Then did she cast flowre from her in a rage,
And passed further to a pearled brooke,
Her language stopt, as byrd pent up in cage,
Yet gaining freedome, bondage hath forsooke.
  Thus with an inward horror cleane amazed,
  Shee speakes these words as on the streame she gazed:

125

Oh well of woe, that canst not wash with water,
Nor drowne the trilling teares of my bemonings.
Oh bewteous brooke, where oft Diana sate her,
Beare record of my griefe, and ghastly gronings.
  Carrie my cares, my cause, my bitter anguish,
  Unto the strond, where sinnefull soules doe languish.

126

Thou marsh-god Pales, (soveraigne of these fennes)
Depart with proude Apollo from these meades.
You Hagges & Goblings, leave your darkesome dennes,
And unfrequented pathes where no man treades.
   Leave your sad caves, & haunt these hateful grounds,
   And hand in hand hoppe out your divelish roundes.

127

When Paris went, the gods went from these fieldes,
When hee tooke leave, the aged Pan departed.
No grapes the vine, no sappe the soyle nowe yeeldes.
(Oh who would thinke that fayre could be false hearted?)
   You gods that guide the earth, and every creature,
   Returne the soyle his sappe, the fieldes their feature.

128

Yee ragged cliffes of never touched rockes,
Helpe to recount my sorrowes and my crosses,
You huntresses tricked up in tucked frockes,
Helpe to lament yours, theirs, mine, all our losses.
   Howle, & lament, you cliffes, rocks, clowdy mountaines,
   Clear-chrystal streams, wels, brooks, & lovely fountaines.

129

Nowe leaving these, (for these would take no pittie)
Shee runnes like hynde, or Roe-bucke to the heardes,
And like a turtle chaunting out a dittie,
Beginnes with those that shake their hayrie beardes:
   Yee goats (quoth she), that kneppe these flowring stalks,
   Pittie my woes, my wordes, my wandring walkes.

130

You stottes, & steeres, throughout these pastures ranging,
Yong kiddes, and sheepe, on these fat lees fast grazing,
Rough pated Rammes, your valour never chaunging,
You light-foote stagges that stand aloofe a-gazing,
   Goates, bulles, young hecfers, kids, and simple sheepe,
   Vine spoyling beasts, helpe me to mourne and weepe.

131

But when shee sawe her cheekes in vaine were watred,
Her pearled teares to no intent were scattered,
Shee then recordes his too disdainefull hatred,
Scorning the fortresse (fayre fort) he had battered.
    When wandring through the desarts, dennes, and dailes,
    Her late lost love she inwardly bewayles.

132

Like to a shippe with tempestes all too dashed,
Beaten with billowes and almost over-turned,
Whose hollowe wombe with watrie waves is washed,
So wandereth shee with flaming fancie burned.
    Or to a passenger that lost his way,
    Feareth his steppes, yet wotes not where to stray.

133

Or likest to a new strooke bleeding hart
That runnes to seeke Dictamus flower to cure it,
And nighly wasted with the pinching smart,
Restes as hee runnes, not able to endure it:
    Yet runnes againe when hunters hup, & showte him,
    Striving for life, yet deaths wound beares about him.

134

So wanders poore Oenone through the thickets,
Uncertaine where to stay, or where to rest her,
Nowe sittes she still, now doeth she chace the prickets,
Heaven helpe (poore soule) her new searcht wound doth fester.
    Here leave I her, with loves disdain rewarded,
    Of her selfe forlorne, of Paris unregarded.

133.2 Dictamus flower, dittany

CEPHALUS AND PROCRIS

Thomas Edwards

(1595)

Faire and bright Cynthia, Joves great ornament,[a]
Richly adorning nightes darke firmament,
Scoured amidst the starry Canapie
Of heavens celestiall governement, well nie
Downe to the ever over-swelling tide,   5
Where old Oceanus was wont t'abide,
At last began to crie, and call amaine,
Oh what is he, my love so long detaines!
Or i'st Joves pleasure Cynthia shall alone,
Obscure by night, still walke as one forlorne: 10
Therewith away she headlong postes along
Salt washing waves, rebellious cloudes among,
So as it seem'd minding the heavens to leave,
And them of light, thus strangely to bereave.
  With that Aurora starting from her bed[b]   15
As one that standes devising, shakes his head,
Not minding either this or that to doe,
So are her thoughtes, nor quicke, nor overflow;
  Phebus halfe wrothe to see the globe stand still,
The world want light, a woman have her will: 20
To post foorth gan another Phaeton,
And swore once more, he should the world uppon,
Or as tis thought to trie th'adventrous boy;
Yet some suppose, he meant upon this day,
A Sympathy of sorrowes to advaunce.   25
The boy thus proude-made, hotly gan to praunce,

[a] A pariphrisis of the Night.
[b] A description of the Morning.

And now heavens coape, Joves pallace chrystaline
Downe dingeth Atlas, and straight doth decline
In such aboundant measure, as tis said,
Since that same day the light of heaven's decaide;   30
A metamorphosis on earth mong'st men,
As touching constancy hath bene since then:
And this is, true maidens since that same day,
Are saide for lovers never more to pray.
     But to returne, Phebe in million teares,   35
Moanes to her selfe, and for a time forbeares,
Aurora she her swift bright shining rayes,
On Phebus charyot tosse, and oft assayes,
With her sweete lookes, her fathers wroth t'appease,
But all she doth, he tels her, doth disease,   40
Like to the uncorrected headstrong childe,
That never felt his parentes strokes but milde,
Growne up to ryper yeares, disdaines a checke:
(For nature overgon comes to defect:)
     So now Aurora having felt the pride   45
Of heaven and earth, turning her selfe a side,
Rapt with a suddaine extasie of minde,
Unto her selfe (thus said) Goddesse divine:
How hapt that Phebus mov'd amid his chase,
Should such kinde frendship scorne for to imbrace,   50
I will no more (quoth she) godd it along
Such unaccustom'd wayes, ne yet among
Such as is Titan, better fittes it me,
With Vesper still to live, then such as he,
Though well I wot, honor is set on high,   55
Yet gentle *Humilitie* is best, say I.
No more she spake, but like the swelling tide,
That having passage skymes, scorning a guide,
Untill the vaste receipte of Neptunes bower,
Kils the hoat fume, even so, away she skoures,   60
Lawlesse, as twere sans thought or any dread,
Like to banditos mong'st the mountaine heard.
     And now upon her gentle lovely mother,°
Bright as the morning, comes the mornings honor,
     ° Aurora filia Titanis & Terræ.
     51 godd, to play the god

All snowy white, save purpled heere and there,   65
So beautifull as beauty might despaire,
And stand amaz'd, noting her wanton eie,
Which at a trice could all the world espie;
Upon her head, a coronet did stand,
Of severall flowers gathered by Titan.   70
A vale she wore downe trayling to her thighes,[d]
The stuffe whereof, I gesse, of such emprize,
As Gods themselves are doubtfull of the arte,
Seeming as aire with otomie disperst,
Her handes, a meny Poets dead and gone,[e]   75
Have heretofore (excelling) wrote upon,
It shall suffize Venus doth grace to her,
In that she waites before, like to a Starre,
Directing of her steps along'st the zone,
Never overtaken by the *Horizon*,   80
Ne yet in daunger put of any Lake,
The frozen Pole she warnes her to forsake:
And all Licurgus daughters[f] Dion noates,
Base in respect of duetie, and out-coates
Each God and Goddesse, such is beauties pride,   85
That Neptunes honor hath no larger tide:
One lastes but a time, till time is come againe,
The other ever over-rules too certaine.
    Thus at the last, Aurora vanquishing
Heavens glory, and earthes cause of mourning: 90
"For now the sparckling vault of Joves high seate,
"Was not so fild with over-swaying heate:
"Red-hoat disdaine gave beauty place, for why?
"Venus had conquered base necessitie.
Along'st she passed by Hesperides,   95
Laden with honor of those golden eies:
And stately bode them stoupe to honor us,
And stoupe they did, thinking twas Venus.
Then from this golden Orchard to the Tower,

[d] An imitation taken from the Thracians called Acroconiæ [for Ἀκρόκομοι, *Iliad* IV, 533], that usually weare long haire downe to their wasts.
[e] Dead as men.
[f] Pleiades, the seaven starres, supposed to be the daughters of Licurgus
74 otomie, atomy   83 Licurgus, i.e., Atlas
84 out-coates, surpasses

Where Jove in likenes of a golden shower,   100
Ravisht faire Danae,[g] she in ravishment
Of strange delightes, the day there almost spent.
Thence to th'Idalian mount, where Venus doves
Plume on the feathers, sent by their true loves:
As Itis Pheasant feathers, Progne, and   105
Tereus,[h] they the Lapwincke winges did send:
Faire Philomela from the Nightingale
Sent likewise feathers, plucked from her taile,
And many others that denying love,
Dide with despight, and here their cause did move.   110
Then on her swift-heeld Pegasus, amaine
Of Colchos golden Fleece a sight to gaine,
And with the swift windes Harrould Mercury,
The golden Sonne-beames of Apolloes tree:
Where valorous warlike Knightes, for feates ydone   115
Are registred, yclept Knightes of the Sonne:
Knightes of the Garter, auncient knightes of Rhodes,
She mainely postes, and there a time abodes.
    I do not tell you all that she did see,
In honor done of this same golden tree.   120
Knightes did their due, and Poets had no lesse,
Then what for Triumphes every one can gesse.
Hence twas that Hermes stole from heaven the power,
To soveranize on schollers idle howres,
And had not Jove bene favourable then,   125
They never should have bene accounted men,
But liv'd as pesants, shaddowes, imagies,
And nere have had the princes *similies*.
    Hence post we foorth unto an Ocean
That beats against the bankes of Helycon,   130
Whereon if so the ruler of the East,
But cast an eie, we are not meanely blest;
No more but so, for more were over much,
Gold is approv'd but by a slender touch.
    And now bright Phebus mounted, gan display   135
His Orient sunne-beames, on the lively day;
Aurora made unto the Silvan shore,

[g] Ovid lib. 2, *de Tristibus.*
[h] Ovid *Metam.* [lib. 6]

158

Where Satyres, Goat-heardes, Shepheards kept of yore,
A sacred and most hallowed cristall spring,
Long'st which oft Cephalus yode on hunting,   140
And much delighted in the murmyring water,
Whose silent noates gave Eccho of their author,
And as in Rondelaies of love they sung,
It aunsweare made, yet bod them hold their toung:
No base groome durst his case here to bemoane,   145
But quench his thirst, and so part, and be gone.
But Cephalus, a man of some compare,
Bore hound, and horse, through depth without despaire,
And when the heate of Sommer stung him thro,
His yvorie limbes heere bath'd, and washt he to;   150
His Steede orecome with anger in the chase,
His dogs halfe tir'd, or put unto disgrace,
Heere, and but here, he sought for remedie,
Nor durst the Silvans shrincke, but aide him presently.
What shall I say in pride of him and his?   155
Man, horse, and dogs, pleasd th'inamored Procris:
But how with him Aurora was in love,
A richer braine the taske would highly move.
   Upon a milke white courser swift as winde,
Betrapt with yssyckles of gold, that chim'bde,   160
By sweete Zephirus, and the gentle aire,
That breathed life (as twere) to kill despaire,
Rode he upright as any heisell wan,
His Steede was wrought, & now would needes be gon:
Whose over head-strong prauncing checkt the earth,   165
In scornefull sorte, and whose loude neighing breath
Rent throgh the clouds, like Joves swift quickning thunder,
And passage bod, or it would pash't in sunder.
So war-like, Mars-like, fit for Venus Court,
Hotly the gallant gentleman did sort,   170
Now here, now there; his Steede began to rage,
And sent foorth fome to bid the cloudes a badge
Of his proud stomacke; who would not be proude,
That is well backt, and in his pride alloude?
"Heere could I tell you many a prettie storie,   175

163 heisell wan, hazel wand; cf. 'straight as Circes wand,' *Hero and Leander* I,
61 (Buckley)

"Of some eterniz'd by an others glory,
"Of men transfourm'd to apes, of womens evils,
"Of fiendes made Angels, and of angels divels,
"Of many brave knightes done to shame, and more,
"How schollers favourites waxe over poore,   180
"But oh faire Muse, let slip to treate of such,
"A taske thou hast, that tyres thee too too much,
"And none (Gods know) thy boldnesse will out backe,
"But naked trueth, that garded coates doth lacke.
"Heroicke Parramore of Fairie land,   185
"That stately built, with thy immortall hand,
"A golden, Angellike, and modest Aulter,
"For all to sacrifice on, none to alter.
"Where is that vertuous Muse of thine become?
"It will awake, for sleepe not prooves it dumme.   190
"And thou Arcadian knight, earthes second Sunne,
"Reapt ere halfe ripe, finisht ere halfe begunne,
"And you that tread the pathes, where these have gone,
"Be your soules agentes in our tragicke song,
"And when the daughter of dispaire is dead,   195
"And ougly nightes blacke Æthiopian head,
"Ycoucht, and woxen pale, for griefe and shame,
"Then shall our quill, lift honor to your name.
O high Apollo, give thou skill to us,
That we may queintly follow Cephalus,   200
That now is mounted, ready to surprize
What game so ere is seaz'd-on by his eies;
Aurora met him, in his furious chase,
As winde doth reigne, so did she him embrace,
And his fierce courage, on the harmefulle Boare,   205
Ere he did part, should be asswag'd she swore.
His amber-couloured tresses, ne'er yet cut,
Into her luke-warme bussome she did put.
She wringes his handes, and hugges him twixt her armes,
(Apes die by culling) yet he tooke no harme: 210
Anone with smiles, she threates his chast conceites,
And (looking on his eies) him she entreates,

---

184 garded, ornamented   185 ff. Allusion to Spenser and the
still unpublished continuation of the *Faerie Queene*
191 Sidney   207 ne'er] never

With kisses, sighes, and teares revying them,
As though their sexe of duetie should woe men,
He striving to be gone, she prest him downe: 215
She striving to kisse him, he kist the growne,
And evermore on contrarieties,
He aunsweare made, unto her Deitie.
Her garland deckt with many a prettie gemme,
And flowers sweete as May, she gave to hem: 220
Her feete (immodest dame) she bear'd to show him,
And askt him, yea, or no, if he did know them,
And therewithall, she whispers in his eare,
Oh, who so long, is able to forbeare!
A thousand prettie tales she tels him too,   225
Of Pan his Sirinx, of Joves Io,
Of Semele, the Arcadian Nimphes disport,
Their stealth in love, and him in covert sorte
Like to th'unhappie Spider, would intangle;
He flie-like strives, and to be gone doth wrangle: 230
And tels, he can no more of love or beautie,
Then ruffe-beard Satyres, that nere heard of duetie.
Therefore to cut of all disquietnesse,
Rudely he throwes her from his down-soft brest:
And with his Steede cuts through the riotouse thornes,   235
That shipwracke make of what is not their owne:
His speare halfe bleeding, with a sharpe desire,
To taint the hot-Boare seemed to aspire:
The ruffe and hidious windes, twixt hope and feare,
Whisle amaine into his greedie eares,   240
His Steede upstartes, and courage freshly takes,
The Rider fiercely after, hotly makes.
Halfe droncke, with spitefull mallice gainst the Boare,
He prickt him forward, never prickt before.
The toyling dogs therewith do mainely runne,   245
And having found the game, their Lord to come
They yalpe couragiously, as who would say,
Come maister come, the footing serves this way.
Therewith more fierce then Aoris did hie

213 revying, countering   227 Arcadian Nimphes disport, Calisto
231 can, knows   249 Aoris, a famous hunter of Corinth

In his swift chase the game for to espie,   250
He gets him gon, nor neede wa'st to say goe,
O cruell men, that can leave wemen so!
    By this the sport grew hot on either part,
Aurora she was bitten to the hart,
A dogged part it was, she telleth oft,   255
To bite so deadfully a hart so soft.
Aie me, had Cupid bene a rightfull lad,
He never should have shot a dart so bad.
But what prevailes? a meny sad laments,
And Madrigals with dolefull tunes she sent,   260
Unto the heavens Lampe Phebus mournefully,
All balefull, treating pittie from his eies,
She does her orizons, and tels how many
Have loved her, before nere scorn'd by any:
Her handes so white as yvorie streame,   265
That through the rockes makes passage unto him:
Halfe blacke with wrathfull wringing them together
She reares to heaven, and downe unto her mother,
Anon she faintly lets them fall againe,
To heaven, earth, father, mother, all in vaine,   270
"For love is pittilesse, rude, and impartiall,
"When he intends to laugh at others fall.
    Afresh the sport of Cephalus began,
Erewhile at fault, his dogs now lively ran,
And he quicke-listed, when he list to heare,   275
Ore tooke them straight, and with his venum'd speare,
Gashly did wound the Boare couragiously.
The dogs upon him likewise lively flie,
His entrals bleeding-ripe before for feare,
Now twixt their grim chaps, *pel mel* they do teare: 280
The master proude at such a stately prize,
Fils his high thoughtes, and gluts his greedie eies,
He bathes himselfe, (as twere) in Seas of blisse;
But what is victorie, where no praise is?
Pittilesse he scornes the plaintes Aurora sendeth,   285
For where her love beginneth, his love endeth,
And seeme she never so ore-gone with griefe,
He treble joyes; o bare and base reliefe!
"Even like two Commets at one instant spred,

"The one of good, the other shame and dread: 290
"Pestering th'aire with vapours multiplying,
"So is our Theame now quicke, and then a dying.
 Once more she met him, and thus gently spake,
(If wemen had no tounges, their hartes would breake,)
Oh Cephalus, for pittie love me, sweete!   295
Or if not love, yet do me gently greete,
Tis Action shewes th'intent, but smile upon me,
Or give a kisse, a kisse hath not undone thee:
(Quoth he), these desertes have I meny a time,
In winters rage, and in the Sommers prime,   300
Mounted as now with horse, and houndes good store,
Chaste and encountred with the gag-tooth'd Boare,
Rousd up the fearefull Lion from his cave,
(That duld the heavens, when he began to rave)
Pursu'd the Lizard, Tyger and a crew   305
Of untam'd beastes; yet none tam'd me as yew.
Admit that woemen have preheminence,
To make men love; yet for so foule offence,
As for to violate the marriage bed,
Were over much to be inamored;   310
Her who I honor, and am tied to,
Would deeply scorne, I should another woe:
Admit the contrary is it no sinne,
In love to end, where I did not begin?
Oh tis a fault, a sinne exceeding any!   315
Then pardon me, for I scorne to love many.
 Twixt shame and feare, scorn'd, and denied so,
Poore soule she blusht, not wotting what to do,
Her teares were issuelesse, her speech was done,
"The spring being stopt, how can the river runne? 320
Her hart (poore hart) was overcharg'd with griefe,
"Tis worse then death to linger on reliefe.
 At last she spake, and thus she mildly said,
Oh, who to choose, would live, and die a maide!
What heavenly joy may be accounted better, 325
Then for a man to have a woman debter?
Now thou art mine in love; Love me againe,
Then I am thine; is it not heartie gaine,

305 Lizard, for libbard (Buckley)

Upon advantage to take double fee?
Thou shalt have double, treble, pleaseth thee: 330
These curled, and untewed lockes of thine,
Let me but borrow upon pawne of mine.
These (oh immortall) eies, these sacred handes,
Lend me I pray thee, on sufficient bandes:
Wilt thou not trust me? By the sacred throne,   335
That Phebus in the mid day sits upon,
I will not kepe them past a day or twaine,
But Ile returne them safely home againe.

    These lockes (quoth he) that curled I do weare,
Within their folding billowes they do beare,   340
The deere remembrance twixt my love and mee:
Therefore I cannot lend them unto thee.
These eies delight, those eies did them mainetaine,
And therefore can not lend them foorth againe.
These handes gave faith of my true faithfulnesse,   345
And therefore will not lend them; pardons us.
"All sad, and in her widdow-hood of sorrow,
"Like to the Pilgrim longing for the morrow,
"Tires on the tedious day, and tels his case
"Unto the ruthelesse Eccho what he was,   350
    So doth Aurora rioteously complaine
Of love, that hath her hart unjustly slaine,
And furiously she throwes her armes about him,
As who would say, she could not be without him;
Fast to his girted side she neately clinges,   355
Her haire let loose about his shoulders flinges:
Nay twere immodest to tell the affection
That she did show him, least it draw to action.
    "Faire Cytherea, mistris of delight,
"Heere was accompanied with foule despight,   360
"The boy woxt proude to see the morning pale,
"And hence it was Jove plucked of his vale,
"That he might pittie her, and note his wrath,
"But scornefully he smiles, and helpeth nothe:
"Whereat revengefully to love he gave,   365
"Perpetuall blindnes in his choice to have,

331 untewed, unrumpled   361 The boy, Cupid
364 nothe, naught

"And too too true we finde it every day;
"That love since then hath bene a blinded boy,
"And knowes not where (unhappy wegg) to dart,
"But desperately, uncounceld slayes the hart.   370
By this deepe chat on either part was one,
And Cephalus would now perforce be gone.
What can a woman more then to entreate?
Is it for men to practise on deceite?
Like to the toiling Sisiphus in vaine,   375
She roules the stone, that tumbleth backe againe,
And strive she ne're so much to conquer him,
It will not be, for he hates such, so sinne:
Againe she pleades, his constancie to misse
Requitall in the lowest degree by Procris;   380
Inferring more to prove her argument,
That woemen cannot be with one content.
    Cephalus as now unto her speech gave heede,
Againe (quoth she), attir'd in marchants weede,
Home to thy faire spouse, move her unto ruth,   385
Pleade tediously on love, boast of thy youth,
And if nor youth, nor love, can her obtaine,
Promise rewardes for some consent, for gaine:
I say no more, but if I were a man,
These cheekes for love should never look so wan.   390
    Drown'd in a sea of overswelling hate,
As one that lies before his enimie prostrate,
Willing to live, yet scorning to beg life,
So feares he now (as twere) with his false wife;
Sometimes he cals her faire, chast, wise, and grave,   395
Anon with too too wrathfull tauntes he raves,
(Quoth he), shall I, where erst I might commaunde,
Goe and intreate with knee, and cap in hand?
Or shall I die, tormented thus in minde?
Just Radamanth, what torture canst thou finde,   400
For woemen that disloyall, counterfeite,
Love to their peeres, and yet would slay their hartes?
Hast thou no more tubs bottomelesse to fill?
Hast thou no more stones to rowle up the hill?
Hast thou no more wheeles to teare of their flesh,   405

369 wegg, wag; cf. hegg for hag l. 657

165

That so disloyally in love transgresse?
Hast thou no torment, never yet inflicted
On woemens flesh, and all this while neglected?
If so I pray thee graunt this boone to mee,
That Procris therewith may tormented be: 410
Oh! he is deafe, and damned let him live,
He will not heare, his kingdome too well thrives.
Proserpina, great goddesse of the Lake,
Some pittie sweete on the distressed take:
And when the Chaos of this worldes disdaine,   415
Hath sent this bodie to th'Elizium plaine,
And left this Center barren of repast,
Ile honor thee eternall with my ghost,
Which said, "as one that banisht doth remaine,
"Would rather die then longing be detained,   420
Desperate he goes unto his innocent wife,
What's she would wed t'abide so bad a life?
And now the tombe that closeth rotten bones,
(Deceitfull man) disguised is come home.
He asketh for himselfe, himselfe being there,   425
Would it not make a thousand woemen feare?
He tels her of his long indur'd laments,
By sea and land, that he for her hath spent,
And would have said more, but she straight was gone,
Is not the fault especiall in the man?   430
Then after takes he by her slender vale,
He holdes her fast, and tels her meny a tale,
He threw her downe upon the yeelding bed,
And swore he there would loose his maiden-head.
She (as some say, all woemen stricktly do,)   435
Faintly deni'd what she was willing too:
But when he saw her won to his desire,
(Discourteous man) did heape flax on the fire;
What there did want in wordes most subtilly,
By liberall giftes he did the same supply.   440
Having pursued so egerly his drift,
Procris unarm'd, suspecting not his shifte,
What for desire of stealth in love commended,
Or gold s'aboundant dealt, she him befrended:

431 takes] makes

166

At least gave notice of her willing minde,   445
(Æsopian snakes will alwaies prove unkind,)
At first content to parley hand in hand,
After steale kisses, talke of Cupids band,
And by degrees applide the tex so well,
As (cunning counter-feite) he did excell,   450
And what but now gently he might obtaine,
O what but now, she wisht cald backe againe.
"The duskie vapours of the middle earth,
"Drawne from contagious dewes, & noisome breathes,
"Choakt the cleere day; and now from Acheron,   455
"Blacke dismall night was come the world uppon,
"Fitting true lovers, and their sweete repast,
"Cinthia arose from Neptunes couch at last.
Oh! then this scape of Cephalus was spide,
Treason may shadowed be but never hid;   460
Unhappy woman, she the dull night spent
In sad complaintes, and giddie merrymentes,
Sometimes intending to excuse her crime,
By vowes protesting, and an other time,
(Remotive woman) would have done worse harme: 465
Hymen therewith sent forth a fresh alarme,
But Chauntecleere that did the morne bewray,
With his cleere noates gave notice of the day,
Whereat she starts, and in a desperate moode,
Skipt from the bed, all wrathfull where she stoode,   470
Vow'd to herselfe perpetuall banishment,
Mournefull complaintes, out-cries, and languishment;
Then to the craggie vaulted caves, whose sound
Small mourning doth a treble griefe resound,
Amid the thickest of the desertes, she   475
Distressed woman, forlorne, sollitarie,
With many a direfull song fits the thicke grove,
And heere and there in uncouth pathes doth rove.
Cephalus we leave unto his secrete muse.
    Lamie by chaunce some sacred herbe to use,   480
On deere compassion of some lovers plaintes,
Among the woods and moorie fennes she hauntes,
Such evill pleasing humours, fairie elves,

465 Remotive, disturbed   477 fits, befits

Observe and keepe autenticke mong'st themselves;
And now was she of purpose travailing,   485
Intending quietly to be a gathering
Some unprophane, or holy thing, or other:
Good Faierie Lady, hadst thou bene loves mother,
Not halfe so meny gallants had bene slaine,
As now in common are with endlesse paine.   490
This Lady compassing her secret favour
Procris espi'd, wondring at her behaviour,
Amaz'd she stoode at such a heavenly sight,
To see so debonary a saint at such a hight,
Her haire downe trailing, and her robes loose worne,   495
Rushing through thickets, and yet never torne,
Her brest so white as ever womans was,
And yet made subject to the Sunnes large compasse:
Each so officious, and became her so,
As Thames doth Swannes, or Swans did ever Po,   500
    Procris in steede of tearmes her to salute,
With teares and sighes, (shewing her toung was mute)
She humbly downe unto her lovely feete,
Bow'd her straight bodie Lamie to greete:
Therewith the Lady of those pretie ones,   505
That in the twylight mocke the frozen zone,
And hand in hand daunce by some silver brooke,
One at an other pointing, and up looke,
(Like rurall Faunes) upon the full fa'st Moone,
Intreating Venus some heroicke boone,   510
Gently gan stoupe, and with her sacred haire,
Her lovely eies, and face so over faire,
She neately covers, and her ungirt gowne,
Deafely commits unto the lowly growne,
She dandleth Procris thereon prettily,   515
And chaunteth soveraigne songs full merrily,
And gins to prancke her up with many a flower,
And vow'd she should be Oboron's parramore.
"Even like to one thats troubled in his sleepe,
"Amazed startes, of nothe scarce taking keepe,   520
"But in a furie tels what he hath done,
So she of Cephalus a tale begun:

    514 Deafely, deftly

Whereby the Lady quickely understood,
The cause she was so grieved and so wood.
Aie me, who can (quoth Lamie) be so cruell,   525
As to convert the building Oake to fuell?
Or rob the Ceder from his royall armes,
That spread so faire, or do a woman harme?
Wast not inough for Læda's Swanly scape,
That Jupiter was author of the rape?   530
What can be more for Cephalus then this,
That Cephalus was author of thy misse?
The fault ydone must be to him alluded,
That in the complot hath thee so abused;
I pray thee tell me, who would not consent,   535
Amourously boorded, and in merriment?
Say that thou hadst not yeelded thereunto,
As one unknowne, unmaskt thou would'st it do:
Methinkes the pastime had bene over pleasing,
So sweetely stolne, and won by such false leasing;   540
A wonder sure that Cephalus a man,
Given to hunting, with the game not ran:
But thou wilt say, he gave thee too much law,
Whereby to course, his dogs the game not saw;
Tut, twas in thee to bring the sport to passe,   545
Knowing his dogs, and where the huntsman was;
In soothe, if he had hunted cunningly,
He should have prickt out where the game did lie,
But peradventure, I will not say so,
His dogs were tir'd: and if new sport not kno,   550
For some a moneth, and many men a weeke,
Cherrish their curs before for game they seeke,
And then no marvaile though they backe did beate,
When they were strengthlesse, and orecome with heate;
If it be royall too, I heard some say,   555
Till warrant had, there's none must coorse or play:
But it is wonder, he on his owne land,
Would not strik't dead, having't so faire at stand;
A was not halfe couragious on the sport,
For who would yeeld when he hath won the fort?   560
An other time he vowes (perhaps) to kill,
But in meane while poore Procris wants her will.

It is but game (quoth she) doth stand betweene you,
And what but sporting doth he disallow?
To end which controversie, (quoth she) againe,   565
Shew him an other course upon the plaine,
And if he then beate backe, or sleeping follow,
Once more give notice by a silver hollow.
It may be he will have some deepe surmize,
That ther's new footing; note his greedie eies,   570
For thei'le be pliant, shevering in his head,
Like to a greedie Priapus in bed,
For pittie, ruthe, compassion, love, or lust,
He can not choose but yeeld; perforce he must.
Perswade thy selfe, a womans wordes can wound,   575
Her teares, oh they are able to confound:
Then Procris cease, and prey thee, mourne no more,
There be that have done ten times worse before.
   Carelesse of what the elvish wanton spake,
Procris begins a fresh her plaintes to make: 580
She kneeleth downe close by the rivers side,
And with her teares did make a second tide,
She up to heaven heaves her immortall eies,
Casting them downe againe she seem'd to die;
No shew of pleasance from her face did come,   585
Except the teares joyd on her cheekes to runne;
Her handes full often would have helpt each other,
But were so weake they could not meete together:
Some orizons I gesse she would have done,
But they, alack, were finisht ere begun.   590
Thus for a season livelesse she doth live,
And prayes to death, but deafe he nothing gives;
Continuing for a space thus desolate,
The new sprung flowers her sences animate;
Her head and eies then she ginnes to mainteine,   595
As one halfe sorrowing that she liv'd againe;
Their former strength her handes possesse at last,
Which serve to drie the teares that she doth wast.
   Thus in distressefull wise, as though she had
Bene ravisht, wounded, or at least halfe mad,   600
(Like a Thessalian Metra, of our storie

601 Metra, evasive because of her ability to change form

To have no part, nor rob us of our glory,)
She fiercely raves, and teares in carelesse sorte,
The lovely flowers (God wot) that hurteth not.
At length the silent Morpheus with his lute,   605
About her tyring braine gan to salute
Her unto rest; the Driades consent,
With downe of thissels they made her a tent,
Where softly slumbering, shadowed from the Sunne,
To rest herselfe devoutly she begun.   610
    But note the sequel: an uncivill Swaine,
That had bene wandring from the scorched plaines,
Espi'd this Amoretta where she lay,
(Conceited deedes base Clownes do oft bewray.)
Rude as he was in action, roughe, and harsh,   615
Dull, sluggish, heavie, willfull, more then rash,
He paces long'st and round about her tent,
And which way he had gone, againe he went:
His rude borne basenesse holdes him thus excus'd,
In age, we do the like in youth we us'd.   620
Nor stood he long on tearmes, but rusheth in,
And boldly thus to boord her doth begin:
    O gentle Goddesse, Loves owne lovely mother!
(For fairer then thy selfe, I know no other,)
What sacrilegious obsequies undone,   625
Art thou perfourming to thy winged Sonne?
Or are these cloistred willow walles the show,
Of thy fell hate to him that thou doest owe?
Tis mercenary toyling thus alone,
Tell me (I pray thee), wherefore doest thou moane?   630
Amid extreames who would not show his griefe?
The river pent seldome yeeldes reliefe:
But being devided flowes and nurseth many,
Sorrow (I gesse) did never good to any.
Thou art too peevish, faith, be rul'd by me;   635
Who lives content, hath not securitie,
And sooner fades the flower then the weede,
Woemen are onely made on for their deedes;
Few reape the stubble, when the corne is gon;
A Hermitage compared to a region,   640
Hath no exceede, but takes disgrace therein:

So woemen living sollitarie, sin,
More by the wrong they do commit thereby,
Then mong'st many acting the contrary:
This said, he bow'd his body to embrace her,   645
Thinking thereby, that he should greatly grace her,
And would have told her something in her eare,
But she orecome with melancholy feare,
Div'd downe amid the greene and rosey briers,
Thinking belike with teares to quench desire.   650
Aie me (I wot), who ever the like tried,
Knowes tis a hell to love, and be denied.
And who so is most politicke, true love
Will send his wits, or headlong, or to Jove.
The dowdy yongster had by this so well   655
Perswaded Procris from her solemne Cell,
That now as heeretofore through thicke and thin,
Like some pernitious hegg surpriz'd with sin,
Cutting the aire with braine-sick shreekes and cries,
Like a swift arrow with the winde she highes,   660
For that same Swaine yspoken of, did tell her,
Where and with what Nimphe Cephalus did err.
Still doth the morning add unto our muse,
And of Auroraes sweete some sweete to use,
Lets mount couragiously; ha done with hate,   665
Tis servile still on sorrow to dilate.
"The staring massacres, blood-dronken plots,
"Hot riotous hell-quickeners, Italian-nots:
"That tup their wits with snaky Nemesis,
"Teate-sucking on the poyson of her mis,   670
"With ougly fiendes ytasked let them bee,
"A milder fury to enrich seeke wee.
"If Homer did so well the feates ypaint
"Of an Ulysses, then how much more quaint,
"Might his sweete verse th'immortall Hector graced,   675
"And praise deserving all, all have imbraced?
"But what is more in ure, or getteth praise,
"Then sweete Affection tun'd in homely layes?
"Gladly would our Cephalian muse have sung
"All of white love, enamored with a tounge,   680
"That still Styll musicke, sighing, teares together,

172

"Could one conceite have made beget an other,
"And so have ransackt this rich age of that,
"The muses wanton favourites have got.
"Heavens-gloryfier, with thy holy fire,   685
"O thrise immortall quickener of desire,
"That scorn'st this vast and base prodigious clime,[1]
"Smyling at such as beg in ragged rime,
"Powre from above, or favour of the prince,
"Distilling wordes to hight the quintessence   690
"Of fame and honor: such I say doest scorne,
"Because thy stately verse was Lordly borne,
"Through all Arcadia, and the Fayerie land,
"And having smale true grace in Albion,
"Thy native soyle, as thou of right deserved'st,   695
"Rightly adornes one now, that's richly served:
"O to that quick sprite of thy smooth-cut quill,
"Without surmise of thinking any ill,
"I offer up in duetie and in zeale,[1]
"This dull conceite of mine, and do appeale,   700
"With reverence to thy (*Affection*)
"On will I put that brest-plate and there on,
"Rivet the standard boare in spite of such
"As thy bright name condigne or would but touch,
"Affection is the whole Parenthesis,   705
"That here I streake, which from our taske doth misse.
     And now conclude we in a word or twaine,
Viragon-like, Procris the woods containe;
Where, by direction from the Swaine she lay,
Shrowded with smale bowes from the scorching day,   710
Close by th'accustom'd harbour of her love,
Where he to sollace did him selfe approve;
It was his guize through melancholy anger,
Heere to oppose his body, as no straunger,
But well affected, and acquainted too,   715
With strange perfourmances, that oft did doo

---

[1] He mindes in respect of Poets and their favourites.
[1] He thinkes it the duetie of every one that sailes, to strike maine-top, before that great & mighty Poet COLLYN.

696 Spenser in Ireland   701 (*Affection*)] om.
703 boare, borne

173

Him honor, service, in respect of her,
That in the skie sits honoured as a Starre.
Soft stealing bare-foote Faieries now and then,
(That counted are as Jewels worne of men,)   720
Together with the scornefull mocking Eccho,
Nymphes, Driades, and Satyres many mo
Then I can tell you, would full oft most trim,
Like gliding ghoastes about his cabine swim;
As what might seeme to imitate delight,   725
Sweete thoughts by day, and musicke in the night,
Causing the one so to confirme the other,
As Revels, Maskes, and all that Cupids mother,
Could summon to the earth, heere was it done,
A second heaven, (aie me) there was begunne.   730
    She waves herselfe, supposing that thereby,
Aurora to embrace he would come nie;
But he mistrusting some devouring beast,
Till he could finde some pray, himselfe did rest,
Under that thicket; eft-soone with the dart,   735
He of Aurora had acted a part,
Fitter for some rude martialist then one,
That should have bene the accent of her moane.
Now in her bowels bathes the dart a good,
The lively, fresh, and rosey couloured blood   740
Then did rebate; in steade whereof pale death,
Lay with his surquedie to draw her breath,
Her speach past sence, her sences past all speaking;
Thus for prolonged life he fals entreating:
Thou saffron God (quoth he), that knits the knot   745
Of marriage, do'st, heavens know, thou knowest not what,
How art thou wrath, that mak'st me of this wrong
Author and Actor, and in tragicke song
Doest binde my temples, eke in sable cloudes,
Encamps the honor thereto is allowde;   750
O Hymen hast thou no remorse in love?
Then Hyems hencefoorth be till I approove
Againe the fruites, and comfort issuelesse
Of Jealousie in marriage had a mis.
    Heere was no want of hate, foule Achoron,   755

731 waves herself, moves restlessly   739 a good, in good earnest

Styx, and Cocytus, duskie Phlegyton,
Eumenydes, and all the hell houndes then,
Spued foorth disgrace, oh what hath Cupid done!
Pherecydes, Puppius, and Philocles mourne,
Mourne with Cephalus, and your Hymni turne   760
To dismall nightes darke ougly stratagems,
To tragicke out-cries, wonderment of men;
And those that take delight in amorous love,
Be their Heraclian wits subject to move
An other Sunne to grace our Theater,   765
That sadly mournes in blacke, with heavy cheere,
Duld with a still continuing heavinesse;
O! in extreames who comes to visite us?

L'ENVOY

Betwixt extreames
Are ready pathes and faire,
On straight and narrow went
    Leades passengers in dreames,
And ever as the aire,
Doth buzze them with content,
    A cruelle ougly fenne;
    Hated of Gods and men,

    Cals out amaine,
O whether but this way:
Or now, or never bend,
    Your steps this goale to gaine,
The tother tels you stray,
And never will finde ende,
    Thus hath the Gods decreed,
    To paine soules for their deedes.

    These monsters tway,
Ycleeped are of all,
Dispaire and eke debate,
    Which are (as Poets say)

759 Three tragic writers

Of Envies whelpes the fall,
And never come too late:
  By Procris it appeeres,
  Whose proofe is bought so deere.

Debate a foote,
And Jealousie abroade,
For remedie, dispaire
  Comes in a yellow coate,
And actes where wysardes troade,
To shew the gazers faire,
  How subtilly he can cloake,
  The tale an other spoake.

O time of times,
When monster-mongers shew,
As men in painted cloathes,
  For foode even like to pine,
And are in weale Gods know,
Upheld with spiced broathes,
  So as the weakest seeme,
  What often we not deeme.

Abandon it,
That breedes such discontent,
Foule Jealousie the sore,
  That vile despight would hit,
Debate his Chorus spent,
Comes in a tragicke more
  Then Actors on this Stage,
  Can plausively engage.

Oh Cephalus,
That nothe could pittie move,
To tend Auroraes plaintes,
  Now sham'd to tell unto us,
How thou would'st gladly love,
So Procris might not faint,
  Full oft the like doth hap,
  To them that thinke to scape.

But aie me, shee,
Unmercifully glad,
To spie her wedded mate,
   Rest from all woemen free,
Yet amorously clad,
Thought on her bended knee,
   Of him to be receav'd
   But aie me, was deceiv'd.

Oft hits the same,
For who the innocent,
To catch in secrete snares,
   (And laughes at their false shame,)
Doth covertly invent,
Themselves not throughly ware,
   Are oft beguil'd thereby,
   Woemen especially.

Faire Procris fall,
The merriment of moe,
That tread in uncouth wents,
   Remaine for sample shall,
And learne them where to goe,
Their eares not so attent,
   To vile disloyaltie,
   Nurse unto Jealousie.

Aurora shee,
Too amorous and coye,
Toyde with the hunters game,
   Till loving not to see,
Spide love cloth'd like a boy;
Whereat as one asham'd,
   She starts, and downe-ward creepes,
   Supposing all a sleepe.

"The servitor,
"That earst did bravely skoure,
"Against the frontier heate,
   "For fame and endlesse honor,

"Retir'd for want of power,
"Secure himselfe would seate,
   So she but all too soone,
   Her honor ere begun,

   Did famish cleane:
For where she sought to gaine,
The type of her content,
   By fatall powers divine,
Was suddainely so stain'd,
As made them both repent,
   And thus enamoured,
   The morning since look't red,

   As blushing thro,
Some tinssell weav'd of lawne,
Like one whose tale halfe spent,
   His coulour comes and goes,
Desirous to be gone,
In briefe, shewes his intent,
   Not halfe so stately done,
   As what he erst begun,

   Even so, and so,
Aurora pittiously,
For griefe and bitter shame,
   Cries out, oh let me goe,
(For who but sluggards eie,
The morning seekes to blame?)
   Let schollers only mourne,
   For this same wretched tourne.

   A just reward
To such as seeke the spoyle,
Of any wedded state,
   But what do we regard?
So live by others toyle,
And reape what they have got,
   No other reckoning wee,
   Suppose but all of glee.

Aie me, the Sonne,
Ere halfe our tale is quit,
His strength rebates amaine,
A clymate cold and wan,
That cannot strength a wit,
By Arte to tell the same,
Faire Cynthia shine thou bright,
Hencefoorth Ile serve the night.

ENDIMION AND PHŒBE: IDEAS LATMUS

Michael Drayton

(1595)

In I-onia whence sprang old Poets fame,
From whom that Sea did first derive her name,
The blessed bed whereon the Muses lay,
Beauty of Greece, the pride of Asia,
Whence Archelaus whom times historifie,   5
First unto Athens brought Phylosophie.
In this faire Region on a goodly Plaine,
Stretching her bounds unto the bordring Maine,
The Mountaine Latmus over-lookes the Sea,
Smiling to see the Ocean billowes play: 10
Latmus, where young Endimion usd to keepe
His fairest flock of silver-fleeced sheepe.
To whom Silvanus often would resort,
At barly-breake to see the Satyres sport;
And when rude Pan his Tabret list to sound,   15
To see the faire Nymphes foote it in a round,
Under the trees which on this Mountaine grew,
As yet the like Arabia never knew:
For all the pleasures Nature could devise,
Within this plot she did imparadize;   20
And great Diana of her speciall grace,
With Vestall rytes had hallowed all the place:
Upon this Mount there stood a stately Grove,
Whose reaching armes, to clip the Welkin strove,
Of tufted Cedars, and the branching Pine,   25
Whose bushy tops themselves doe so intwine,
As seem'd when Nature first this work begun,

Shee then conspir'd against the piercing Sun;
Under whose covert (thus divinely made)
Phœbus greene Laurell florisht in the shade: 30
Faire Venus Mirtile, Mars his warlike Fyrre,
Minervas Olive, and the weeping Myrhe,
The patient Palme, which thrives in spite of hate,
The Popler, to Alcides consecrate;
Which Nature in such order had disposed, 35
And there-withall these goodly walkes inclosed,
As serv'd for hangings and rich Tapestry,
To beautifie this stately Gallery:
Imbraudring these in curious trailes along,
The clustred Grapes, the golden Citrons hung, 40
More glorious then the precious fruite were these,
Kept by the Dragon in Hesperides;
Or gorgious Arras in rich colours wrought,
With silk from Affrick, or from Indie brought:
Out of thys soyle sweet bubling Fountaines crept, 45
As though for joy the sencelesse stones had wept;
With straying channels dauncing sundry wayes,
With often turnes, like to a curious Maze:
Which breaking forth, the tender grasse bedewed
Whose silver sand with orient Pearle was strewed, 50
Shadowed with Roses and sweet Eglantine,
Dipping theyr sprayes into this christalline:
From which the byrds the purple berries pruned,
And to theyr loves their small recorders tuned.
The Nightingale, woods Herauld of the Spring, 55
The whistling Woosell, Mavis carroling,
Tuning theyr trebbles to the waters fall,
Which made the musicque more angelicall:
Whilst gentle Zephyre murmuring among,
Kept tyme, and bare the burthen to the song. 60
About whose brims, refresht with dainty showers,
Grew Amaranthus, and sweet Gilliflowers,
The Marigold, Phœbus beloved frend,
The Moly, which from sorcery doth defend:
Violet, Carnation, Balme and Cassia, 65
Ideas Primrose, coronet of May.
Above this Grove a gentle faire ascent,

Which by degrees of Milk-white Marble went:
Upon the top, a Paradise was found,
With which Nature this miracle had crownd; 70
Empald with Rocks of rarest precious stone,
Which like the flames of Aetna brightly shone;
And serv'd as Lanthornes furnished with light,
To guide the wandring passengers by night:
For which fayre Phœbe sliding from her Sphere, 75
Used oft times to come and sport her there.
And from the Azure starry-painted Sky,
Embalmd the bancks with precious lunary:
That now her Menalus shee quite forsooke,
And unto Latmus wholy her betooke, 80
And in this place her pleasure us'd to take,
And all was for her sweet Endimions sake:
Endimion, the lovely Shepheards boy,
Endimion, great Phœbes onely joy,
Endimion, in whose pure-shining eyes, 85
The naked Faries daunst the heydegies.
The shag-haird Satyrs Mountain-climing race,
Have been made tame by gazing in his face.
For this boyes love, the water-Nymphs have wept
Stealing oft times to kisse him whilst he slept: 90
And tasting once the Nectar of his breath,
Surfet with sweet, and languish unto death;
And Jove oft-times bent to lascivious sport,
And comming where Endimion did resort,
Hath courted him, inflamed with desire, 95
Thinking some Nymph was cloth'd in boyes attire.
And often-times the simple rural Swaines,
Beholding him in crossing or'e the Plaines,
Imagined Apollo from above
Put on this shape, to win some Maidens love. 100
This Shepheard, Phœbe ever did behold,
Whose love already had her thoughts controld;
From Latmus top (her stately throne) shee rose,
And to Endimion downe beneath shee goes.
Her Brothers beames now had shee layd aside, 105
Her horned cressent, and her full-fac'd pride:

79 Menalus, for Maenalus, a mountain in Arcadia

For had shee come adorned with her light,
No mortall eye could have endur'd the sight;
But like a Nymph, crown'd with a flowrie twine,
And not like Phœbe, as herselfe divine.   110
An Azur'd Mantle purfled with a vaile,
Which in the Ayre puft like a swelling saile,
Embosted Rayne-bowes did appeare in silk,
With wavie streames as white as mornings Milk:
Which ever as the gentle Ayre did blow,   115
Still with the motion seem'd to ebb and flow:
About her neck a chayne twise twenty fold,
Of Rubyes, set in lozenges of gold;
Trust up in trammels, and in curious pleats,
With spheary circles falling on her teats.   120
A dainty smock of Cipresse, fine and thin,
Or'e cast with curls next to her Lilly skin:
Throgh which the purenes of the same did show
Lyke Damaske-roses strew'd with flakes of snow,
Discovering all her stomack to the waste,   125
With branches of sweet circling veynes enchaste.
A Coronet she ware of Mirtle bowes,
Which gave a shadow to her Ivory browes.
No smother beauty maske did beauty smother
"Great lights dim lesse yet burn not one another,   130
Nature abhorrs to borrow from the Mart,
"Simples fit beauty, fie on drugs and Art.
    Thus came shee where her love Endimion lay,
Who with sweet Carrols sang the night away;
And as it is the Shepheards usuall trade,   135
Oft on his pype a Roundelay he playd.
As meeke he was as any Lambe might be,
Nor never lyv'd a fayrer youth then he:
His dainty hand, the snow it selfe dyd stayne,
Or her to whom Jove showr'd in golden rayne: 140
From whose sweet palme the liquid Pearle dyd swell,
Pure as the drops of Aganippas Well:
Cleere as the liquor which fayre Hebe spylt;
Hys sheephooke silver, damask'd all with gilt.
The staffe it selfe, of snowie Ivory,   145

111 purfled, bordered   129 smother, ? smothering

Studded with Currall, tipt with Ebony;
His tresses, of the Ravens shyning black,
Stragling in curles along his manly back.
The balls which nature in his eyes had set,
Lyke Diamonds inclosing Globes of Jet: 150
Which sparkled from their milky lids out-right,
Lyke fayre Orions heaven-adorning light.
The stars on which her heavenly eyes were bent,
And fixed still with lovely blandishment,
For whom so oft disguised shee was seene, 155
As shee Celestiall Phœbe had not beene:
Her dainty Buskins lac'd unto the knee,
Her pleyted Frock, tuck'd up accordingly:
A Nymph-like huntresse, arm'd with bow & dart
About the woods she scoures the long-liv'd Hart. 160
She climes the mountains with the light-foot Fauns
And with the Satyrs scuds it or'e the Launes.
In Musicks sweet delight shee shewes her skill,
Quavering the Cithron nimbly with her quill,
Upon each tree she carves Endimions name 165
In Gordian knots, with Phœbe to the same:
To kill him Venson now she pitch'd her toyles,
And to this lovely Raunger brings the spoyles;
And thus whilst she by chaste desire is led
Unto the Downes where he his fayre Flocks fed, 170
Neere to a Grove she had Endimion spide,
Where he was fishing by a River side
Under a Popler, shadowed from the Sun,
Where merrily to court him she begun:
Sweet boy (qd. she) take what thy hart can wish, 175
When thou doost angle would I were a fish,
When thou art sporting by the silver Brooks,
Put in thy hand, thou need'st no other hooks;
Hard harted boy Endimion, looke on mee,
Nothing on earth I hold too deere for thee: 180
I am a Nimph and not of humaine blood,
Begot by Pan on Isis sacred flood:
When I was borne upon that very day,
Phœbus was seene the Reveller to play:
In Joves hye house the Gods assembled all, 185

And Juno held her sumptuous Festivall,
Oceanus that hower was dauncing spy'de,
And Tython seene to frolick with his Bride,
The Halcions that season sweetly sang,
And all the shores, with shouting Sea-Nymphes rang, 190
And on that day, my birth to memorize,
The Shepheards hold a solemne sacrifice:
The chast Diana nurst mee in her lap,
And I suckt Nectar from her Downe-soft pap.
The Well wherein this body bathed first, 195
Who drinks thereof, shall never after thirst;
The water hath the Lunacie appeased,
And by the vertue, cureth all diseased;
The place wherein my bare feete touch the mold,
Made up in balls, for Pomander is sold. 200
See, see, these hands have robd the Snow of white,
These dainty fingers, organs of delight:
Behold these lyps, the Load-stones of desire,
Whose words inchant, like Amphyons well-tun'd lyre,
This foote, Arts just proportion doth reveale, 205
Signing the earth with heavens own manuel seale.
Goe, play the wanton, I will tend thy flock,
And wait the howres as duly as a clock;
Ile deck thy Ram with bells, and wreathes of Bay,
And gild his hornes upon the sheering day; 210
And with a garlond crown thee Shepheards king,
And thou shalt lead the gay Gyrles in a ring;
Birds with their wings shall fan thee in the Sun,
And all the fountaynes with pure Wine shall run;
I have a Quier of dainty Turtle-doves, 215
And they shall sit and sweetly sing our loves:
Ile lay thee on the Swans soft downy plume,
And all the Winde shall gently breath perfume,
Ile plat thy locks with many a curious pleate,
And chafe thy temples with a sacred heate; 220
The Muses still shall keepe thee company,
And lull thee with inchaunting harmony;
If not all these, yet let my vertues move thee,
A chaster Nymph Endimion cannot love thee.

206 manuel seale, signature

But he imagin'd she some Nymph had been,   225
Because shee was apparrelled in greene;
Or happily, some of fayre Floras trayne,
Which oft did use to sport upon the Plaine:
He tels her, he was Phœbes servant sworne,
And oft in hunting had her Quiver borne,   230
And that to her virginity he vowed,
Which in no hand by Venus was alowed;
Then unto her a Catalogue recites
Of Phœbes Statutes, and her hallowed Rites,
And of the grievous penalty inflicted,   235
On such as her chast lawes had interdicted:
Now, he requests, that shee would stand aside,
Because the fish her shadow had espide;
Then he intreats her that she would be gone,
And at this time to let him be alone;   240
Then turnes him from her in an angry sort,
And frownes and chafes that shee had spoil'd his sport.
And then he threatens her, if she did stay,
And told her great Diana came this way.
But for all this, this Nymph would not forbeare,   245
But now she smoothes his crispy-curled haire,
And when hee (rudely) will'd her to refrayne,
Yet scarcely ended, she begins agayne:
Thy Ewes (qd. she) with Milk shall daily spring,
And to thy profit yeerely Twins shall bring,   250
And thy fayre flock, (a wonder to behold)
Shall have their fleeces turn'd to burnisht gold;
Thy batefull pasture to thy wanton Thewes,
Shall be refresht with Nectar-dropping dewes,
The Oakes smooth leaves, sirropt with hony fall,   255
Trickle down drops to quench thy thirst withall:
The cruell Tygar will I tame for thee,
And gently lay his head upon thy knee;
And by my spells, the Wolves jawes will I lock,
And (as good Sheepheards) make them gard thy flock,   260
Ile mount thee bravely on a Lyons back,
To drive the fomy-tusked Bore to wrack:
The brazen-hoofed yelling Bulls Ile yoke,

253 Thewes, for theaves, ewes

186

And with my hearbs, the scaly Dragon choke.
Thou in great Phœbes Ivory Coche shalt ride,   265
Which drawne by Eagles, in the ayre shall glide:
Ile stay the time, it shall not steale away,
And twenty Moones as seeming but one day.
Behold (fond boy), this Rozen-weeping Pine,
This mournfull Larix, dropping Turpentine,   270
This mounting Teda, thus with tempests torne,
With incky teares continually to mourne;
Looke on this tree, which blubbereth Amber gum,
Which seemes to speak to thee, though it be dumb,
Which being senceles blocks, as thou do'st see,   275
Weepe at my woes, that thou might'st pitty mee:
O thou art young, and fit for loves profession,
Like wax which warmed quickly takes impression,
Sorrow in time, with floods those eyes shall weare,
Whence pitty now cannot extort a teare.   280
Fond boy, with words thou might'st be overcome,
"But love surpriz'd the hart, the tongue is dumbe,
But as I can, Ile strive to conquer thee;
Yet teares, & sighes, my weapons needs must bee.
My sighs move trees, rocks melting with my tears,   285
But thou art blind; and cruell, stop'st thine eares:
Looke in this Well, (if beautie men alow)
Though thou be faire, yet I as fayre as thou;
I am a Vestall, and a spotles Mayd,
Although by love to thee I am betrayd: 290
But sith (unkinde) thou doost my love disdayne,
To rocks and hills my selfe I will complaine.
   Thus with a sigh, her speeches of she broke,
The whilst her eyes to him in silence spoke;
And from the place this wanton Nymph arose,   295
And up to Latmus all in hast shee goes;
Like to a Nymph on shady Citheron,
The swift Ismænos, or Thirmodoon,
Gliding like Thetis, on the fleet waves borne,
Or which trips upon the eares of Corne;   300
Like Swallowes when in open ayre they strive,

270 Larix, the larch   271 Teda, the torch pine
273 this tree, the poplar
187

Or like the Foule which towring Falcons drive.
But whilst the wanton thus pursu'd his sport,
Deceitfull Love had undermin'd the Fort,
And by a breach (in spight of all deniance,)   305
Entred the Fort which lately made defiance:
And with strong siedge had now begirt about
The mayden Skonce which held the souldier out.
"Love wants his eyes, yet shoots he passing right,
His shafts our thoughts, his bowe hee makes our sight.   310
His deadly piles are tempred by such Art,
As still directs the Arrowe to the hart:
He cannot love, and yet forsooth he will,
He sees her not, and yet he sees her still,
Hee goes unto the place shee stood upon,   315
And asks the poore soyle whether she was gon;
Fayne would he follow her, yet makes delay,
Fayne would he goe, and yet fayne would he stay,
Hee kist the flowers depressed with her feete,
And swears from her they borrow'd all their sweet.   320
Faine would he cast aside this troublous thought,
But still like poyson, more and more it wrought,
And to himselfe thus often would he say,
Heere my Love sat, in this place did shee play,
Heere in this Fountaine hath my Goddesse been,   325
And with her presence hath she grac'd this green.
　　Now black-brow'd Night plac'd in her chaire of Jet,
Sat wrapt in clouds within her Cabinet,
And with her dusky mantle over-spred,
The path the Sunny Palfrayes us'd to tred;   330
And Cynthia sitting in her Christall chayre,
In all her pompe now rid along her Spheare,
The honnied dewe descended in soft showres,
Drizled in Pearle upon the tender flowers;
And Zephyre husht, and with a whispering gale,   335
Seemed to harken to the Nightingale,
Which in the thorny brakes with her sweet song,
Unto the silent Night bewrayd her wrong.
　　Now fast by Latmus neere unto a Grove,
Which by the mount was shadowed from above,   340

308 Skonce, fort　　　　　　　311 piles, arrowheads

Upon a banck Endimion sat by night,
To whom fayre Phœbe lent her frendly light:
And sith his flocks were layd them downe to rest,
Thus gives his sorrowes passage from his brest:
Sweet leaves (qd. he) which with the ayre do tremble,   345
Oh how your motions do my thoughts resemble,
With that milde breath, by which you onely move,
Whisper my words in silence to my Love:
Convay my sighes, sweet Civet-breathing ayre,
In dolefull accents to my heavenly fayre;   350
You murmuring Springs, like doleful Instruments
Upon your gravell sound my sad laments,
And in your silent bubling as you goe,
Consort your selves like Musick to my woe.
And lifting now his sad and heavy eyes   355
Up, towards the beauty of the burnisht skies,
Bright Lamps (qd. he), the glorious Welkin bears,
Which clip about the Plannets wandring Sphears,
And in your circled Maze doe ever role,
Dauncing about the never-mooving Pole: 360
Sweet Nymph, which in fayre Elice doost shine,
Whom thy surpassing beauty made divine,
Now in the Artick constellation,[a]
Smyle sweet Calisto on Endimion:
And thou brave Perseus in the Northern ayre,   365
Holding Medusa by the snaky hayre,
Joves showre-begotten Son, whose valure tryed,
In seaventeene glorious lights art stellified;
Which won'st thy love, left as a Monsters pray;
And thou the lovely fayre Andromida,   370
Borne of the famous Etheopian lyne,
Darting these rayes from thy transpiercing eyne
To thee the bright Cassiopey, with these,
(Whose beauty strove with the Neriedes,)
With all the troupe of the celestiall band,   375
Which on Olimpus in your glory stand;
And you great wandring lights, if from your Sphears

[a] The constellations neere the Pole Artick.
347 you] om.
361 Elice, for Helice, named from the home of Calisto

You have regard unto a Sheepeheards teares,
Or as men say, if over earthly things
You onely rule as Potentates and Kings,   380
Unto my loves event sweet Stars direct
Your kindest revolution and aspect,
And bend your cleere eyes from your Thrones above
Upon Endimion, pyning thus in love.
   Now, ere the purple dauning yet did spring,   385
The joyfull Lark began to stretch her wing,
And now the Cock, the mornings Trumpeter,
Playd hunts-up for the day starre to appeare,
Downe slydeth Phœbe from her Christall chayre,
Sdayning to lend her light unto the ayre,   390
But unto Latmus all in haste is gon,
Longing to see her sweet Endimion;
At whose departure all the Plannets gazed,
As at some seld-seene accident amazed,
Till reasoning of the same, they fell at ods,   395
So that a question grew amongst the Gods,
Whether without a generall consent
She might depart their sacred Parliament.
But what they could doe was but all in vaine,
Of liberty they could her not restraine: 400
For of the seaven sith she the lowest was,
Unto the earth she might the easiest passe;
Sith onely by her moysty influence,
Of earthly things she hath preheminence,
And under her, mans mutable estate,   405
As with her changes doth participate;
And from the working of her waning source,
Th'uncertaine waters held a certaine course,
Throughout her kingdome she might walk at large
Whereof as Empresse she had care and charge,   410
And as the Sunne unto the Day gives light,
So is she onely Mistris of the Night;
Which whilst shee in her oblique course dooth guide,
The glittering stars apeare in all their pride,
Which to her light their frendly Lamps do lend,   415
And on her trayne as Hand-maydes doe attend,

388 hunts-up, an early-morning song

190

And thirteene times she through her Sphere doth run,
Ere Phœbus full his yearly course have don:
And unto her of women is assign'd,
Predominance of body and of mind,   420
That as of Plannets shee most variable,
So of all creatures they most mutable.
But her sweet Latmus which she lov'd so much,
No sooner once her dainty foote doth touch,
But that the Mountaine with her brightnes shone   425
And gave a light to all the Horizon:
Even as the Sun which darknes long did shroud,
Breakes suddainly from underneath a clowd,
So that the Nimphs which on her still attended,
Knew certainly great Phœbe was discended;   430
And all aproched to this sacred hill,
There to awayt their soveraigne Goddesse will,
And now the little Birds whom Nature taught,
To honour great Diana as they ought,
Because she is the Goddesse of the woods,   435
And sole preserver of their hallowed floods,
Set to their consort in their lower springs,
That with the Musicke all the mountaine rings;
So that it seemd the Birds of every Grove
Which should excell and passe each other strove,   440
That in the higher woods and hollow grounds,
The murmuring Eccho every where resounds,
The trembling brooks their slyding courses stayd,
The whilst the waves one with another playd,
And all the flocks in this rejoycing mood,   445
As though inchaunted do forbeare their food:
The heards of Deare downe from the mountains flew,
As loth to come within Dianas view,
Whose piercing arrowes from her Ivory bowe,
Had often taught her powerfull hand to knowe;   450
And now from Latmus looking towards the plains
Casting her eyes upon the Sheepheards swaines,
Perceiv'd her deare Endimions flock were stray'd
And he himselfe upon the ground was layd;
Who late recald from melancholy deepe,   455
The chaunting Birds had lulled now asleepe:

For why the Musick in this humble kinde,
As it first found, so doth it leave the minde;
And melancholy from the Spleene begun,
By passion moov'd, into the veynes doth run;   460
Which when this humor as a swelling Flood
By vigor is infused in the blood;
The vitall spirits doth mightely apall;[b]
And weakeneth so the parts organicall,
And when the sences are disturbd and tierd,   465
With what the hart incessantly desierd,
Like Travellers with labor long opprest,
Find release, eft-soones they fall to rest.
    And comming now to her Endimion,
Whom heavy sleepe had lately ceas'd upon,   470
Kneeling her downe, him in her armes she clips,
And with sweet kisses sealeth up his lips,
Whilst from her eyes, teares streaming downe in showrs
Fell on his cheekes like dew upon the flowrs,
In globy circles like pure drops of Milk,   475
Sprinckled on Roses, or fine crimson silk:
Touching his brow, this is the seate (quoth she)
Where Beauty sits in all her Majestie,
She calls his eye-lids those pure Christall covers
Which do include the looking Glasse of Lovers,   480
She calls his lips the sweet delicious folds
Which rare perfume and precious incense holds,
Shee calls his soft smooth Allablaster skin,
The Lawne which Angels are attyred in,
Sweet face (qd. she), but wanting words I spare thee   485
Except to heaven alone I should compare thee:
And whilst her words she wasteth thus in vayne,
Sporting herselfe the tyme to entertayne,
The frolick Nymphes with Musicks sacred sound,
Entred the Meddowes dauncing in a round: 490
And unto Phœbe straight their course direct,
Which now their joyfull comming did expect,
Before whose feet their flowrie spoyles they lay,
And with sweet Balme his body doe imbay.
And on the Laurels growing there along,   495

    [b] The effect of Melancholie.

Their wreathed garlonds all about they hung:
And all the ground within the compasse load,
With sweetest flowers, wheron they lightly troad.
With Nectar then his temples they be dew,
And kneeling softly kisse him all arew;   500
Then in brave galiards they themselves advaunce,
And in the Thyas, Bacchus stately daunce;
Then following on fayre Floras gilded trayne,
Into the Groves they thus depart agayne,
And now to shew her powerfull deitie,   505
Her sweet Endimion more to beautifie,
Into his soule the Goddesse doth infuse,
The fiery nature of a heavenly Muse,
Which in the spyrit labouring by the mind
Pertaketh of celestiall things by kind: 510
For why the soule being divine alone,°
Exempt from vile and grosse corruption,
Of heavenly secrets comprehensible,
Of which the dull flesh is not sensible,
And by one onely powerfull faculty,   515
Yet governeth a multiplicity,
Being essentiall, uniforme in all;
Not to be sever'd nor dividuall,
But in her function holdeth her estate,
By powers divine in her ingenerate,   520
And so by inspiration conceaveth
What heaven to her by divination breatheth;
But they no sooner to the shades were gone,
Leaving their Goddesse by Endimion,
But by the hand the lovely boy shee takes,   525
And from his sweet sleepe softly him awakes,
Who being struck into a sodayne feare,
Beholding thus his glorious Goddesse there,
His hart transpiersed with this sodayne glance,
Became as one late cast into a trance: 530
Wiping his eyes not yet of perfect sight,
Scarcely awak'd, amazed at the light,
His cheekes now pale, then lovely blushing red,

° The excellency of the soule.

502 Thyas, from θίασος] (sugg. Tillotson); Tryas
H*   193

Which oft increasd, and quickly vanished,
And as on him her fixed eyes were bent, 535
So to and fro his colour came and went;
Like to a Christall neere the fire set,
Against the brightnes rightly opposet,
Now doth reteyne the colour of the flame,
And lightly moved againe, reflects the same; 540
For our affection quickned by her heate,[d]
Alayd and strengthned by a strong conceit,
The minde disturbed forth-with doth convart,
To an internall passion of the hart,
By motion of that sodaine joy or feare, 545
Which we receive either by the eye or eare,
For by retraction of the spirit and blood,
From those exterior parts where first they stood,
Into the center of the body sent,
Returnes againe more strong and vehement: 550
And in the like extreamitie made cold,
About the same, themselves doe closely hold,
And though the cause be like, in this respect
Works by this meanes a contrary effect.

    Thus whilst this passion hotely held his course, 555
Ebbing and flowing from his springing source,
With the strong fit of this sweet Fever moved,
At sight of her which he intirely loved,
Not knowing yet great Phœbe this should be,
His soveraigne Goddesse, Queene of Chastitie, 560
Now like a man whom Love had learned Art,
Resolv'd at once his secrets to impart:
But first repeats the torments he had past,
The woes indur'd since tyme he saw her last;
Now he reports he noted whilst she spake, 565
The bustling windes their murmure often brake,
And being silent, seemd to pause and stay,
To listen to her what she ment to say:
Be kind (quoth he) sweet Nymph, unto thy lover,
My soules sole essence, and my sences mover, 570
Life of my life, pure Image of my hart,
Impressure of Conceit, Invention, Art,

    [d] The causes of the externall signes of passion.

My vitall spirit, receves his spirit from thee,
Thou art that all which ruleth all in me,
Thou art the sap, and life whereby I live,   575
Which powerfull vigor doost receive and give;
Thou nourishest the flame wherein I burne,
The North wherto my harts true tuch doth turne.
Pitty my poore flock, see their wofull plight,
Theyr Maister perisht living from thy sight,   580
Theyr fleeces rent, my tresses all forlorne,
I pyne, whilst they theyr pasture have forborne;
Behold (quoth he) this little flower belowe,
Which heere within this Fountayne brim dooth grow;
With that, a solemne tale begins to tell   585
Of this fayre flower, and of this holy Well,
A goodly legend, many Winters old,
Learn'd by the Sheepheards sitting by their folde,
How once this Fountayne was a youthfull swaine,
A frolick boy and kept upon the playne,   590
Unfortunate it hapt to him (quoth he)
To love a fayre Nymph as I nowe love thee,
To her his love and sorrow he imparts,
Which might dissolve a rock of flinty harts;
To her he sues, to her he makes his mone,   595
But she more deafe and hard then steele or stone;
And thus one day with griefe of mind opprest,
As in this place he layd him downe to rest,
The Gods at length uppon his sorrowes looke,
Transforming him into this pirrling Brooke,   600
Whose murmuring bubles softly as they creepe,
Falling in drops, the Channell seems to weepe,
But shee thus careles of his misery,
Still spends her dayes in mirth and jollity;
And comming one day to the River side,   605
Laughing for joy when she the same espyde,
This wanton Nymph in that unhappy hower,
Was heere transformd into this purple flower,
Which towards the water turnes it selfe agayne,
To pitty him by her unkindnes slayne.   610
    She, as it seemd, who all this time attended,
Longing to heare that once his tale were ended,

Now like a jealous woman she repeats,
Mens subtilties, and naturall deceyts;
And by example strives to verifie,   615
Their ficklenes and vaine inconstancie:
Their hard obdurate harts, and wilfull blindnes,
Telling a storie wholy of unkindnes;
But he, who well perceived her intent,
And to remove her from this argument,   620
Now by the sacred Fount he vowes and sweares,
By Lovers sighes, and by her halowed teares,
By holy Latmus now he takes his oath,
That all he spake was in good fayth and troth;
And for no frayle uncertayne doubt should move her,   625
Vowes secrecie, the crown of a true Lover.
    She hearing this, thought time that she reveald,
That kind affection which she long conceald,
Determineth to make her true Love known,
Which shee had borne unto Endimion;   630
I am no Huntresse, nor no Nymph (quoth she)
As thou perhaps imagin'st me to be,
I am great Phœbe, Latmus sacred Queene,
Who from the skies have hether past unseene,
And by thy chast love hether was I led,   635
Where full three yeares thy fayre flock have I fed,
Upon these Mountaines and these firtile plaines,
And crownd thee King of all the Sheepheards swaines:
Nor wanton, nor lacivious is my love,
Nor never lust my chast thoughts once could move.   640
But sith thou thus hast offerd at my Shrine,
And of the Gods hast held me most divine,
Mine Altars thou with sacrifice hast stord,
And in my Temples has my name ador'd,
And of all other, most hast honor'd mee,   645
Great Phœbes glory thou alone shalt see.
    Thys spake, she putteth on her brave attire,
As being burnisht in her Brothers fire,
Purer then that Celestiall shining flame
Wherein great Jove unto his Lemmon came,   650
Which quickly had his pale cheekes over-spred,

650 his Lemmon, Aegina

196

And tincted with a lovely blushing red.
Which whilst her Brother Titan for a space,
Withdrew himself, to give his sister place,
Shee now is darkned to all creatures eyes,   655
Whilst in the shadow of the earth she lyes,
For that the earth of nature cold and dry,
A very Chaos of obscurity,
Whose Globe exceeds her compasse by degrees,
Fixed upon her Superficies;   660
When in his shadow she doth hap to fall,
Dooth cause her darknes to be generall.
   Thus whilst he layd his head upon her lap,
Shee in a fiery Mantle doth him wrap,
And carries him up from this lumpish mould,   665
Into the skyes, whereas he might behold,
The earth in perfect roundnes of a ball
Exceeding globes most artificiall:
Which in a fixed poynt Nature disposed,
And with the sundry Elements inclosed,   670
Which as the Center permanent dooth stay,
When as the skies in their diurnall sway,
Strongly maintaine the ever-turning course,
Forced alone by their first moover sourse,
Where he beholds the ayery Regions,   675
Whereas the clouds and strange impressions,
Maintaynd by coldnes often doe appeare,
And by the highest Region of the ayre,
Unto the cleerest Element of fire,
Which to her silver foot-stoole doth aspire.   680
Then dooth she mount him up into her Sphere,
Imparting heavenly secrets to him there,
Where lightned by her shining beames, he sees
The powerfull Plannets, all in their degrees,
Their sundry revolutions in the skies,   685
And by their working how they simpathize;
All in theyr circles severally prefixt,
And in due distance each with other mixt:
The mantions which they hold in their estate,
Of which by nature they participate;   690
And how those signes their severall places take,

197

Within the compasse of the Zodiacke:
And in their severall triplicities consent,^e
Unto the nature of an Element,
To which the Plannets do themselves disperce,   695
Having the guidance of this univers,
And do from thence extend their severall powers,
Unto this little fleshly world of ours:
Wherin her Makers workmanship is found,
As in contriving of this mighty round,   700
In such strange maner and such fashion wrought,
As doth exceede mans dull and feeble thought,
Guiding us still by their directions;
And that our fleshly frayle complections,
Of Elementall natures grounded bee,   705
With which our dispositions most agree,
Some of the fire and ayre participate,
And some of watry and of earthy state,
As hote and moyst, with chilly cold and dry,
And unto these the other contrary;   710
And by their influence powerfull on the earth,
Predominant in mans fraile mortall bearth,
And that our lives effects and fortunes are,
As is that happy or unlucky Starre,
Which reigning in our frayle nativitie,   715
Seales up the secrets of our destinie,
With frendly Plannets in conjunction set,
Or els with other meerely opposet:
And now to him her greatest power she lent,
To lift him to the starry Firmament,   720
Where he beheld that milky stayned place,
By which the Twynns & heavenly Archers trace
The dogge which doth the furious Lyon beate,
Whose flaming breath increaseth Titans heate,
The teare-distilling mournfull Pliades,   725
Which on the earth the stormes & tempests raise,
And all the course the constellations run,
When in conjunction with the Moone or Sun,
When towards the fixed Articke they arise,
When towards the Antarticke, falling from our eyes;   730

^e The signes in their triplicities participate with the Elements.

198

And having impt the wings of his desire,
And kindled him, with this cœlestiall fire,
She sets him downe, and vanishing his sight,
Leaves him inwrapped in this true delight:
Now wheresoever he his fayre flock fed,   735
The Muses still Endimion followed;
His sheepe as white as Swans or driven snow,
Which beautified the soyle with such a show,
As where hee folded in the darkest Night,
There never needed any other light;   740
If that he hungred and desired meate,
The Bees would bring him Honny for to eate,
Yet from his lyps would not depart away,
Tyll they were loden with Ambrosia;
And if he thirsted, often there was seene   745
A bubling Fountaine spring out of the greene,
With Christall liquor fild unto the brim,
Which did present her liquid store to him.
If hee would hunt, the fayre Nymphs at his will,
With Bowes & Quivers would attend him still: 750
And what-soever he desierd to have,
That he obtain'd, if hee the same would crave.
   And now at length, the joyful tyme drew on,
Shee meant to honor her Endimion,
And glorifie him on that stately Mount   755
Whereof the Goddesse made so great account.
Shee sends Joves winged Herauld to the woods,
The neighbour Fountains, & the bordring floods,
Charging the Nymphes which did inhabit there,
Upon a day appoynted to appeare,   760
And to attend her sacred Majestie
In all theyr pompe and great solemnity.
Having obtaynd great Phœbus free consent,
To further her divine and chast intent,
Which thus imposed as a thing of waight,   765
In stately troupes appeare before her straight.
The Faunes and Satyres from the tufted Brakes,
Theyr brisly armes wreath'd al about with snakes;
Their sturdy loynes with ropes of Ivie bound,
Theyr horned heads with Woodbine Chaplets crownd,   770

With Cipresse Javelens, and about their thyes,
The flaggy hayre disorder'd loosely flyes:
Th'Oriades like to the Spartan Mayd,
In Murrie-scyndall gorgiously arayd:
With gallant greene Scarfes girded in the wast,   775
Theyr flaxen hayre with silken fillets lac'd,
Woven with flowers in sweet lascivious wreathes,
Mooving like feathers as the light ayre breathes,
With crownes of Mirtle, glorious to behold,
Whose leaves are painted with pure drops of gold: 780
With traines of fine Bisse checker'd al with frets
Of dainty Pincks and precious Violets,
In branched Buskins of fine Cordiwin,
With spangled garters downe unto the shin,
Fring'd with fine silke, of many a sundry kind,   785
Which lyke to pennons waved with the wind.
The Hamadriads from their shady Bowers,
Deckt up in Garlonds of the rarest flowers,
Upon the backs of milke-white Bulls were set,
With horne and hoofe as black as any Jet,   790
Whose collers were great massy golden rings,
Led by their swaynes in twisted silken strings;
Then did the lovely Driades appeare,
On dapled Staggs, which bravely mounted were,
Whose velvet palmes with nosegaies rarely dight,   795
To all the rest bred wonderfull delight;
And in this sort accompaned with these,
In tryumph rid the watry Niades,
Upon Sea-horses, trapt with shining finns,
Arm'd with their male impenitrable skinns,   800
Whose scaly crests like Raine-bowes bended hye;
Seeme to controule proud Iris in the skye;
Upon a Charriot was Endimion layd,
In snowy Tissue gorgiously arayd,
Of precious Ivory covered or'e with Lawne,   805
Which by foure stately Unicornes was drawne.
Of ropes of Orient pearle their traces were,
Pure as the path which dooth in heaven appeare,
With rarest flowers inchaste and over-spred,

774 Murrie-scyndall, purple silk   781 Bisse, fine linen

Which serv'd as Curtaynes to this glorious bed,   810
Whose seate of Christal in the Sun-beames shone,
Like thunder-breathing Joves celestiall Throne;
Upon his head a Coronet instald,
Of one intire and mighty Emerald,
With richest Bracelets on his lilly wrists,   815
Of Hellitropium, linckt with golden twists;
A bevy of fayre Swans, which flying over,
With their large wings him from the Sun do cover,
And easily wafting as he went along,
Doe lull him still with their inchaunting song,   820
Whilst all the Nimphes on solemne Instruments,
Sound daintie Musick to their sweet laments.
   And now great Phœbe in her tryumph came,
With all the tytles of her glorious name,
Diana, Delia, Luna, Cynthia,   825
Virago, Hecate, and Elythia,
Prothiria, Dictinna, Proserpine,
Latona, and Lucina, most divine;
And in her pompe began now to approch,
Mounted aloft upon her Christall Coach,   830
Drawn or'e the playnes by foure pure milk-white Hinds,
Whose nimble feete seem'd winged with the winds,
Her rarest beauty being now begun,
But newly borrowed from the golden Sun,
Her lovely cressant with a decent space,   835
By due proportion beautifi'd her face,
Till having fully fild her circled side,
Her glorious fulnes now appeard in pride;
Which long her changing brow could not retaine,
But fully waxt, began againe to wane;   840
Upon her brow (like meteors in the ayre)
Twenty & eyght great gorgious lamps shee bare;
Some, as the Welkin, shining passing bright,
Some not so sumptuous, others lesser light,
Some burne, some other let theyr faire lights fall,   845
Composd in order Geometricall;
And to adorne her with a greater grace,
And ad more beauty to her lovely face,
Her richest Globe shee gloriously displayes,

Now that the Sun had hid his golden rayes: 850
Least that his radiencie should her suppresse,
And so might make her beauty seeme the lesse;
Her stately trayne layd out in azur'd bars,
Poudred all thick with troopes of silver stars:
Her ayrie vesture yet so rare and strange,   855
As every howre the colour seem'd to change,
Yet still the former beauty doth retaine,
And ever came unto the same againe.
Then fayre Astrea, of the Titans line,
Whom equity and justice made divine,   860
Was seated heer upon the silver beame,
And with the raines guides on this goodly teame,
To whom the Charites led on the way,
Aglaia, Thalia, and Euphrozine,
With princely crownes they in the triumph came,   865
Imbellished with Phœbes glorious name:
These forth before the mighty Goddesse went,
As Princes Heraulds in a Parliament.
And in their true consorted symphony,
Record sweet songs of Phœbes chastity;   870
Then followed on the Muses, sacred nyne,
With the first number equally divine,
In Virgins white, whose lovely mayden browes,
Were crowned with tryumphant Lawrell bowes;
And on their garments paynted out in glory,   875
Their offices and functions in a story,
Imblazoning the furie and conceite
Which on their sacred company awaite;
    For none but these were suffered to aproch,
Or once come neere to this celestiall Coach,   880
But these two of the numbers, nine and three,
Which being od include an unity,
Into which number all things fitly fall,
And therefore named Theologicall:
And first composing of this number nine,   885
Which of all numbers is the most divine,
From orders of the Angels dooth arise,
Which be contayned in three Hirarchies,
And each of these three Hirarchies in three,

The perfect forme of true triplicity;   890
And of the Hirarchies I spake of erst,
The glorious Epiphania is the first,
In which the hie celestiall orders been,
Of Thrones, Chirrup, and the Ciraphin;
The second holds the mighty Principates,   895
The Dominations and the Potestates,
The Ephionia, the third Hirarchie,
Which Vertues Angels and Archangels be;
And thus by threes we aptly do define,
And do compose this sacred number nyne,   900
Yet each of these nyne orders grounded be,
Upon some one particularity,
Then as a Poet I might so infer,
An other order when I spake of her.
From these the Muses onely are derived,   905
Which of the Angels were in nyne contrived;
These heaven-inspired Babes of memorie,
Which by a like attracting Sympathy,
Apollos Prophets in theyr furies wrought,
And in theyr spirit inchaunting numbers taught,   910
To teach such as at Poesie repine,
That it is onely heavenly and divine,
And manifest her intellectuall parts,
Sucking the purest of the purest Arts;
And unto these as by a sweet consent,   915
The Sphery circles are equivalent,
From the first Moover, and the starry heaven,
To glorious Phœbe, lowest of the seaven,
Which Jove in tunefull Diapazons fram'd,
Of heavenly Musick of the Muses nam'd,   920
To which the soule in her divinitie,
By her Creator made of harmony,
Whilst she in frayle and mortall flesh dooth live,
To her, nyne sundry offices doe give,
Which offices united are in three,   925
Which like the orders of the Angels be,
Prefiguring thus by the number nyne,
The soule, like to the Angels is divine:

904 of her, his tenth Worthy, Muse, and Angel: *Ideas Mirrour*, No. 8.

And from these nines those Conquerers renowned,
Which with the wreaths of triumph oft were crowned.   930
Which by their vertues gain'd the worthies name
First had this number added to their fame,
Not that the worthiest men were onely nine,
But that the number of it selfe divine,
And as a perfect patterne of the rest,   935
Which by this holy number are exprest;
Nor Chivalrie this title onely gaynd;
But might as well by wisedome be obtaynd,
Nor in this number men alone included,
But unto women well might be aluded,   940
Could wit, could worlds, coulde times, could ages find,
This number of Elizas heavenly kind;
And those rare men which learning highly prized
By whom the Constellations were devised,
And by their favours learning highly graced,   945
For Orpheus harpe nine starres in heaven placed:
This sacred number to declare thereby,
Her sweet consent and solid harmony,
And mans heroique voyce, which doth impart,
The thought conceaved in the inward hart,   950
Her sweetnes on nine Instruments doth ground,
Else doth she fayle in true and perfect sound.
Now of this three in order to dispose,
Whose trynarie doth justly nyne compose,
First in the forme of this triplicitie   955
Is shadowed that mighty Trinitie,
Which still in stedfast unity remayne,
And yet of three one Godhead doe containe;
From this eternall living deitie,
As by a heaven-inspired prophecy,   960
Divinest Poets first derived these,
The fayrest Graces Jove-borne Charites;
And in this number Musick first began,
The Lydian, Dorian, and the Phrigian,
Which ravishing in their soule-pleasing vaine,   965
They made up seaven in a higher strayne;
And all those signes which Phœbus doth ascend,
Before he bring his yearely course to end,

Their several natures mutually agree,
And doe concurre in thys triplicitie;   970
And those interior sences with the rest,
Which properly pertaine to man and Beast,
Nature herselfe in working so devised,
That in this number they should be comprized.
  But to my tale I must returne againe,   975
Phœbe to Latmus thus convayde her swayne,
Under a bushie Lawrells pleasing shade,
Amongst whose boughs the Birds sweet Musick made,
Whose fragrant branch-imbosted Cannapy,
Was never pierst with Phœbus burning eye;   980
Yet never could thys Paradise want light,
Elumin'd still with Phœbes glorious sight:
She layd Endimion on a grassy bed,
With sommers Arras ritchly over-spred,
Where from her sacred Mantion next above,   985
She might descend and sport her with her love,
Which thirty yeeres the Sheepheards safely kept,
Who in her bosom soft and soundly slept;
Yet as a dreame he thought the tyme not long,
Remayning ever beautifull and yong,   990
And what in vision there to him be fell,
My weary Muse some other time shall tell.

Deare Collin, let my Muse excused be,
Which rudely thus presumes to sing by thee,
Although her straines be harsh untun'd & ill,   995
Nor can attayne to thy divinest skill.
  And thou the sweet Museus of these times,
Pardon my rugged and unfiled rymes,
Whose scarce invention is too meane and base,
When Delias glorious Muse dooth come in place.   1000
  And thou my Goldey which in Sommer dayes,
Hast feasted us with merry roundelayes,
And when my Muse scarce able was to flye,
Didst imp her wings with thy sweete Poesie.
  And you the heyres of ever-living fame,   1005

993 Allusion to Spenser; Daniel (l. 997); Lodge (l. 1001); and Anne Goodere
(l. 1011)

The worthy titles of a Poets name,
Whose skill and rarest excellence is such,
As spitefull Envy never yet durst tuch,
To your protection I this Poem send,
Which from proud Momus may my lines defend.   1010
    And if sweet mayd thou deign'st to read this story,
Wherein thine eyes may view thy vertues glory,
Thou purest spark of Vesta's kindled fire,
Sweet Nymph of Ankor, crowne of my desire,
The plot which for their pleasure heaven devis'd,   1015
Where all the Muses be imparadis'd,
Where thou doost live, there let all graces be,
Which want theyr grace if onely wanting thee,
Let stormy winter never touch the Clyme,
But let it florish as in Aprils prime,   1020
Let sullen night, that soyle nere over-cloud,
But in thy presence let the earth be proud.
If ever Nature of her worke might boast,
Of thy perfection she may glory most,
To whom fayre Phœbe hath her bow resign'd,   1025
Whose excellence doth lyve in thee refin'd,
And that thy praise Time never should impayre,
Hath made my hart thy never moving Spheare.
Then if my Muse give life unto thy fame,
Thy vertues be the causers of the same.   1030
And from thy Tombe some Oracle shall rise,
To whom all pens shall yearely sacrifice.

OVIDS BANQUET OF SENCE

George Chapman

(1595)

THE ARGUMENT

OVID, newly enamoured of Julia, (daughter to Octavius Augustus Cæsar, after by him called Corynna,) secretly convaid himselfe into a Garden of the Emperors Court: in an Arbor whereof, Corynna, was bathing; playing upon her Lute, and singing: which Ovid over-hearing, was exceedingly pleasde with the sweetnes of her voyce, & to himselfe uttered the *Auditus* comfort he conceived in his sence of Hearing.

Then the odors shee usde in her bath, breathing a rich savor, *Olfactus* hee expresseth the joy he felt in his sence of Smelling.

Thus growing more deeplie enamoured, in great contentation with himselfe, he venters to see her in the pride of her naked-nesse: which dooing by stealth, he discovered the comfort hee *Visus* conceived in Seeing, and the glorie of her beautie.

Not yet satisfied, he useth all his Art to make knowne his being there, without her offence: or (being necessarily offended) to appease her: which done, he entreats a kisse to serve for *Gustus* satisfaction of his Tast, which he obtaines.

Then proceedes he to entreaty for the fift sence and there is interrupted. *Tactus*

NARRATIO

I

The Earth, from heavenly light conceived heat,
Which mixed all her moyst parts with her dry,
When with right beames the Sun her bosome beat,

And with fit foode her Plants did nutrifie;
They (which to Earth, as to theyr Mother cling
In forked rootes) now sprinckled plenteously
With her warme breath; did hasten to the spring,
 Gather their proper forces, and extrude
 All powre but that, with which they stood indude.

2

Then did Cyrrhus[a] fill his eyes with fire,
Whose ardor curld the foreheads of the trees,
And made his greene-love burne in his desire,
When youth, and ease, (Collectors of loves fees)
Entic'd Corynna to a silver spring,
Enchasing a round Bowre; which with it sees[b]
(As with a Diamant dooth an ameld Ring.)
 Into which eye, most pittifully stood
 Niobe, shedding teares, that were her blood.

3

Stone Niobe, whose statue to this Fountaine,
In great Augustus Cæsars grace was brought
From Sypilus, the steepe Mygdonian Mountaine:
That statue tis, still weepes for former thought
Into thys spring, Corynnas bathing place;
So cunningly to optick reason wrought,
That a farre of, it shewd a womans face,
 Heavie, and weeping; but more neerely viewed,
 Nor weeping, heavy, nor a woman shewed.

4

In Sommer onely wrought her exstasie;
And that her story might be still observed,
Octavius caus'd in curious imagrie,
Her fourteene children should at large be carved,
Theyr fourteene brests, with fourteene arrowes gored,

 [a] Cyrrhus is a surname of the Sun, from a towne called Cyrrha, where he was honored.
 [b] By Prosopopaeia, he makes the fountaine the eye of the round Arbor, as a Diamant seemes to be the eye of a Ring: and therefore sayes, the Arbor sees with the Fountaine.

And set by her, that for her seede so starved,
To a stone Sepulcher herselfe deplored,
  In Ivory were they cut, and on each brest,
  In golden Elements theyr names imprest.

5

Her sonnes were Sypilus, Agenor, Phædimus,
Ismenus, Argus, and Damasicthen,
The seaventh calde like his Grandsire, Tantalus.
Her Daughters, were the fayre Astiochen,
Chloris, Næera, and Pelopie,
Phaeta, proud Phthia, and Eugigen,
All these apposde to violent Niobe
  Had lookes so deadly sad, so lively doone,
  As if Death liv'd in theyr confusion.

6

Behind theyr Mother two Pyramides
Of freckled Marble, through the Arbor viewed,
On whose sharp brows, Sol, and Tytanides
In purple and transparent glasse were hewed,
Through which the Sun-beames on the statues staying,
Made theyr pale bosoms seeme with blood imbrewed,
Those two sterne Plannets rigors still bewraying
  To these dead forms, came living beauties essence
  Able to make them startle with her presence.

7

In a loose robe of Tynsell foorth she came,
Nothing but it betwixt her nakednes
And envious light. The downward-burning flame,
Of her rich hayre did threaten new accesse,
Of ventrous Phaeton to scorch the fields:
And thus to bathing came our Poets Goddesse,
Her handmaides bearing all things pleasure yeelds
  To such a service; Odors most delighted,
  And purest linnen which her lookes had whited.

8

Then cast she off her robe, and stood upright,
As lightning breakes out of a laboring cloude;
Or as the Morning heaven casts off the Night,
Or as that heaven cast off it selfe, and showde
Heavens upper light, to which the brightest day
Is but a black and melancholy shroude:
Or as when Venus striv'd for soveraine sway
 Of charmfull beautie, in yong Troyes desire,
 So stood Corynna vanishing her tire.

9

A soft enflowered banck embrac'd the founte;
Of Chloris ensignes, an abstracted field;
Where grew Melanthy, great in Bees account,
Amareus, that precious Balme dooth yeeld,
Enameld Pansies, us'd at Nuptials still,
Dianas arrow, Cupids crimson shielde,
Ope-morne, night-shade, and Venus navill,
 Solemne Violets, hanging head as shamed,
 And verdant Calaminth, for odor famed.

10

Sacred Nepenthe, purgative of care,
And soveraine Rumex that doth rancor kill,
Sya, and Hyacinth, that Furies weare,
White and red Jessamines, Merry, Melliphill:
Fayre Crowne-imperiall, Emperor of Flowers,
Immortall Amaranth, white Aphrodill,
And cup-like Twillpants, stroude in Bacchus Bowres,
 These cling about this Natures naked Jem,
 To taste her sweetes, as Bees doe swarme on them.

9.4 Amareus, pinks or perhaps for amaracus, sweet marjoram, which produces an 'excellent oyle,' Gerarde, *Herbal*
9.6 Dianas arrow, ? artemisia; Cupids crimson shielde, love-in-idleness
9.7 Venus navill, pennywort
10.2 Rumex, garden dock   10.3 Sya, for syue, chive
10.4 Merry, black cherry; Melliphill, (honey leaf) ? balm
10.5 Crowne-imperiall, fritillary

11

And now shee usde the Founte, where Niobe,
Toomb'd in her selfe, pourde her lost soule in teares,
Upon the bosome of this Romaine Phœbe;
Who, bathd and Odord, her bright lyms she rears,
And drying her on that disparent rounde;
Her Lute she takes t'enamoure hevenly eares,
And try if with her voyces vitall sounde,
   She could warme life through those colde statues spread,
   And cheere the Dame that wept when she was dead.

12

And thus she sung, all naked as she sat,
Laying the happy Lute upon her thigh,
Not thinking any neere to wonder at
The blisse of her sweete brests divinitie:

THE SONG OF CORYNNA

T'is better to contemne then love,
And to be fayre then wise;
For soules are rulde by eyes:
And Joves Bird, ceaz'd by Cypris Dove,
It is our grace and sport to see,
Our beauties sorcerie,
That makes (like destinie)
Men followe us the more wee flee;
That sets wise Glosses on the foole,
And turns her cheekes to bookes,
Where wisdome sees in lookes
Derision, laughing at his schoole,
   Who (loving) proves, prophanenes, holy;
   Nature, our fate, our wisdome, folly.

13

While this was singing, Ovid yong in love
With her perfections, never proving yet
How mercifull a Mistres she would prove,
Boldly embrac'd the power he could not let,

And like a fiery exhalation
Followd the sun he wisht might never set;
Trusting heerein his constellation
   Rul'd by loves beames, which Julias eyes erected,
   Whose beauty was the star his life directed.

14

And having drencht his anckles in those seas,
He needes woulde swimme, and car'd not if he drounde:
Loves feete are in his eyes; for if he please
The depth of beauties gulfye floodd to sounde,
He goes upon his eyes, and up to them,
At the first steap he is; no shader grounde
Coulde Ovid finde; but in loves holy streame
   Was past his eyes, and now did wett his eares,
   For his high Soveraignes silver voice he heares.

15

Whereat his wit assumed fierye wings,
Soring above the temper of his soule,
And he the purifying rapture sings
Of his eares sence, takes full the Thespian boule
And it carrouseth to his Mistres health,
Whose sprightfull verdure did dull flesh controle,
And his conceipt he crowneth with the wealth
   Of all the Muses in his pleased sences,
   When with the eares delight he thus commences:

16

Now Muses come, repayre your broken wings,
(Pluckt, and prophan'd by rusticke Ignorance,)
With feathers of these notes my Mistres sings;
And let quick verse hir drooping head advance
From dungeons of contempt to smite the starrs;
In Julias tunes, led forth by furious trance
A thousand Muses come to bid you warrs,
   Dive to your Spring, and hide you from the stroke,
   All Poets furies will her tunes invoke.

17

Never was any sence so sette on fire
With an immortall ardor, as myne eares;
Her fingers to the strings doth speeche inspire
And numberd laughter; that the deskant beares
To hir sweete voice; whose species through my sence
My spirits to theyr highest function reares;
To which imprest with ceaseles confluence
   It useth them, as propper to her powre
   Marries my soule, and makes it selfe her dowre;

18

Me thinks her tunes flye guilt, like Attick Bees
To my eares hives, with hony tryed to ayre;
My braine is but the combe; the wax, the lees;
My soule the Drone, that lives by their affayre.
O so it sweets, refines, and ravisheth,
And with what sport they sting in theyr repayre:
Rise then in swarms, and sting me thus to death
   Or turne me into swounde; possesse me whole,
   Soule to my life, and essence to my soule.

19

Say gentle Ayre, ô does it not thee good
Thus to be smit with her correcting voyce?
Why daunce ye not, ye daughters of the wood?
Wither for ever, if not now rejoyce.
Rise stones, and build a Cittie with her notes,
And notes, infuse with your most Cynthian noyse,
To all the Trees, sweete flowers, and christall Flotes,
   That crowne, and make this cheerefull Garden quick,
   Vertue, that every tuch may make such Musick.

20

O that as man is cald a little world
The world might shrink into a little man,
To heare the notes about this Garden hurld,
That skill disperst in tunes so Orphean

18.2 tryed, refined

Might not be lost in smiting stocks and trees
That have no eares; but growne as it began,
Spred theyr renownes, as far as Phœbus sees
    Through earths dull vaines; that shee like heaven might move,
    In ceaseles Musick, and be fill'd with love.

21

In precious incense of her holy breath,
My love doth offer Hecatombs of notes
To all the Gods; who now despise the death
Of Oxen, Heifers, Wethers, Swine, and Goates.
A Sonnet in her breathing sacrifiz'd,
Delights them more then all beasts bellowing throates,
As much with heaven, as with my hearing priz'd.
    And as guilt Atoms in the sunne appeare,
    So greete these sounds the grissells of myne eare.

22

Whose pores doe open wide to theyr regreete,
And my implanted ayre, that ayre embraceth
Which they impresse; I feele theyr nimble feete
Tread my eares Labyrinth; theyr sport amazeth
They keepe such measure; play themselves and dance.
And now my soule in Cupids Furnace blazeth,
Wrought into furie with theyr daliance:
    And as the fire the parched stuble burns,
    So fades my flesh, and into spyrit turns.

23

Sweete tunes, brave issue, that from Julia come;
Shooke from her braine, armd like the Queene of Ire;
For first conceived in her mentall wombe,°

   ° In this allusion to the birth of Pallas, he shewes the conceit of her Sonnet;
both for matter and note, and by Metaphor hee expresseth how shee delivered
her words, & tunes, which was by commision of the order Philosophers set
downe in apprehension of our knoweledge, and effection of our sences, for first
they affirme, the species of every object propagates it selfe by our spirites to our
common sence, that delivers it to the imaginative part, that to the Cogitative:
the Cogitative to the Passive Intelect: the Passive Intelect to that which is
called Dianoia, or Discursus, and that delivers it up to the minde, which order
hee observes in her utterance.

And nourisht with her soules discursive fire,
They grew into the power of her thought;
She gave them dounye plumes from her attire,
And them to strong imagination brought:
    That, to her voice; wherein most movinglye
    Shee (blessing them with kysses) letts them flye.

24

Who flye rejoysing; but (like noblest mindes)
In giving others life, themselves do dye,
Not able to endure earthes rude unkindes,
Bred in my soveraigns parts too tenderly;
O that as Intellects[d] themselves transite
To eache intellegible quallitie,
My life might passe into my loves conceit,
    Thus to be form'd in words, her tunes, and breath,
    And with her kysses, sing it selfe to death.

25

This life were wholy sweete, this onely blisse,
Thus would I live to dye; Thus sence were feasted,
My life that in my flesh a Chaos is
Should to a Golden worlde be thus dygested;
Thus should I rule her faces Monarchy,
Whose lookes in severall Empires are invested
Crown'd now with smiles, and then with modesty,
    Thus in her tunes division I should raigne,
    For her conceipt does all, in every vaine.

26

My life then turn'd to that, t'each note, and word
Should I consorte her looke; which sweeter sings,
Where songs of solid harmony accord,
Rulde with Loves rule; and prickt with all his stings;
Thus should I be her notes, before they be;[e]

[d] The Philosopher saith, *Intellectus in ipsa intellegibilia transit*, upon which is grounded thys invention, that in the same manner his life might passe into hys Mistres conceite, intending his intellectuall life, or soule: which by this Analogie, should bee *Intellectus*, & her conceit, *Intellegibilis*.
[e] This hath reference to the order of her utterance, exprest before.

While in her blood they sitte with fierye wings
Not vapord in her voyces stillerie,
　　Nought are these notes her breast so sweetely frames,
　　But motions, fled out of her spirits flames.

27

For as when steele and flint together smit,
With violent action spitt forth sparkes of fire,
And make the tender tynder burne with it;
So my loves soule doth lighten her desire
Uppon her spyrits in her notes^f pretence;
And they convaye them (for distinckt attire)
To use the Wardrobe of the common sence:
　　From whence in vailes of her rich breath they flye,
　　And feast the eare with this felicitye.

28

Me thinks they rayse me from the heavy ground
And move me swimming in the yeelding ayre;
As Zephirs flowry blasts doe tosse a sounde;
Upon their wings will I to Heaven repayre,
And sing them so, Gods shall descend and heare:
Ladies must bee ador'd that are but fayre,
But apt besides with art to tempt the eare
　　In notes of Nature, is a Goddesse part,
　　Though oft, men Natures notes please more then Art.

29

But heere are Art and Nature both confinde,
Art casting Nature in so deepe a trance
That both seeme deade, because they be divinde,
Buried is Heaven in earthly ignorance.
Why breake not men then strumpet Follies bounds,
To learne at this pure virgine utterance?
No; none but Ovids eares can sound these sounds,
　　Where sing the harts of Love and Poesie,
　　Which make my Muse so strong she works too hye.

^f So is thys lykewise referd to the order abovesaid, for the more perspicuitie.
28.9 men] (sugg. G. Loane); mens

30

Now in his glowing eares her tunes did sleepe,
And as a silver Bell, with violent blowe
Of Steele or Iron, when his soundes most deepe
Doe from his sides and ayres soft bosome flowe,
A great while after murmures at the stroke,
Letting the hearers eares his hardnes knowe,
So chid the Ayre to be no longer broke:
    And left the accents panting in his eare
    Which in this Banquet his first service were.

31

Heerewith, as Ovid something neerer drew,
Her Odors, odord with her breath and brest,   *Olfactus*
Into the sensor of his savor flew,
As if the Phenix, hasting to her rest
Had gatherd all th'Arabian Spicerie
T'enbalme her body in her Tombe, her nest,
And there lay burning gainst Apollos eye,
    Whose fiery ayre straight piercing Ovids braine
    Enflamde his Muse with a more odorouse vaine.

32

And thus he sung: come soveraigne Odors, come
Restore my spirits now in love consuming,
Wax hotter ayre, make them more savorsome,
My fainting life with fresh-breath'd soule perfuming,
The flames of my disease are violent,
And many perish on late helps presuming,
With which hard fate must I yet stand content,
    As Odors put in fire most richly smell,
    So men must burne in love that will excell.

33

And as the ayre is rarefied with heate
But thick and grosse with Summer-killing colde,
So men in love aspire perfections seate,
When others, slaves to base desire are sold,
And if that men neere Ganges liv'd by sent

Of Flowres, and Trees, more I a thousand fold
May live by these pure fumes that doe present
   My Mistres quickning, and consuming breath
   Where her wish flyes with power of life and death.

34

Me thinks, as in these liberall fumes I burne,
My Mistres lips be neere with kisse-entices,
And that which way soever I can turne,
She turns withall, and breaths on me her spices,
As if too pure for search of humaine eye
She flewe in ayre disburthening Indian prizes,
And made each earthly fume to sacrifice.
   With her choyse breath fell Cupid blowes his fire,
   And after, burns himselfe in her desire.

35

Gentle, and noble are theyr tempers framde,
That can be quickned with perfumes and sounds,
And they are cripple-minded, Gowt-wit lamde,
That lye like fire-fit blocks, dead without wounds,
Stird up with nought, but hell-descending gaine,
The soule of fooles that all theyr soules confounds,
The art of Pessants and our Nobles staine,
   The bane of vertue and the blisse of sinne.
   Which none but fooles and Pessants glorie in.

36

Sweete sounds and Odors, are the heavens, on earth
Where vertues live, of vertuous men deceast,
Which in such like, receive theyr second birth
By smell and hearing endlesly encreast;[g]
They were meere flesh were not with them delighted,

[g] By this allusion drawne from the effects of sounds and Odors, hee imitates
the eternitie of Vertue: saying, the vertues of good men live in them, because
they stir up pure enclinations to the like, as if infusde in perfumes & sounds:
Besides, he infers, that such as are neyther delighted with sounds (intending
by sounds all utterance of knowledge, as well as musicall affections,) nor with
Odors, (which properly drye the braine & delight the instruments of the soule,
making them the more capable of her faculties) such saith hee, perrish without
memorie.

And every such is perisht like a beast
As all they shall that are so foggye sprighted,
 Odors feede love, and love cleare heaven discovers,
 Lovers weare sweets; then sweetest mindes, be lovers.

37

Odor in heate and drynes is consite,
Love then a fire is much thereto affected;
And as ill smells do kill his appetite,
With thankful savors it is still protected;
Love lives in spyrits, and our spyrits be
Nourisht with Odors, therefore love refected;
And ayre lesse corpulent in quallitie
 Then Odors are, doth nourish vitall spyrits,
 Therefore may they be prov'd of equall merits;

38

O soveraigne Odors; not of force to give
Foode to a thing that lives nor let it dye,
But to ad life to that did never live;
Nor to ad life, but immortallitie.
Since they pertake her heate that like the fire
Stolne from the wheeles of Phœbus waggonrie
To lumps of earth, can manly lyfe inspire;
 Else be these fumes the lives of sweetest dames
 That (dead) attend on her for novell frames;

39

Rejoyce blest Clime, thy ayre is so refinde
That while shee lives no hungry pestilence
Can feede her poysoned stomack with thy kynde;
But as the Unicorns pregredience
To venomd Pooles, doth purdge them with his horne,
And after him the desarts Residence
May safely drinke, so in the holesome morne
 After her walke, who there attends her eye,
 Is sure that day to tast no maladye.

40

Thus was his course of Odors sweet and sleight,
Because he long'd to give his sight assaye,
And as in fervor of the summers height,
The sunne is so ambitious in his sway
He will not let the Night an howre be plast,
So in this Cupids Night (oft seene in day)
Now spred with tender clouds these Odors cast,
  Her sight, his sunne, so wrought in his desires,
  His savor vanisht in his visuale fires.

41

So vulture love on his encreasing liver,
And fruitfull entrails egerly did feede,
And with the goldnest Arrow in his Quiver,
Wounds him with longings, that like Torrents bleeds,
To see the Myne of knowledge that enricht
His minde with povertie, and desperate neede:
A sight that with the thought of sight bewitcht,
  A sight taught Magick his deepe misterie,
  Quicker in danger then Dianas eye.[h]

42

Stay therefore Ovid, venter not; a sight
May prove thy rudenes, more then shew thee loving,
And make thy Mistres thinke thou think'st her light:
Which thought with lightest Dames is nothing moving.
The slender hope of favor thou hast yet
Should make thee feare, such grosse conclusions proving:
Besides, the Thicket Floras hands hath set
  To hide thy theft, is thinne and hollow harted,
  Not meete to have so high a charge imparted.

43

And should it keepe thy secrets, thine owne eye
Would fill thy thoughts so full of lightenings,

[h] Allusion to the transformation of Acteon with the sight of Diana.
40.8 Cf. Musaeus, l. 403.

That thou must passe through more extremitie,
Or stand content to burne beneath theyr wings;
Her honor gainst thy love, in wager layde,
Thou wouldst be prickt with other sences stings,
To tast, and feele, and yet not there be staide:
    These casts he cast, and more, his wits more quick
    Then can be cast, by wits Arithmetick.

44

Forward, and back, and forward went he thus,
Like wanton Thamysis,[1] that hastes to greete
The brackish Court of old Oceanus;
And as by Londons bosome she doth fleet
Casts herselfe proudly through the Bridges twists,
Where (as she takes againe her Christall feete:)
She curls her silver hayre like Amorists,
    Smoothes her bright cheekes, adorns her browes with ships
    And Empresse-like along the Coast she trips.

45

Till comming neere the Sea, she heares him rore,
Tumbling her churlish billowes in his face,
Then, more dismaid then insolent before,
Charg'd to rough battaile, for his smooth embrace,
She crowcheth close within her winding bancks,
And creepes retreate into her peacefull Pallace;
Yet straite high-flowing in her female prancks
    Againe she will bee wanton, and againe,
    By no meanes stayde, nor able to containe.

46

So Ovid with his strong affections striving,
Maskt in a friendly Thicket neere her Bowre,
Rubbing his temples, fainting, and reviving,
Fitting his garments, praying to the howre,

---

[1] A simile, expressing the manner of his minds contention in the desire of her sight, and feare of her displeasure.

45.2 his] her

Backwards, and forwards went, and durst not venter,
To tempt the tempest of his Mistres lowre,
Or let his eyes her beauties ocean enter;
    At last, with prayer he pierceth Junos eare,
    Great Goddesse of audacitie and feare:

47

Great Goddesse of audacitie, and feare,
Queene of Olympus, Saturns eldest seede,
That doost the scepter over Samos beare,
And rul'st all Nuptiale rites with power, and meede,
Since thou in nature art the meane to mix
Still sulphure humors, and canst therefore speede
Such as in Cyprian sports theyr pleasures fix,
    Venus herselfe, and Mars by thee embracing,
    Assist my hopes, me and my purpose gracing.

48

Make love within me not too kinde but pleasing,
Exiling Aspen feare out of his forces,
My inward sight, with outward seeing, easing,
And if he please, further to stretch his courses,
Arme me with courage to make good his charges;
Too much desire to please, pleasure divorces,
Attemps, and not entreats get Ladies larges,
    Wit is with boldnes prompt, with terror danted,
    And grace is sooner got of Dames then graunted.

49

Visus This sayde, he charg'd the Arbor with his eye,
Which pierst it through, and at her brests reflected,
Striking him to the hart with exstasie:
As doe the sun-beames gainst the earth prorected,
With their reverberate vigor mount in flames,
And burne much more then where they were directed.
He saw th'extraction of all fayrest Dames:
    The fayre of Beauty, as whole Countries come
    And shew theyr riches in a little Roome.

222

50

Heere Ovid sold his freedome for a looke,
And with that looke was ten tymes more enthralde,
He blusht, lookt pale, and like a fevour shooke,
And as a burning vapor[1] being exhalde,
Promist by Phœbus eye to be a star,
Heavens walles denying to be further scalde
The force dissolves that drewe it up so far:
    And then it lightens gainst his death and fals,
    So Ovids powre, this powrefull sight appals.

51

This beauties fayre is an enchantment made
By natures witchcraft, tempting men to buy
With endles showes, what endlessly will fade,
Yet promise chapmen all eternitie:
But like to goods ill got a fate it hath,
Brings men enricht therewith to beggerie
Unlesse th'enricher be as rich in fayth,
    Enamourd (like good selfe-love) with her owne,
    Seene in another, then tis heaven alone.

52

For sacred beautie is the fruite of sight,
The curtesie that speakes before the tongue,
The feast of soules, the glory of the light,
Envy of age, and everlasting young,
Pitties Commander, Cupids richest throne,
Musick intransed, never duely sung,
The summe and court of all proportion:
    And that I may dull speeches best afforde,
    All Rethoricks flowers, in lesse then in a worde.

53

Then in the truest wisdome can be thought,
Spight of the publique *Axiom* worldlings hold,

---

[1] This simile expresseth the cause and substance of those exhalations which vulgarly are called falling starres: so Homer and Virgill calls them *Stellas cadentes*, Homer comparing the descent of Pallas among the Troyans to a falling Starre.

That nothing wisdome is, that getteth nought,
This all-things-nothing, since it is no gold,
Beautie enchasing love, love gracing beautie,
To such as constant simpathies enfold,
To perfect riches dooth a sounder duetie
    Then all endevours, for by all consent
    All wealth and wisdome rests in true Content.

54

Contentment is our heaven, and all our deedes
Bend in that circle, seld or never closde,
More then the letter in the word preceedes,
And to conduce that compasse is reposde;
More force and art in beautie joyned with love,
Then thrones with wisdome; joyes of them composde
Are armes more proofe gainst any griefe we prove,
    Then all their vertue-scorning miserie
    Or judgments graven in Stoick gravitie,

55

But as weake colour alwayes is allowde
The proper object of a humaine eye,
Though light be with a farre more force endowde
In stirring up the visuale facultie,
This colour being but of vertuous light
A feeble Image; and the cause dooth lye
In th'imperfection of a humaine sight,
    So this for love, and beautie, loves cold fire
    May serve for my praise, though it merit higher.

56

With this digression, wee will now returne
To Ovids prospect in his fancies storme:
Hee thought hee sawe the Arbors bosome burne,
Blaz'd with a fire wrought in a Ladyes forme:
Where silver past the least, and Natures vant
Did such a precious miracle performe,
Shee lay, and seemd a flood of Diamant
    Bounded in flesh: as still as Vespers hayre,
    When not an Aspen leafe is styrrd with ayre.

57

Shee lay at length, like an immortall soule
At endlesse rest in blest Elisium:[k]
And then did true felicitie enroule
So fayre a Lady, figure of her kingdome.
Now Ovids Muse as in her tropicke shinde,
And hee (strooke dead) was meere heaven-borne become,
So his quick verse in equall height was shrinde:
    Or els blame mee as his submitted debter,
    That never Mistresse had to make mee better.

58

Now as shee lay, attirde in nakednes,
His eye did carve him on that feast of feasts:
Sweet fields of life[1] which Deaths foote dare not presse,
Flowred with th'unbroken waves of my Loves brests,
Unbroke by depth of those her beauties floods:
See where with bent of Gold curld into Nests
In her heads Grove, the Spring-bird Lameate broods:
    Her body doth present those fields of peace
    Where soules are feasted with the soule of ease.

59

To prove which Parradise that nurseth these,
See, see the golden Rivers that renowne it:
Rich Gehon, Tigris, Phison, Euphrates,
Two from her bright Pelopian shoulders crowne it,
And two out of her snowye Hills doe glide,
That with a Deluge of delights doe drowne it:
The highest two, theyr precious streames divide
    To tenne pure floods, that doe the body dutie
    Bounding themselves in length, but not in beautie.

---

[k] The amplification of this simile is taken from the blisfull state of soules in Elisium, as Virgill faines: and expresseth a regenerate beauty in all life & perfection, not intimating any rest of death. But in place of that eternall spring, he poynteth to that life of life, thys beauty-clad naked Lady.

[1] He calls her body (as it were divided with her breasts,) the fields of Paradise, and her armes & legs the famous Rivers in it.

Note *k*, place] (sugg. J. Kermode); peace

1*   225

60

These[m] winde theyr courses through the painted bowres,
And raise such sounds in theyr inflection,
As ceaseles start from Earth fresh sorts of flowers,
And bound that booke of life with every section.
In these the Muses dare not swim for drowning,
Theyr sweetnes poisons with such blest infection,
And leaves the onely lookers on them swouning;
    These forms so decks, and colour makes so shine,
    That Gods for them would cease to be divine.

61

Thus though my love be no Elisium
That cannot move from her prefixed place;
Yet have her feete no powre from thence to come,
For where she is, is all Elisian grace:
And as those happy men are sure of blisse
That can performe so excellent a race
As that Olympiad where her favor is,
    So shee can meete them, blessing them the rather
    And give her sweetes, as well as let men gather.

62

Ah how should I be so most happy then
T'aspire that place, or make it come to mee?
To gather, or be given, the flowre of women?
Elisium must with vertue gotten bee,
With labors of the soule and continence,
And these can yeeld no joy with such as she,
Shee is a sweet Elisium for the sence
    And Nature dooth not sensuall gifts infuse
    But that with sence, shee still intends their use.

63

The sence is given us to excite the minde,
And that can never be by sence exited

---

[m] Hee intends the office of her fingers in attyring her, touching thys of theyr
courses, in theyr inflection following, theyr playing upon an Instrument.
    Note *m* of her] her

But first the sence must her contentment finde,
We therefore must procure the sence delighted,
That so the soule may use her facultie;
Mine Eye then to this feast hath her invited;
That she might serve the soveraigne of mine Eye,
   Shee shall bid Time, and Time so feasted never,
   Shall grow in strength of her renowne for ever.

64

Betwixt mine Eye and object, certayne lynes,
Move in the figure of a Pyramis,
Whose chapter in mine eyes gray apple shines,
The base within my sacred object is:
On this will I inscribe in golden verse
The mervailes raigning in my soveraigns blisse,
The arcks of sight, and how her arrowes pierse:
   This in the Region of the ayre shall stand
   In Fames brasse Court, and all her Trumps commaund.

65

Rich Beautie, that ech Lover labors for,
Tempting as heapes of new-coynd-glowing Gold,
(Rackt of some miserable Treasurer)
Draw his desires, and them in chaynes enfold,
Urging him still to tell it, and conceale it,
But Beauties treasure never can be told:
None can peculier joy, yet all must steale it.
   O Beautie, this same bloody siedge of thine
   Starves me that yeeld, and feedes mee till I pine.

66

And as a Taper burning in the darke
(As if it threatned every watchfull eye
That viewing burns it,) makes that eye his marke,
And hurls guilt Darts at it continually,
Or as it envied any eye but it
Should see in darknes, so my Mistres beautie

63.3 finde] (sugg. Bush); minde   63.8 bid]; (bide, Bartlett)

From foorth her secret stand my hart doth hit:
And like the Dart of Cephalus dooth kill
Her perfect Lover, though shee meane no ill.

67

Thus, as the innocence of one betraide
Carries an Argus with it, though unknowne,
And Fate, to wreake the trecherie bewraide;
Such vengeance hath my Mistres Beautie showne
On me the Traitor to her modestie,
So unassailde, I quite am overthrowne,
And in my tryumph bound in Slaverie.
O Beauty, still thy Empire swims in blood,
And in thy peace, Warre stores himselfe with foode.

68

O Beautie, how attractive is thy powre?
For as the lives heate clings about the hart,
So all Mens hungrie eyes do haunt thy Bowre,
Raigning in Greece, Troy swum to thee in Art;
Remov'd to Troy, Greece followd thee in feares;
Thou drewst each Syreles sworde, each childles Dart
And pulld'st the towres of Troy about thine eares:
Shall I then muse that thus thou drawest me?
No, but admire I stand thus farre from thee.

69

Heerewith shee rose like the Autumnale Starre
Fresh burnisht in the loftie Ocean floode,
That darts his glorious influence more farre
Then any Lampe of bright Olympus broode;
Shee lifts her lightning arms above her head,
And stretcheth a Meridian from her blood,
That slept awake in her Elisian bed:
Then knit shee up, lest loose, her glowing hayre
Should scorch the Center and incense the ayre.

68.6 Thou]; (Thy, Bartlett)

70

Thus when her fayre hart-binding hands had tied
Those liberall Tresses, her high frontier part,
Shee shrunk in curls, and curiously plied
Into the figure of a swelling hart:
And then with Jewels of devise it graced:
One was a Sunne graven at his Eevens depart,
And under that a Mans huge shaddow placed,[n]
    Wherein was writ, in sable Charectry,
    Decrescente nobilitate, crescunt obscuri.

71

An other was an Eye in Saphire set,
And close upon it a fresh Lawrell spray.
The skilfull Posie was, *Medio caret,*[o]
To showe not eyes, but meanes must truth display.
The third was an Apollo with his Teme[p]
About a Diall and a worlde in way,
The Motto was, *Teipsum et orbem,*
    Graven in the Diall; these exceeding rare
    And other like accomplements she ware.

72

Not Tygris, Nilus, nor swift Euphrates,
Quoth Ovid now, can more subdue my flame,
I must through hell adventure to displease,
To tast and touch, one kisse may worke the same:
If more will come, more then much more I will;
Each naturall agent doth his action frame,
To render that he works on like him styll:
    The fire on water working doth induce
    Like qualitie unto his owne in use.

[n] At the Sun going downe, shadowes grow longest, whereupon this Embleme is devised.

[o] Sight is one of the three sences that hath his medium extrinsecally, which now (supposed wanting,) lets the sight by the close apposition of the Lawrell: the application wherof hath many constructions.

[p] The Sun hath as much time to compasse a Diall as the world, & therfore the world is placed in the Dyall, expressing the conceite of the Emprese morally which hath a far higher intention.

73

But Heaven in her a sparckling temper blewe
(As love in mee) and so will soone be wrought,
Good wits will bite at baits most strang and new,
And words well plac'd, move things were never thought;
What Goddesse is it Ovids wits shall dare
And he disgrace them with attempting nought?
My words shall carry spirits to ensnare,
    The subtelst harts affecting sutes importune,
    "Best loves are lost for wit when men blame Fortune.

74

Narratio With this, as she was looking in her Glasse,
She saw therein[q] a mans face looking on her:
Whereat she started from the frighted Grasse,
As if some monstrous Serpent had been shown her:
Rising as when (the sunne in Leos signe)
Auriga with the heavenly Goate upon her,
Shows her horn'd forehead with her Kids divine,
    Whose rise, kils Vines, Heavens face with storms disguising;
    No man is safe at sea, the Hædy rising.

75

So straight wrapt shee her body in a Clowde,
And threatned tempests for her high disgrace,
Shame from a Bowre of Roses did unshrowde
And spread her crimson wings upon her face;
When running out, poore Ovid humbly kneeling
Full in the Arbors mouth, did stay her race
And saide: faire Nimph, great Goddesse, have some feeling
    Of Ovids paines; but heare: and your dishonor
    Vainely surmisde, shall vanish with my horror.

76

Traytor to Ladies modesties (said shee)
What savage boldnes hardned thee to this?
Or what base reckoning of my modestie?
What should I thinke thy facts proude reason is?

[q] Ovid standing behind her, his face was seene in the Glasse.

Love (sacred Madam) love exhaling mee
(Wrapt in his Sulphure,) to this clowde of his
Made my affections his artillerie,
   Shot me at you his proper Cytadell,
   And loosing all my forces, heere I fell.

77

This Glosse is common, as thy rudenes strange
Not to forbeare these private times, (quoth she)
Whose fixed Rites, none shoulde presume to change
Not where there is adjudg'd inchastitie;
Our nakednes should be as much conceald
As our accomplishments desire the eye:
It is a secrete not to be revealde,
   But as Virginitie, and Nuptialls clothed,
   And to our honour all to be betrothed.

78

It is a want, where our aboundance lyes,
Given a sole dowre t'enrich chast Hymens Bed,
A perfect Image of our purities,
And glasse by which our actions should be dressed,
That tells us honor is as soone defild
And should be kept as pure, and incompressed,
But sight attainteth it: for Thought, Sights childe
   Begetteth sinne; and Nature bides defame,
   When light and lawles eyes bewray our shame.

79

Deere Mistresse (answerd Ovid,) to direct
Our actions, by the straitest rule that is,
We must in matters Morrall, quite reject
Vulgar Opinion, ever led amisse,
And let autentique Reason be our guide,
The wife of Truth, and Wisdoms Governisse:
The nature of all actions must be waide,
   And as they then appeare, breede love or loathing,
   Use makes things nothing huge, and huge things nothing.

80

As in your sight, how can sight, simply beeing
A sence-receiving essence to his flame
Sent from his object, give it harme by seeing,
Whose action[r] in the Seer hath his frame?
All excellence of shape is made for sight,
Else, to be like a Beast were no defame;
Hid Beauties lose theyr ends, and wrong theyr right:
 And can kinde love, (where no harms kinde can be)
 Disgrace with seeing that is given to see?

81

Tis I (alas) and my hart-burning Eye
Doe all the harme, and feele the harme wee doo:
I am no Basiliske, yet harmles I
Poyson with sight, and mine owne bosome too;
So am I to my selfe a Sorceresse
Bewitcht with my conceites in her I woo:
But you unwrongd, and all deshonorlesse
 Nor ill dares touch; affliction, sorcerie,
 One kisse of yours can quickly remedie.

82

I could not times observe, as others might
Of cold affects, and watry tempers framde,
Yet well assurde the wounder of your sight
Was so farre of from seeing you defamde,
That ever in the Phane of Memorie
Your love shall shine by it, in mee enflamde.
Then let your powre be clad in lenitie,
 Doe not (as others would) of custome storme,
 But prove your wit as pregnant as your forme.

83

Nor is my love so suddaine, since my hart
Was long loves Vulcan, with his pants unrest
Ham'ring the shafts, bred this delightsome smart:
And as when Jove at once from East and West

[r] Actio cernendi in homine vel animali, vidente collocanda est. Aristot.

Cast off two Eagles, to discerne the sight
Of this world Center, both his Byrds joynd brest
In Cynthian Delphos, since *Earths navill* hight:
  So casting off my ceaseles thoughts to see
  My harts true Center, all doe meete in thee.

84

Cupid that acts in you, suffers in mee
To make himselfe one tryumph-place of twaine,
Into your tunes and odors turned hee,
And through my sences flew into my braine
Where rules the Prince of sence,[s] whose Throne hee takes,
And of my Motions engines framd a chaine
To leade mee where hee list; and heere hee makes
  Nature (My fate)[t] enforce mee: and resignes
  The raines of all, to you, in whom hee shines.

85

For yeelding love then, doe not hate impart,
Nor let mine Eye, your carefull Harbengere
That hath purvaide your Chamber in my hart,
Be blamde for seeing who it lodged there;
The freer service merrits greater meede,
Princes are serv'd with unexpected chere,
And must have things in store before they neede:
  Thus should faire Dames be wise and confident,
  Not blushing to be noted excellent.

86

Now, as when Heaven is muffled with the vapors
His long since just divorced wife, the Earth
In envie breath's, to maske his spurrie Tapers
From the unrich aboundance of her birth,
When straight the westerne issue of the Ayre
Beates with his flowrie wings those Brats of dearth,
And gives Olympus leave to shew his fayre,

[s] In Cerebro est principium sentiendi, et inde nervi, qui instrumenta sunt motus voluntarij oriuntur.
  [t] Natura est uniuscuiusque Fatum, ut Theophr.
  86.7 leave]; (league, Bartlett)

So fled th'offended shaddowes of her cheere,
And showd her pleased count'nance full as cleere.

Which for his fourth course made our Poet court her &c.

87

Gustus This motion of my soule, my fantasie
Created by three sences put in act,
Let justice nourish with thy simpathie,
Putting my other sences into fact;
If now thou grant not, now changde that offence;
To suffer change, doth perfect sence compact:[u]
Change then, and suffer for the use of sence;
    Wee live not for our selves, the Eare, and Eye,
    And every sence, must serve societie.

88

To furnish then, this Banquet where the tast
Is never usde, and yet the cheere divine,
The neerest meane deare Mistres, that thou hast
To blesse me with it, is a kysse of thine,
Which grace shall borrow organs of my touch
T'advance it to that inward[v] taste of mine
Which makes all sence, and shall delight as much
    Then with a kisse (deare life) adorne thy feast
    And let (as Banquets should) the last be best.

89

Corynna I see unbidden Guests are boldest still,
And well you showe how weake in soule you are
That let rude sence subdue your reasons skill
And feede so spoilefully on sacred fare;
In temper of such needles feasts as this
We show more bounty still, the more we spare,
Chiefly where birth and state so different is:
    Ayre too much rarefied breakes forth in fire,
    And favors too farre urg'd do end in ire.

[u] Alterationem pati est sentire.
[v] He intends the common sence which is *centrum sensibus et speciebus*, & cals it last because it dooth, *sapere in effectione sensuum.*

90

The difference of our births (imperiall Dame)
Is heerein noted with too triviall eyes
For your rare wits; that should your choices frame
To state of parts, that most doth royalize,
Not to commend mine owne; but that in yours
Beyond your birth, are perrils soveraignties
Which (urgd) your words had strook with sharper powers;
    Tis for mere looke-like Ladies, and for men
    To boast of birth that still be childeren,

91

Running to Father straight to helpe theyr needs;
True dignities and rites of reverence,
Are sowne in mindes, and reapt in lively deedes,
And onely pollicie makes difference
Twixt States, since vertue wants due imperance;
Vertue makes honor, as the soule doth sence,
And merit farre exceedes inheritance,
    The Graces fill loves cup, his feasts adorning,
    Who seekes your service now, the Graces scorning.

92

Pure love (said she), the purest grace pursues,
And there is contact, not by application
Of lips or bodies, but of bodies vertues,
As in our elementale Nation
Stars by theyr powers, which are theyr heat and light
Do heavenly works, and that which hath probation
By vertuall contact hath the noblest plight,
    Both for the lasting and affinitie
    It hath with naturall divinitie.

93

Ovid replied: in thys thy vertuall presence
(Most fayre Corynna) thou canst not effuse
The true and solid parts of thy pure essence
92.8 divinitie]; (diunitie, Bartlett)

235

But doost the superficiall beames produce
Of thy rich substance; which because they flow
Rather from forme then from the matters use
Resemblance onely of thy body showe
    Whereof they are thy wondrous species,
    And t'is thy substance must my longings ease.

94

Speake then sweet ayre, that giv'st our speech event,
And teach my Mistres tractabilitie,
That art to motion most obedient,
And though thy nature, swelling be and high
And occupiest so infinite a space,
Yet yeeldst to words, and art condeust thereby
Past nature prest into a little place;
    Deare soveraigne then, make ayre thy rule in this,
    And me thy worthy servant with a kisse.

95

Ovid (sayd shee) I am well pleasd to yeeld:
Bountie by vertue cannot be abusde:
Nor will I coylie lyft Minervas shielde
Against Minerva; honor is not brusde
With such a tender pressure as a kisse,
Nor yeelding soone to words, though seldome usde,
Nicenes in civill favours, folly is:
    Long sutes make never good a bad detection,
    Nor yeelding soone, makes bad, a good affection.

96

To some I know, (and know it for a fault)
Order and reverence are repulst in skaling,
When pryde and rudenes enter with assault,

93.4 the] (Bartlett); thy
93.5–8 Cf.   for as colour flowes
      From superficies of each thing we see,
      Even so with colours formes emitted bee:
      And where Loves forme is, love is, love is forme;
                          Hero and Leander v, 224–27
94.6 condeust]; (condenst, Bartlett)

Consents to fall are worse to get then falling:
Willing resistance takes away the will,
And too much weakenes tis to come with calling:
Force in these frayes is better man then skyll.
   Yet I like skill, and Ovid if a kis
   May doe thee so much pleasure, heere it is.

97

Her mooving towards him, made Ovids eye
Beleeve the Firmament was comming downe
To take him quick to immortalitie,
And that th'Ambrosian kisse set on the Crowne:
Shee spake in kissing, and her breath infusde
Restoring syrrop to his tast, in swoune:
And hee imaginde Hebes hands had brusde
   A banquet of the Gods into his sence,
   Which fild him with this furious influence:

98

The motion of the Heavens that did beget
The golden age, and by whose harmonie
Heaven is preservd, in mee on worke is set,
All instruments of deepest melodie
Set sweet in my desires to my loves liking
With this sweet kisse in mee theyr tunes apply,
As if the best Musitians hands were striking:
   This kisse in mee hath endlesse Musicke closed,
   Like Phœbus Lute, on Nisus Towrs imposed.

99

And as a Pible cast into a Spring,
Wee see a sort of trembling cirkles rise,
One forming other in theyr issuing
Till over all the Fount they circulize,
So this perpetuall-motion-making kisse,
Is propagate through all my faculties,
And makes my breast an endlesse Fount of blisse,
   Of which, if Gods could drink, theyr matchlesse fare
   Would make them much more blessed then they are.

100

But as when sounds^w doe hollow bodies beate,
Ayre gatherd there, comprest, and thickned,
The selfe same way shee came doth make retreate,
And so effects the sounde reechoed
Onely in part, because shee weaker is
In that redition, then when first shee fled:
So I alas, faint eccho of this kisse,
    Onely reiterate a slender part
    Of that high joy it worketh in my hart.

101

And thus with feasting, love is famisht more,
Without my touch are all things turnd to gold,
And till I touch, I cannot joy my store:
To purchase others, I my selfe have sold;
Love is a wanton famine, rich in foode,
But with a richer appetite controld,
An argument in figure and in Moode,
    Yet hates all arguments: disputing still
    For Sence, gainst Reason, with a sencelesse will.

102

Tactus Then sacred Madam, since my other sences
Have in your graces tasted such content,
Let wealth not to be spent, feare no expences,
But give thy bountie true eternizement:
Making my sences ground-worke, which is, Feeling,
Effect the other, endlesse excellent,
Their substance with flint-softning softnes steeling:
    Then let mee feele, for know, sweet beauties Queene,
    Dames may be felt, as well as heard or seene.

103

For if wee be allowd to serve the Eare
With pleasing tunes, and to delight the Eye
With gracious showes, the Taste with daintie cheere,
The Smell with Odors, ist immodestie

^w Qua ratione fiat Eccho.

To serve the sences Emperor, sweet Feeling,
With those delights that fit his Emperie?
Shall Subjects free themselves, and bind theyr King?
  Mindes taint no more with bodies touch or tyre,
  Then bodies nourish with the mindes desire.

104

The minde then cleere, the body may be usde,
Which perfectly your touch can spritualize;
As by the great elixer is trans-fusde
Copper to Golde, then grant that deede of prise:
Such as trans-forme into corrupt effects
What they receave from Natures purities,
Should not wrong them that hold her due respects:
  To touch your quickning side then give mee leave,
  Th'abuse of things, must not the use bereave.

105

Heere-with, even glad his arguments to heare,
Worthily willing to have lawfull grounds
To make the wondrous power of Heaven appeare,
In nothing more then her perfections found,
Close to her navill shee her Mantle wrests,
Slacking it upwards, and the foulds unwound,
Showing Latonas Twinns, her plenteous brests
  The Sunne and Cynthia in theyr tryumph-robes
  Of Lady-skin; more rich then both theyr Globes.

106

Whereto shee bad, blest Ovid put his hand:
Hee, well acknowledging it much too base
For such an action, did a little stand,
Enobling it with tytles full of grace,
And conjures it with charge of reverend verse,
To use with pietie that sacred place,
And through his Feelings organ to disperse
  Worth to his spirits, amply to supply
  The porenes of his fleshes facultie.

107

And thus hee sayd: King of the King of Sences,
Engine of all the engines under heaven,
To health, and life, defence of all defences,
Bountie by which our nourishment is given,
Beauties bewtifier, kinde acquaintance maker,
Proportions odnes that makes all things even,
Wealth of the laborer, wrongs revengement taker,
    Patterne of concord, Lord of exercise,
    And figure of that power the world did guise:

108

Deere Hand, most dulie honored in this
And therefore worthy to be well employde:
Yet know, that all that honor nothing is,
Compard with that which now must be enjoyd:
So thinke in all the pleasures these have showne
(Likened to this) thou wert but meere anoyde,
That all hands merits in thy selfe alone
    With this one touch, have more then recompence,
    And therefore feele, with feare and reverence.

109

See Cupids Alps which now thou must goe over,
Where snowe that thawes the Sunne doth ever lye:
Where thou maist plaine and feelingly discover
The worlds fore-past, that flow'd with Milke and Honny:
Where, (like an Empresse seeing nothing wanting
That may her glorious child-bed bewtifie)
Pleasure her selfe lyes big with issue panting:
    Ever deliverd, yet with childe still growing,
    Full of all blessings, yet all blisse bestowing.

110

This sayd, hee layde his hand upon her side,
Which made her start like sparckles from a fire,
Or like Saturnia from th'Ambrosian pride
Of her morns slumber, frighted with admire

107.2 Engine] Engines

When Jove layd young Alcydes to her brest,
So startled shee, not with a coy retire,
But with the tender temper shee was blest,
　　Proving her sharpe, unduld with handling yet,
　　Which keener edge on Ovids longings set.

III

And feeling still, he sigh'd out this effect:
Alas why lent not heaven the soule a tongue?
Nor language, nor peculier dialect,
To make her high conceits as highly sung,
But that a fleshlie engine must unfold
A spirituall notion; birth from Princes sprung
Pessants must nurse, free vertue waite on gold
　　And a profest though flattering enemie,
　　Must pleade my honor, and my libertie.

112

O nature how doost thou defame in this
Our humane honors? yoking men with beasts
And noblest mindes with slaves? thus beauties blisse,
Love and all vertues that quick spirit feasts
Surfet on flesh; and thou that banquests mindes,
Most bounteous Mistresse, of thy dull-tongu'd guests
Reapst not due thanks; thus rude frailetie bindes
　　What thou giv'st wings; thus joyes I feele in thee
　　Hang on my lips and will not uttered be.

113

Sweete touch the engine that loves bow doth bend,
The sence wherewith he feeles him deified,
The object whereto all his actions tend,
In all his blindenes his most pleasing guide,
For thy sake will I write the Art of love,
Since thou doost blow his fire and feede his pride,
Since in thy sphere his health and life doth move,
　　For thee I hate who hate societie
　　And such as self-love makes his slaverie.

112.9 my]; (thy, Bartlett)

114

In these dog-dayes how this contagion smoothers
The purest bloods with vertues diet fined,
Nothing theyr owne, unlesse they be some others,
Spite of themselves are in themselves confined
And live so poore they are of all despised,
Theyr gifts, held down with scorne should be divined,
And they like Mummers mask, unknowne, unprised:
    A thousand mervailes mourne in some such brest
    Would make a kinde and worthy Patrone blest.

115

To mee (deere Soveraigne) thou art Patronesse,
And I, with that thy graces have infused,
Will make all fat and foggy braines confesse,
Riches may from a poore verse be deduced:
And that Golds love shall leave them groveling heere,
When thy perfections shall to heaven be Mused,
Deckt in bright verse, where Angels shall appeare,
    The praise of vertue, love, and beauty singing,
    Honor to Noblesse, shame to Avarice bringing.

116

Heere Ovid interupted with the view
Of other Dames, who then the Garden painted,
Shrowded himselfe, and did as death eschew
All note by which his loves fame might be tainted:
And as when mighty Macedon had wun
The Monarchie of Earth, yet when hee fainted,
Griev'd that no greater action could be doone,
    And that there were no more worlds to subdue,
    So loves defects, loves Conqueror did rue.

117

But as when expert Painters have displaid,
To quickest life a Monarchs royall hand
Holding a Scepter, there is yet bewraide
But halfe his fingers; when we understand

The rest not to be seene; and never blame
The Painters Art, in nicest censures skand:
So in the compasse of this curious frame,
  Ovid well knew there was much more intended,
  With whose omition none must be offended.

Intentio, animi actio.

THE METAMORPHOSIS OF PIGMALIONS IMAGE

John Marston

(1598)

PIGMALION whose chast mind all the beauties in Cyprus could not ensnare, yet at the length having carved in Ivorie an excellent proportion of a beauteous woman, was so deeplie enamored on his owne workmanship, that he would oftentimes lay the Image in bedde with him, and fondlie use such petitions and dalliance, as if it had been a breathing creature. But in the end, finding his fond dotage, and yet persevering in his ardent affection, made his devout prayers to Venus, that shee would vouchsafe to enspire life into his Love, and then joyne them both together in marriage. Whereupon Venus graciously condiscending to his earnest sute, the Mayde, (by the power of her Deitie) was metamorphosed into a living Woman. And after, Pigmalion (beeing in Cyprus) begat a sonne of her, which was called Paphus, wherupon, that Iland Cyprus, in honor of Venus, was after, and is now, called by the inhabitants, Paphos.

I

Pigmalion, whose hie love-hating minde
Disdain'd to yeeld servile affection,
Or amorous sute to any woman-kinde,
Knowing their wants, and mens perfection.
   Yet Love at length forc'd him to know his fate,
   And love the shade, whose substance he did hate.

2

For having wrought in purest Ivorie,
So faire an Image of a Womans feature,

244

That never yet proudest mortalitie
Could show so rare and beautious a creature.
   (Unlesse my Mistres all-excelling face,
    Which gives to beautie, beauties onely grace.)

3

Hee was amazed at the wondrous rarenesse
Of his owne workmanships perfection.
He thought that Nature nere produc'd such fairenes
In which all beauties have their mantion.
   And thus admiring, was enamored
    On that fayre Image himselfe portraied.

4

And naked as it stood before his eyes,
Imperious Love declares his Deitie.
O what alluring beauties he descries
In each part of his faire imagery!
   Her nakednes, each beauteous shape containes.
    All beautie in her nakednes remaines.

5

He thought he saw the blood run through the vaine
And leape, and swell with all alluring meanes:
Then feares he is deceiv'd, and then againe,
He thinks he see'th the brightnes of the beames
   Which shoote from out the fairenes of her eye:
    At which he stands as in an extasie.

6

Her Amber-coloured, her shining haire,
Makes him protest, the Sunne hath spread her head
With golden beames, to make her farre more faire.
But when her cheeks his amorous thoughts have fed,
   Then he exclaimes, such redde and so pure white,
    Did never blesse the eye of mortall sight.

7

Then view's her lips, no lips did seeme so faire
In his conceit, through which he thinks doth flie
So sweet a breath, that doth perfume the ayre.
Then next her dimpled chin he doth discry,
   And views, and wonders, and yet view's her still.
   "Loves eyes in viewing never have their fill.

8

Her breasts, like polisht Ivory appeare,
Whose modest mount, doe blesse admiring eye,
And makes him wish for such a Pillowbeare.
Thus fond Pigmalion striveth to discry
   Each beauteous part, not letting over-slip
   One parcell of his curious workmanship.

9

Untill his eye discended so farre downe
That it discried Loves pavillion:
Where Cupid doth enjoy his onely crowne,
And Venus hath her chiefest mantion:
   There would he winke, & winking looke againe,
   Both eies & thoughts would gladly there remaine.

10

Who ever saw the subtile Citty-dame
In sacred church, when her pure thoughts shold pray,
Peire through her fingers, so to hide her shame,
When that her eye her mind would faine bewray.
   So would he view, and winke, and view againe,
   A chaster thought could not his eyes retaine.

11

He wondred that she blusht not when his eye
Saluted those same parts of secrecie:
Conceiting not it was imagerie
That kindly yeelded that large libertie.
   O that my Mistres were an Image too,
   That I might blameles her perfections view.

12

But when the faire proportion of her thigh
Began appeare: O Ovid would he cry,
Did ere Corinna show such Ivorie
When she appear'd in Venus livorie?
   And thus enamour'd, dotes on his owne Art
   Which he did work, to work his pleasing smart.

13

And fondly doting, oft he kist her lip.
Oft would he dally with her Ivory breasts.
No wanton love-trick would he over-slip,
But still observ'd all amorous beheasts.
   Whereby he thought he might procure the love
   Of his dull Image, which no plaints coulde move.

14

Looke how the peevish Papists crouch, and kneele
To some dum Idoll with their offering,
As if a senceles carved stone could feele
The ardor of his bootles chattering,
   So fond he was, and earnest in his sute
   To his remorsles Image, dum and mute.

15

He oft doth wish his soule might part in sunder
So that one halfe in her had residence:
Oft he exclaimes, ô beauties onely wonder,
Sweet modell of delight, faire excellence,
   Be gracious unto him that formed thee,
   Compassionate his true-loves ardencie.

16

She with her silence, seemes to graunt his sute.
Then he all jocund like a wanton lover,
With amorous embracements doth salute
Her slender wast, presuming to discover
   The vale of Love, where Cupid doth delight
   To sport, and dally all the sable night.

17

His eyes, her eyes, kindly encountered,
His breast, her breast, oft joyned close unto,
His armes embracements oft she suffered,
Hands, armes, eyes, tongue, lips, and all parts did woe.
  His thigh, with hers, his knee playd with her knee,
  A happy consort when all parts agree.

18

But when he saw poore soule, he was deceaved,
(Yet scarce he could beleeve his sence had failed)
Yet when he found all hope from him bereaved,
And saw how fondly all his thoughts had erred,
  Then did he like to poore Ixion seeme,
  That clipt a cloud in steede of heavens Queene.

19

I oft have smil'd to see the foolery
Of some sweet Youths, who seriously protest
That Love respects not actuall Luxury,
But onely joy's to dally, sport, and jest:
  Love is a child, contented with a toy,
  A busk-point, or some favour still's the boy.

20

Marke my Pigmalion, whose affections ardor
May be a mirror to posteritie.
Yet viewing, touching, kissing, (common favour,)
Could never satiat his loves ardencie:
  And therefore Ladies, thinke that they nere love you,
  Who doe not unto more then kissing move you.

21

For my Pigmalion kist, viewd, and imbraced,
And yet exclaimes, why were these women made
O sacred Gods, and with such beauties graced?
Have they not power as well to coole, and shade,
  As for to heate mens harts? or is there none
  Or are they all like mine? relentlesse stone.

248

22

With that he takes her in his loving armes,
And downe within a Downe-bed softly layd her.
Then on his knees he all his sences charmes,
To invocate sweet Venus for to raise her
   To wished life, and to infuse some breath,
   To that which dead, yet gave a life to death.

23

Thou sacred Queene of sportive dallying,
(Thus he begins,) Loves onely Emperesse,
Whose kingdome rests in wanton revelling,
Let me beseech thee show thy powerfulnesse
   In changing stone to flesh, make her relent,
   And kindly yeeld to thy sweet blandishment.

24

O gracious Gods, take compassion.
Instill into her some celestiall fire,
That she may equalize affection,
And have a mutuall love, and loves desire.
   Thou know'st the force of love, then pitty me,
   Compassionate my true loves ardencie.

25

Thus having said, he riseth from the floore,
As if his soule divined him good fortune,
Hoping his prayers to pitty moov'd some power.
For all his thoughts did all good luck importune.
   And therefore straight he strips him naked quite,
   That in the bedde he might have more delight.

26

Then thus, Sweet sheetes he sayes, which nowe doe cover,
The Idol of my soule, the fairest one
That ever lov'd, or had an amorous lover.
Earths onely modell of perfection,
   Sweet happy sheetes, daine for to take me in,
   That I my hopes and longing thoughts may win.

27

With that his nimble limbs doe kisse the sheetes,
And now he bowes him for to lay him downe,
And now each part, with her faire parts doe meet,
Now doth he hope for to enjoy loves crowne:
　　Now doe they dally, kisse, embrace together,
　　Like Leda's Twins at sight of fairest weather.

28

Yet all's conceit. But shadow of that blisse
Which now my Muse strives sweetly to display
In this my wondrous metamorphosis.
Daine to beleeve me, now I sadly say:
　　The stonie substance of his Image feature,
　　Was straight transform'd into a living creature.

29

For when his hands her faire form'd limbs had felt,
And that his armes her naked wast imbraced,
Each part like Waxe before the sunne did melt,
And now, oh now, he finds how he is graced
　　By his owne worke. Tut, women will relent
　　When as they finde such moving blandishment.

30

Doe but conceive a Mothers passing gladnes,
(After that death her onely sonne hath seazed
And overwhelm'd her soule with endlesse sadnes)
When that she sees him gin for to be raised
　　From out his deadly swoune to life againe:
　　Such joy Pigmalion feeles in every vaine.

31

And yet he feares he doth but dreaming find
So rich content, and such celestiall blisse.
Yet when he proves & finds her wondrous kind,
Yeelding soft touch for touch, sweet kisse, for kisse,
　　He's well assur'd no faire imagery
　　Could yeeld such pleasing, loves felicity.

32

O wonder not to heare me thus relate,
And say to flesh transformed was a stone.
Had I my Love in such a wished state
As was afforded to Pigmalion,
   Though flinty hard, of her you soone should see
   As strange a transformation wrought by mee.

33

And now me thinks some wanton itching eare
With lustfull thoughts, and ill attention,
List's to my Muse, expecting for to heare
The amorous discription of that action
   Which Venus seekes, and ever doth require,
   When fitnes graunts a place to please desire.

34

Let him conceit but what himselfe would doe
When that he had obtayned such a favour,
Of her to whom his thoughts were bound unto,
If she, in recompence of his loves labour,
   Would daine to let one payre of sheets containe
   The willing bodies of those loving twaine.

35

Could he, oh could he, when that each to eyther
Did yeeld kind kissing, and more kind embracing,
Could he when that they felt, and clipt together
And might enjoy the life of dallying,
   Could he abstaine midst such a wanton sporting
   From doing that, which is not fit reporting?

36

What would he doe when that her softest skin
Saluted his with a delightfull kisse?
When all things fit for loves sweet pleasuring
Invited him to reape a Lovers blisse?
   What he would doe, the selfe same action
   Was not neglected by Pigmalion.

37

For when he found that life had tooke his seate
Within the breast of his kind beauteous love,
When that he found that warmth, and wished heate
Which might a Saint and coldest spirit move,
  Then arms, eyes, hands, tong, lips, & wanton thigh,
  Were willing agents in Loves luxurie.

38

Who knowes not what ensues? O pardon me
Yee gaping eares that swallow up my lines.
Expect no more. Peace idle Poesie,
Be not obsceane though wanton in thy rimes.
  And chaster thoughts, pardon if I doe trip,
  Or if some loose lines from my pen doe slip.

39

Let this suffice, that that same happy night
So gracious were the Gods of marriage
Mid'st all there pleasing and long wish'd delight
Paphus was got: of whom in after age
  Cyprus was Paphos call'd, and evermore
  Those Ilandars do Venus name adore.

39.5 Cyprus] Cyrus

FAUNUS AND MELLIFLORA

John Weever

(1600)

When Jove ambitious by his former sinnes,
(From him al Muses, so my Muse beginnes)
Deposde his Syre Saturnus from the throne,
And so usurpt the Diadem alone:
Some higher power for aged Saturne strove,   5
Gave him a gift, which angred lust-stung Jove:
A lovely boy, whose beautie at his birth,
Made poore the heav'ns to enrich the earth.
(When Jove no beautie in the heavens found,
Was he not angry? yea, and to the ground   10
Sent Mercurie, to wooe a shepheards swaine,
Whilst he himselfe came in a showre of raine:
Whose drizling drops fell into Danaes lappe,
Which to receive, (maides wil receive such happe)
She held hir skirt, Jove such abundance powred,   15
Twentie to one but Danae was deflowred.)
His name was Pycus, yet surnam'd the Faire,
Whom Circe chaunted in her scorne-gold haire,
Whom Ladies lov'd, and loved of so many,
The wood-Nymphes woo'd him, yet not won of any,   20
Till Canens came, (who when she gan to sing,
The ayrie Bird would hoover with her wing,
To heare her notes, for Canens she was call'd,
Of singing sweete) and Pycus heart enthrall'd:
Not married long, but Canens did enjoy   25
Of fairest father, farre more faire a boy,
(That heav'n, & earth, in bringing forth these two,
Made a great bragge that so much they could do:)

Faunus a boy whose amber-stragling haires,
So strangely trammeld all about his eares,   30
The crispe dishevel'd playing with the winde,
Among the thickest, never way could finde,
But sweetest flowers would leape from Floraes lap,
And so themselves within his tresses wrap.
That glad he was those lockes (those lockes alone,   35
Those lockes that lockt in bondage many one:)
With carelesse art, or artlesse care infolde,
And draw them in a coronet of golde.
If bashfulnesse enveloped his face,
A prettie palenesse damask't such sweet grace,   40
Like Daisie with the Gilliflower distill'd,
Or Roses on a bed of Lillies spill'd:
Or rather when the wood-Nimphs gazing stood,
Love like a tyrant therein threatned blood:
His eies were such, my Muse yet hardly can   45
Emblazon forth the beutie of a man:
My dullard muse to sing it may suffize,
Of his rich coate he wore in wondrous guize:
The ground whereof was velvet, white as snow,
Reaching unto the ankles downe below,   50
With buttons made of Diamonds upon,
Such as our knights of th'order first put on:
Upon the left side it no fastning had,
But on the right side with a pearle staide,
Upon th'one shoulder where the two ends met,   55
Were both together, with a jewell set,
On top whereof in lively forme did stand,
Great Hercules with distaffe in his hand:
To every seame were fastned ribonings,
With stories wrought of Emperours and Kings: 60
And at each ribbon hung a pretious stone;
(Loves chiefe disport consists in these alone)
Which were faire Ladies costly Amatists,
Tide to the tender small leav'de ozear twists,
That so they might his ribbons enterlace,   56
When he pursude the nimble Hart in chace:
And she grew prowd, and held the rest in scorne,
That knew her favour by yong Faunus worne.

Poudred upon so strange, that many thought
With purple coloured silke it had beene wrought: 70
But (ah alas) it was the crimson staine,
Of goddesses, which Faunus lookes had slaine:
About his necke he wore a falling band,
Which tooke it pride from his faire mothers hand:
His ivory feete, appearing unto sight,   75
In murrey velvet buskins rich were dight,
The middle slits with tyrian Bisse were laced,
Whose prettie knots his man-like legge embraced.
In many places bare as use hath bin,
To shew the clearenesse of the naked skin.   80
The wanton boy attired in this sort,
Unto the Latian mountaines did resort,
Whose prowde height garnisht with such stately trees,
Seemde to contemne the vally at his knees,
The humble vally in as good a state: 85
(But loftie Gallants lower minds do hate)
Was still replenisht with a pleasant river,
(Prowd of the gift, and yet more prowd the giver,)
Whose wanton streames the bank so oft do kisse,
That in her lap (at length) he falling is: 90
Her bubbling water with slow gliding pace,
Shews her great griefe to leave that pleasant place:
And with a murmure when she goes away,
Greatly laments she can no longer stay,
Cause th'upper streams by violence would come,   95
To take possession of that joyfull roome,
With swift pursute, and as they gin to chace it,
The bankes like armes doe lovingly imbrace it:
Whose purling noise upon the pibble stones,
For such departure are the dolefull grones: 100
Her teares exhalde such norishment doth give,
As on the tree-fringd banks made Pleasure live.
Among these trees a goodly Cypresse grew,
That all the lofty pines did over-view,
Who bow'd her faire head (in the sunnie gleames,)   105
To tresse her greene locks by those glassie streames.
Her top, her shade, upon the River show'd,

76 murrey, purple

255

For the kind moisture on her root bestow'd,
Running upon so delicate a ground,
As that the truth could never yet be found: 110
Whether it made the gravell pretious looke,
Or else the gravell purifide the brooke:
Whose meddowes greene enameled with roses,
(Twas Paradise some Poet yet supposes)
Added a shew so ruddie, that most deemed   115
The field to blush at his owne beautie seemed.
Neare to this valley Shepheards often met,
And by this valley sheepish squadrons set,
Within this valley past the time away,
With leapes and gamboles, and with other play: 120
Here the Nymphes playd such summer games as Base,
For it was summer alwaies in this place,
And Barlibreake, the which when Faunus saw,
So many wood-Nymphes standing on a row:
The boy, though yong, (yet who so yong that loves not,   125
Or who so old that womens beautie moves not?)
Spide Melliflora: Melliflora was
Among the number sitting on the grasse:
Sweete Melliflora I can tell ye true,
The grasse grew prowd that under her it grew.   130
Faire Melliflora, amorous, and yong,
Whose name, nor story, never Poet sung:
She wore a garland wrought with Amorets,
With orphrates overlaid and violets,
Whose Jacinth love-lockes hanged out so faire,   135
As drest the garland, garland drest the haire,
And enterlaced with a purle band,
(Like cristall Tagus through his golden sand)
Which hiding nowe, then hidden by the haire,
At fast and loose to play it did appeare,   140
Faire was her face yet fairer might have beene,
If that the Sunne so often had not seene
Her lovely face, for halfe the day he spent
In kissing her, yet never was content:
(For God or man thinkes he the Cushion misses,   145
That wooes all day, and winnes nought else but kisses.)

    134 orphrates, for orphreys, gold embroideries

256

Untill the sunne with overmuch desire
Of love (for love is hotter then the fire)
Consumde the wreathe of Diamonds in his throne:
(Ovid's beguilde, it was not Phaeton)   150
For Melliflora was the cause he burned,
His chariot, and the world to cinders turned.
Strange were her weedes to Faunus, yet not strange,
For in such weedes the wood-Nymphes use to range,
A petticote tuckte even with the knees,   155
Garnisht about with leaves of sundry trees:
And sometimes like a net drawne up, and wrought,
(Which net the eagle-Jove might well have cought)
And all her garments made so light and thin,
(Who could restraine, but thinke what was within?)   160
And blacke silke laces whereon silver bells
Did hang above her elbowes, and of shels
Her slippers were; her legges, her armes, her brest,
In many places naked, yet so drest,
As nakednesse another raiment scorned,   165
For she her cloaths, her cloaths not her adorned.
Faunus a farre off stood stone-still and gazed,
The more he lookt, the more Love inly blazed,
He would have quencht it with his teares, but then
(A sparke of beautie burnes a world of men)   170
It burnt the more, yet who can well refraine
From drinking water, when he feeles the paine
Of burning fever, though that water drenches,
And turnes to fire, which like Love never quenches?
But youth may love, and yongmen may admire,   175
If old age cannot, yet it will desire.
For since that time old men of sixty yeeres,
(*Bearing a beard, or rather, beard them beares*)
Will heate their blouds with love and yong wives chuse,
(At such sweete weddings yongmen nothing loose).   180
Faunus kneel'd downe and unto Venus prayde,
Before his prayers were the one halfe said,
He thought it best unto the Nimph to write
And shew his love, but ginning to indite,
He tride the Muses with his often changes,   185
(Love never loves to rest, but alwaies ranges.)

If once on Melliflora he did thinke,
He wet his paper both with teares and inke:
Fearing to end before he had begunne,
Mistrusting each word which his wit had done: 190
One was too darke, another was too plaine,
This word too loftie, and the other vaine.
That set not downe the sorrow of his hart,
This shew'd his passion, but it shew'd no Art:
He tore his papers, cast away his pen,   195
Sore was he grievde, and yet not angrie (men
In true love are not angrie) for he knew,
The more hee studied, still the worse it grew:
Then he resolvde to take the rose-strowne way,
Into the valley where he saw them play,   200
Accosted all with Venus and the Graces:
With white haire hiding their enticing faces,
Which hand in hand would make a circle round,
With often turning, then themselves confound,
In Pyrrhus daunce, like souldiers armed twine them,   205
And wedge-wise yoked in array combine them.
And when he came, that wood-Nymph was most faine,
That to their play might Faunus entertaine.
And if he spake, the Nymphs drew somewhat neare him,
To taste the sirrop of sweete wordes, and heare him.   210
And gray-eyd Dorys she would alwayes eye him,
Till she was strucke purblinde she could not see him:
Some wisht him sooner (though he came too soone)
Before the pleasure of the day was done:
Some saide, the night for Lovers was the day,   215
And Love delighted in the night to play,
For now the day his office gave to night,
To lend our adverse hemisphere his light.
The Nymphs requested Melliflora than,
To move this sute to Faunus; she beganne: 220
I would we had such eloquence as might
Intreate your Highnesse lodge with us all night,
We and our arbour evermore would rest
Content, and honourd with so great a ghest:
You shall but lie upon a bed of roses,   225
Your sheetes white lillies, pillowes fragrant poses,

Your blankets flowerdeluces shall be drawne
With prety pinkes, your curtaines leafie lawne,
And in my bed, *My*, unawares out slipt,
Her face bewraide how that her tongue had tript,   230
Which Faunus seeing, would have kist her then,
To hide those blushes (oh how kind are men!)
Fresh she begins, thinking that word to alter,
The more she speakes, the more her tongue doth falter,
And gainst her will that *My* she spoke againe,   235
(Love will not let such words be spoke in vaine.)
This past as unregarded: Faunus said,
I were inhumane if this were denaid.
Orecome with joy, they in the mid rancke set him,
He thought their arbour in the midway met him,   240
Such force of Musicke conquerd length of way,
With torches making artificiall day.
Above all trees in th'odoriferous meades,
(With greene vine branches, curling their prowd heades,
And honni-suckles) at their lodging doore,   245
Doth grow the pleasing brode leav'de Sycamore:
Her entrances adornd with pretious stone,
Built in the forme of a pavillion:
Ridings cut out, so that the eie might judge,
What Angells did inhabite in the lodge,   250
And like a comet (yet more pretious farre)
Stretching her tale unto a lesser starre:
He pointed at a pleasant summer hall,
Wherein the Nymphes did use to banquet all;
The coloured marble beautified the top,   255
Whose pillars serv'de the house to underprop,
And underneath whereas a river rode,
Was minerall, her streames an handfull broade,
Her shaking Christall was a perfect mirrour,
To all the beauties in the garden neare her,   260
Whose water washt them; rather they did wash it,
For when their snow-white ivorie hands would plash it,
(Like honie-bubbling Ladon, or Pirene,
Cleare Castalie, or luke-warme Hippocrene)
Upon her face she makes ten thousand lines,   265

249 Ridings, lanes

Ten thousand Saphir coloured bubbles shines,
As not content in large to have their pinctures,
In each of them sets forth their lively tinctures:
And comes againe to play, embrace, and threaten,
And laughes, and smiles, and leapes to be so beaten. 270
Behind this brooke or thicket was a greene,
Whereas five hundred grassie rounds had beene
Made one in one, like to these water rings,
Thence to a gallerie Melliflore him brings;
There was Diana: when Acteon saw her, 275
Bathing her selfe (alas he did not know her):
(A goldsmiths wife once nakt without her pearle,
Hard to be knowne is from a countrie gerle.)
A foolish Nimph sate weeping, (for love can
Make goddesses like women love a man) 280
The posture of whose limmes so lively seated,
As Art and Nature Love and Anger freated:
Within this gallerie whenas Faunus comes,
The grapes with childe, and divers coloured plums,
Gave to the eie a pleasant taste, before 285
Unto the mouth they came, and evermore
The coole wine fild into the goblet skips,
And laughes for joy to come unto such lips:
As Faunus drunke, still would he steale a looke,
(Thus Faunus swallowed Cupids golden hooke) 290
Then laide his eies wide ope his love to view,
(Thus he receiv'd the darts which Cupid threw)
Then closde his eie-lids from that glorious light,
(Thus he preserv'd the riches of his sight)
And thus faire words and power attractive beuty, 295
Bring men to women in subjective duety.
But supper ends, and all the Nymphes expected
Some amorous talke of Faunus: he neglected
Untill a Nymph (this order yet we use)
Sayd, let us husbands in the ashes chuse. 300
In lovers rites, Faunus though rude and raw,
It was no dallying yet with Nimphs he saw,
Then smiling said: Faire Nymphs, the shepheards lasses,
Thus chuse them husbands, turning crabs in ashes;
If in these woods good husbands be so scant, 305

Will you sweete Nymphes, with me supplie some want?
But some said nothing; these gave ful consent,
And some said twice No, which affirmes content,
And some said once No; these would grant and give:
In womens mouths, No is no negative: 310
Whereat he blusht, and fearing to offend,
The fondling thus abruptly made an end.
Sorie (God knowes) the Nymphes were hee had done,
Then Deiopeia mongst them all begun
To speake, whose words to Beril straight distilld,   315
As from her lippes the orient pearle trilld,
Looking at Faunus smilingly then said:
A cumbersome companion to a maid
Is modesty; our elders all contemn'd it,
For cowardize most valiant men condemn'd it;   320
Blushing and sighing Theseus never strove,
To woe and winne Antiope his love.
Nor would hee have his time so spent and lavisht,
But laid her downe, and some say shee was ravisht,
And so she was, but ravisht with content,   325
And got with childe, belike both did consent:
Stout Hercules yong Ioles father slew,
And then by force his force faire Iole knew.
Yet this unfathered Ladie would beginne,
Most sportfully put on the Lions skinne,   330
And tooke his clubbe betwixt her hands and viewd it,
Though shee was ravisht, yet she never rewd it.
Soft Menelaus Helen could not brooke,
Yet what inforcing Paris gave, she tooke:
Women are servants, servants unto men,   335
But praise your servants, what will follow then?
A readie horse straight yeeldes when he hath found,
One that will have him yeeld, else falles to bound:
And thus she parl'de, thus she plainely woode,
Yet childish Faunus hardly understood.   340
Untill to bedward all the Nimphes them drest
To take their rest, yet tooke no ease in rest:
The night beginnes be angrie, when she sees
She can distill no sleepe in lovers eies,
Tossing her selfe among the cloudes now hath   345

Sent the red morne as Herald of her wrath,
Whose lover Phœbus rising from his bed,
With his dewie mantle hath the world o'er-spread,
Shaking his tresses over Neptunes ebbe:
And giving tincture to the Spiders webbe: 350
These faire Nimphes rose, seeing the light did call them,
And fairest Faunus equipaged all them.
A fairer bevie of faire virgines never,
The worlds faire eie, the Sunne could yet dissever:
Their prettie pastimes, and their plaies begunne,   355
At Barlibreake yong Faunus needes must runne,
In couples, three, the mid place, called Hell.
But since that time the play is knowne too well:
With Deiopeia it was Faunus lot,
First to be Hell: they ran, and Syrinx got: 360
Syrinx and Spio so pursude the chase,
That Melliflora had the middle place.
Her partner Atte at Deiopeia ran,
But first for Faunus she her course beganne:
He ran, but ranne with eie cast o're his shoulder,   365
Not caring how, so that hee might behold her:
She tooke him straight, about his necke she clang,
And on the grassie carpet Faunus flang.
Willing he was, yet wrastled, strove, and fought,
And fell to feele, and said hee was not cought   370
By law of Barlibreake, because hee fell,
It was his heav'n, though thus to be in Hell:
(For many one for Hell, not Heaven would pray,
If such shee divels were in Hell to play.)
Longer hee strove, that longer hee might stay,   375
But Deiopeia bade her come away:
(For shee poore soule was liver-sicke of love,
And fear'd such strife another strife would move,)
And yeeld to Faunus, then she parts him froe:
(Though she from him, nor he from hir could goe)   380
Let us (she feard againe they would contend)
Of Barlibreake for this time make an end,
Some other play, some other sport begin,
That standers by, and lookers on be in:

    348 o'erspread] overspread

It ended; thus the other play began, 385
Some fiftie maides, (too many for one man)
Tooke hand in hand, which made a spherie round,
Or globe, the perfect'st figure to be found;
Then one (whose lot is first among them all)
Must goe about and let a napkin fall: 390
And whom soe're it lieth next behind,
So soone as ever she the cloth doth find,
Must with swift-running foote the other chace,
Untill she come unto her ranke and place:
If catcht before, the fliers forfeit is, 395
To gratifie the follower with a kisse.
The sport begins, and Arethusa first,
Would have drop-napkin'd Faunus if she durst,
But she tooke Doris, Doris at next bout,
Kist Melliflora, she fetcht Faunus out: 400
She fled (yet tooke); he follow'd (not forsaken);
She ran (yet caught); he follow'd (and was taken):
Upon the backe part, fixed she her eies
So firmely, that before she nothing sees.
But downe she falls (the Nymphes began to wonder) 405
Faunus above (tut women will lie under:)
Gave her the kisse, she (willingly though tooke it,)
Gave it againe, the novice then forsooke it:
White Nisæe next for Deiopeia prest,
And she at Faunus; he could never rest, 410
But either catcht, or else was to be cought,
Untill the freshman faint and breathlesse brought
With tracing was, (the Nymphes much swifter were)
(For love is heavenly light, compact of aire)
So that the slow'st among them never misses, 415
But casts him downe, and smothers him with kisses.
These gamesome Nimphs, welnere sev'n daies had spent
In such like plaies, and sportfull merriment;
Faunus thought oft Loves fire for to display,
Desire was bolde, but Shamefastnesse said nay. 420
If he began to come but somewhat neare her,
His body quak't as though his heart did feare her;
All that he said was, *Nimph, when you are at leasure,*
Faine would I speak, he might have spoke his pleasure:

She found this means, only that he might wooe her,   425
To loose her Necklace; let her Caule forgo her,
Within the woods, that well she could not weare,
Untill she found them, her loose dangling haire,
And as she sought them, softly thus would say:
I prethee Faunus, helpe me, come away,   430
If thou shouldst goe into these woods alone,
Thy Melliflore would follow thee anone:
Wilt thou not come? beleeve me I must chide.
Yet he in love for all this would abide,
When for his love, Love fram'de the time most fit,   435
(Boyes love is foolish, Love to youth brings wit.)
Then to the hedges walke they on a row,
To plucke the sweetes (how sharply sweetes wil grow:)
From sharpest stinging hawthorne as they go,
Fortune to turne their mirth to sodaine woe: 440
From out the woods did send a fierce wild boare,
Which seene (such beasts they never saw before)
A care, or feare, or both, did make them trudge,
Some to the woods, and some towards the lodge:
Some under hedges, some to holes would runne,   445
This way, and that, the best, the beast to shunne:
But Melliflore (whose beautie by that passe,
Like a rubd rubie much augmented was:
Like muske, or civit kept in bosome hot,
Her breath most sweete by running sweetnes got,)   450
Kept on her course, yet never lookt behind,
Whom Faunus follow'd, whilst a wanton wind,
Like to some pleasant civit smelling breath,
Would gently play him with her vaile beneath,
And come, and go, heave up, throw downe, to show   455
Twise-wounded Faunus, what he did not know:
Something he staid his swift pursute with leasure,
Fearing to be deprived of such pleasure,
But what he saw, tis needlesse for to say,
Heere shall your thoughts, and not my pen bewray: 460
But as he gan his swifter running slacke,
The anger-froathing boare was at his backe,
Which made him turne, and at the boare to thrust,

426 caule, head-dress

Into whose heart his hand he guided just:
He was but armed with a little knife,   465
Some destiny belike preserv'd his life:
Yet by this fight he Melliflora lost,
So Faunus thought him worse then ever crost.
In th'unknowne woods, then up and downe he rangeth,
This way for that, that for another changeth: 470
Losing himselfe, within a grove he found
Love-sicke Adonis lying on the ground.
For hating Love, and saying Venus nay,
Yet meeting Melliflora in his way:
Love made (Love weepe to see thy tyrannie,)   475
Adonis frustrate his vow'd chastitie:
Whilst narrowly upon her lookes he spide,
Strooke with loves arrow, he fell downe and dide.
For by the Bore (as all our Poets faine,)
He was not kilde: Faunus the Bore had slaine.   480
But tracing further, who but Venus met him,
Thinking he had beene Adon, thus she gret him:
Welcome Adonis, in thy lovelie breast
Now do I see remorse and pitie rest;
Which to returne my deare Adonis moved,   485
Venus perswades her selfe she is beloved:
Hoping to have some water from the rocke,
Which shee had pierst, she stript her to the smocke,
Wrought all in flames of Chrisolite and gold,
And bout his necke her armes she did enfold: 490
So (at the least) shee meaning to have kist him,
He turn'de aside: then sorie cause shee mist him,
To Faunus said: faire Saint, shun not such kindnesse,
Can these bright eies be blemisht with such blindnesse?
If thou wert blind, and Venus could not see,   495
Yet in the darke best sighted lovers be:
Or give, or take, or both, relent, be kind,
Locke not Love in the paradize of thy mind:
Is Venus lovely? then Adonis love her.
Is she the Queene of love? then what should move her   500
To sue and not command? Is shee Loves mother?
Shall she be loath'd, which brings love to all other?
With that she doft all to the Ivorie skinne,

Thinking her naked glorie would him winne.
The shamefac't Faunus thereat something smiled,   505
Venus lookt on him, knew shee was beguiled:
Yet would have lov'd him for Adonis sake,
(Thus women will one for another take.)
Faunus resisted; Venus would no more
Sollicite him, but mounted as before   510
In her light Chariot, drawne with milke-white Doves,
Away she flies: Faunus left in the groves
No sooner had the wood him passage lent,
But home to see his father Faunus went.
Picus much wondred where his sonne had beene,   515
Whom of seven daies and more he had not seene:
But sleeplesse nights, his being soone revealed,
With sighes and teares (Love cannot be concealed.)
His father by his countenance espide him
To be in love, and mildely thus gan chide him: 520
Fond Boy, quoth hee, and foolish cradle witted,
To let base love with thy yong yeares be fitted:
This upstart love, bewitcher of the wit,
The scorne of vertue, vices parasite:
The slave to weakenesse, friendships false bewrayer,   525
Reasons rebell, Fortitudes betraier:
The Church-mens scoffe, court, camp, and countrie's guiler,
Arts infection, chaste thoughts and youth's defiler.
And what are women? painted weathercocks,
Natures oversight, wayward glittring blocks: 530
True, true-bred cowards, proude if they be coide,
A servile sex, of wit and reason voide:
Shall women move thee, whom so many loathes,
In gaudie plumes trickte, and new-fangled cloathes?
Thus in our find-fault age, many a man   535
Will fondly raile with foule-mouth'd Mantuan.
Some sharpe witted, only in speaking evill,
Would prove a woman worse then any divell
With prating Picus: though that women be,
Fram'd with the same parts of the minde as we.   540
Nay, Nature triumpht in their beauteous birth,
And women made the glorie of the earth:
The life of Beautie, in whose supple breasts,

As in her fairest lodging vertue rests,
Whose towring thoughts attended with remorce,   545
Doe make their fairenesse be of greater force.
But of this subject everie day who reades not,
Which is so praised, as it praises needs not?
And my conceite not able for to reach them,
Might bring forth words for praise, which might impeach
              them: 550
And so with love tis easie to find fault,
Yet not so easie when it gives assault:
Then to resist his force, whose excellence
Is to transforme the verie soule and essence
Of the lover, into the thing beloved: 555
This heavenly love (no doubt) yong Faunus moved:
But (all this while being dumbe) Faunus replide
Unto his father, and withall denide
He lov'd a woman: then his father knew
From whence his griefe and melancholy grew,   560
And that he was by some wood-Nymph accosted,
Because the pleasure of the woods he boasted,
And Latian mountes. Then Picus thus againe
Sharply rebukte his sonne, but all in vaine:
Thou art no souldier for Dianaes garison,   565
Nor twixt her Nymphes and Faunus is comparison:
Nymphes are like Poets, full of wit, but poore,
Unto thy kingdome, adde a kingdome more
By marriage: let Pycus counsel thee,
Looke not (my boy) at wit, and Poetrie.   570
Faunus no reckning of such counsell makes,
(Light is that love which any counsell takes.)
Then like Hermocrates the Phisitian,
Seeing his patient with an incision
Sore vext, in steede of ministring to the sore,   575
Began to chide, bade him be sicke no more.
Or like a friend, that visiting his friend
Loaden with fetters in darke prison pend,
With unkind words, and bitter termes doth move him,
To leave those fetters, or he would not love him: 580
This other way from love would Pycus reave him,
And bade him leave to love, or love to leave him:

Or if such love made Love not to regard him,
His love would love with hatred to reward him.
Remember love, and Pycus would the rather,   585
Forget his sonne he should forgoe his father.
Love all this while on Faunus ey-balls stood,
Whose Envie, palenesse, Anger, caused blood
In Faunus cheekes, to heare such blasphemie
Pronounc'd by Pycus gainst his deitie.   590
With that he leapes from Faunus face and flies
Unto the seld-prevented Destinies.
He found them busie at a Parliament,
Under their feete relentlesse Adamant,
Above their heads the marble was for teele,   595
The ribs of yron, and the raftrie steele,
The walls of flint, and brazen was the gate,
And every one upon a wooll-packe sate.
Whose sterne austere lookes never mov'de to ruth,
By gold, nor favour, beauty, age nor youth: 600
Yet when Love came (what hearts though made of stone,
In which Love cannot make impression?)
Welcome he was; Love then his speech began,
To shew th'unmanlike crueltie of man,
How Nature first ordaining *one for one*,   605
Made woman chiefe for procreation:
But men like drudges, not content to use them,
In blows (sometimes) and speeches will abuse them;
Love's will was this, that maides should have their will,
Not overmuch, but to restraine from ill.   610
Ill kept-in-thoughts, with vertuous companie,
Restraining not from well-rulde libertie.
For maides were made to make such harmlesse plaies,
Such honest sports, as daunce upon the laies:
The hey-de-guise, and run the wild-goose chace,   615
And trie the keeles, the Barlibreake, and base,
But with a barly when the pastimes end,
And maides must needes for milking homewards wend:
As some depart, some are constraind to stay,
For when they end, then Love begins to play: 620
His play is paine, but yet a paine with ease,

595 teele, tile   616 keeles, keelepins (kayles)

His keeles are coales, whose fire doth grieve and please,
From play (for pray) Love takes two loving freeres,
Traind up alike, perhaps of equall yeeres,
Yet such is love of parents such begot,   625
That wealth, nor worth, true love considers not.
Sometime a King dotes on a countrie swaine,
Sometime a Lady loves a lad againe:
Sometime the meaner will the greatst reject,
No not a person Love will once respect.   630
And having pearc'd the soule's seven-doubled shield,
Love makes the one unto the other yeeld.
They yeeld (kind soules) but parents will not grant,
With tedious brawlings still they finde a want,
One is too rich, the other is too poore,   635
(So then twixt Faunus and faire Melliflore,
Love told the Love,) and fearing fathers ire,
Love is defeated of his chiefe desire.
This kind unkindnesse children yet must take,
Untill their parents price of them do make,   640
As in a market: then what man wil crave them,
And give the most, he shalbe sure to have them.
Thus from Loves mouth the honnie as he spoke
Distild, as from the brode-leav'd builder oake,
And opall pearle from his lippes did fall,   645
The Destinies began to gather all
Such pretious jewells, if they fell but neare them,
And prowd of such love-tokens yet do weare them;
His sugred tale thus sweetned by his mouth,
The Destinies did somewhat pittie youth: 650
With one consent and voice they all agreed,
These statutes should for ever be decreed:
That man for his unmanlike treacherie
Should be tormented with vile jealousie,
That maids from honest libertie restrained,   655
Should alway thinke from what they thus refrained:
That twas some treasure from the which th'are tide,
Some Indian jewell which men use to hide,
Some strange conserve, sweete, deare, and pretious,
And women are by nature licorous.   660
These thoughtes awaked, women growe manwood,

Nor can these thoughts from actions be withstood.
What bird is pleasde, though in a silver cage?
A dogge tide up in golden chaines will rage.
That market marriages evermore should be: 665
Content the best, the worst to disagree,
That shrewdnesse should possesse the womans heart,
In stubbornnesse the husband act his part:
Thus drawing opposite in one yoke, alive
Long might they live, but they should never thrive: 670
And since that time, all marriages enforced,
Never agree untill they be devorced.
This sentence given, Love then backe returned,
To lovely Faunus, who in Loves fire burned,
But ere he came, Faunus had turnd to hate   675
His fathers speeches, and grew passionate,
Who in the night (the best meanes for desire)
Got up, and darklings, only his attire,
And naked beautie with a tresse of Amber,
Gave a resplendance to the purle-hung Chamber: 680
Sought for a suite, yet could not well devise,
What garment best might please his faire Nimphs eies:
If costly, then for woddy Nimphs too curious,
If gay or gawdie, that was but penurious:
This was too olde, the other was not new,   685
This the Tailer (Tailers will not be true)
Had cut too short, that hee might have a sharing;
A garment then hee tooke more rich then glaring,
Of gold beat Samite to his heeles which rought,
With knoppes and broches, birdes, and beasts, ywrought. 690
In tuffes of Cypresse hung the Topaze stone,
Which through the Cypresse (yet obscurely) shone:
As when wee see a thinne blacke cloudie clustre,
Through which the stars do yeeld a darksome lustre:
A gorgeous choller of deare chevasall,   695
Set with a white embrodered Pyronall,
And Margarites, with workmans rare devise,
It seemed like unto a shining Ice:
That night (adorned in this princely sort)

678 darklings, in the dark   690 knoppes, studs
695 chevasall, embroidery   696 Pyronall, ? from περόνη brooch

Faunus departed from his fathers Court,   700
And went, untill for wearines he was
Constrainde to lie downe on the yeelding grasse,
And recommended his faire bodies breath,
To Morpheus, the elder borne of death.
There Faunus lie, and cease my pen to tell,   705
What paine those Nimphes abode for thy farewell:
How sops of sorrow drencht in cups of care,
In steede of Nectar and Ambrosia were:
Greefe great in all, yet great'st in Melliflore,
Who thought her Faunus murdred by the Bore: 710
She cut the trees, and carv'de the tender graffes,
With dolefull Sestines, mourning Epitaphes.
And stopt with sighs, and drownd in kisse-cheeke teares,
Her halfe-spoke words. A garment now she weares
Right Raven-blacke, like sorrowes liverie,   715
Cut all in rags, yet joynde so cunningly,
As by her clothes poore raggednesse was braved,
And povertie no greater riches craved.
The Sun this morne before hee did appeare,
Got two houres journey in his Hemisphere.   720
And Melliflora at the Sunnes first peeping,
With loves sharpe-sighted eie the thickets creeping,
Under the broad head of a Pine-tree spies
Faunus asleepe, whose face to heavn-ward lies.
She shrunke aside, aside againe she started,   725
Thinking he had beene Adon, she departed:
But comes againe, (for love lept from his eies
And puld her backe;) twas Faunus then she sees:
She knew and feared, feare she knew before,
Fearing he had beene murdered by the Bore,   730
She layd her eie-liddes to his eies and wept,
Then she perceivde her dearest Faunus slept.
With that she joynd her corrall lips to his,
Sucking his breath, and stealing many a kisse:
Wishing the life of a Camelion,   735
That she might onely live his breath upon:
Which all unwilling his faire body left,
And would not from that paradise be reft,

711 graffes, shoots

Or heavenly mansion, which he did retaine,
But there in hope to be enclosde againe: 740
This soft sound sleepe to Melliflore gave leysure,
To see, to feele, to smell, to taste such pleasure,
As none but onely she could ever know,
And none but Faunus on the earth could show.
Oh for how oft (whilst love her marrow warmes)   745
Would she embrace twixt Alablaster armes,
And hugge, and cull the snow-white fronted Boy,
Call him her love, her life, her soule, her joy?
Then pry more nearely on his necke, with oft
Quicke moving lookes, and with her fingers soft   750
Dimple his breast, and hanging ore his shoulder,
Hold Faunus downe (thrise blest with such an holder.)
And then againe, though yet he sleeping is,
Thus she beganne to woe him for a kisse:
    More gratious farre then dawning of the day,   755
Then Venus starre, or purple coloured Maie:
Let not my begging dearest Faunus, grieve thee,
Upon a note ten thousand kisses give mee:
And then as many busses overplus,
As Cinthia gave her love Propertius.   760
How many Cupids with the Graces trippe
Upon thy left cheeke, and thine upper lippe?
How many lifes, deaths, joyes, hopes, cares, and feares,
Thy quicker moving eie-balles Faunus beares:
So many collings, with kind clippings give mee,   765
As Cupids golden headed arrowes grieve me:
And adde enticements twixt thine amorous kisses,
And pleasant murmures with sweete sounding hisses.
As Doves by turnes be either other nibbing,
And lovingly in blither words be snibbing: 770
And bloudlesse in my bosome when thou lies,
And I turne up my watrie swimming eies:
Then will I glew thee in my limber arme,
If cold as lead, my breast shall make thee warme;
And Melliflora with her kisses breath,   775
Shall give her Faunus life in lookt-for death:
Untill my spirit in dewie kisses altring,

770 snibbing, rebuking

272

Within my body faint and fall a faultring.
Then take me Faunus, twixt thy naked armes,
And use thy hugging and thy kissing charmes: 780
And in thy hearts spoone coll me least I perish,
As twixt thy breasts my frozen bloud Ile cherish:
And then, like mine, thy moistie kisses dew,
At poynt of death life will againe renew:
Thus shall we enjoy the heaven of our age,   785
And both together both our lives will swage.
This said, she gathered fragrant smelling posies,
And strewd him o're with violets and roses:
Then with a kisse faine would she him have raised,
Yet stood stone still, and wishly on him gazed: 790
And forth his sleepe, as though she feard to feare him,
She fixt her kisses to the roses neare him.
The roses warme by Mellifloraes mouth,
A whispering gale of wind came West by South,
How many roses then before she kist,   795
(If she had knowne this, none she would have mist:)
Her former kisses kisses gainde such plentie,
That she receiv'de for one kisse more then twentie.
Such store of kisses on the sodaine found,
Some (slipping from her) fell upon the ground,   800
That such an harvest came upon the earth,
As since, we had of kisses never dearth.
But stirring once, his pillow made of grasse,
Faunus awakt, and Venus thought she was:
With that he rose, and like the blushing morne,   805
Having all night the loathsome burden borne
Of aged Tython (old men do no good,
Yet will be fumbling,) angrie then and wood,
Among the clowdes herselfe shee headlong throwes,
To meete with Phœbus; what they do, all knowes: 810
Headlong he ran, such gamesome love he scorned,
As Venus lov'd, to have his love suborned.
But Melliflora ranne and overtooke him,
And held him hard, and never once forsooke him,
Until his name was honour'd by her tongue: 815
As one that findes great treasure standeth long,
Doubting hee sleepes, so stood the lovely boy,

273

Love-sicke, amaz'd, and surfeited with joy.
But when he knew her, O what amorous greeting
Faunus devisde to entertaine his sweeting!   820
Like to the elme enclaspt with wanton vine,
Or as the ivie doth the oake combine,
About her necke his ivorie armes did twine,
Faint, feeble, weake, and languishing: in fine,
A moystie kisse seald up their lippes, as never   825
Injurious death should their embracements sever,
But with their kisses make two bodies one,
And so their hearts with kisses live alone:
Some teares betwixt them (teares of joy againe)
Did fall like silver drops in sun-shine raine: 830
Then Faunus told her how he scapt the bore,
And both related th'accidents before:
His ey-browes touch her roundie speaking eyne,
Kissing her necke and lippes like Corraline:
Then busseth she his cheeke, his chin, and brow,   835
Red, comely-short, and like to Cupids bow:
Yet in this union thus displeasde they be,
Because themselves they kissing cannot see:
Then like two culvers once againe they cleave,
Hugge, cull, and clippe, and sory for to leave.   840
She carries kisses on her doubtfull eies,
In those two Diamonds prettie babes he spies:
Untill they smile, which as the sunne doth chace,
The mist-hung clowdes, then shewes his cheerefull face,
From eies, and cheekes, did drive away the teares,   845
The sighs, the sobs, the cares and doubtfull feares.
Faunus resolv'd now had intention,
To wooe (how love refines invention)
And thus he courted: Faunus thus begunne
To wooe a Nymph, who was already wonne.   850
   Sweete namelesse Saint, (no name can set thee forth,
All titles are but staines to such thy worth:)
Whose ornaments and beautie pure divine,
Do make the cittie at these woods repine,
If that great highnesse can discend so low,   855
Vouchsafe those eies to see their overthrow,
Disdaine him not whose wit, whose life, whose daies,

Doth studie, live, and serve, to shew thy praise.
Thinke not my sute of small weight in thine eares,
Nor lesse regarded for my boyish yeares.   860
With that in his he tooke her moisty hand,
(How white God knowes) and gently did demand:
Shall these white hands (quoth he) (and then he kist them,
And turnde and lookte as though his kisses mist them)
Become as withered grasse, drie, leane, and yellow,   865
And these ripe yeeres be fruitlesse rotten mellow?
Shall such a field lie leyes and not be tilled?
Shall such rare sweetes be spent and never spilled?
Shall beautie fade, and earth enjoy this cover,
And not remaine and flourish in your lover?   870
The heavens prevent from woman-kind that fall,
Women were borne to beare, and borne withall,
That burdens borne that they might beare another,
A mothers childe must be a childes faire mother.
Deare Nymph, enjoy the spring-tide of your age,   875
These Aprill flowers in winter will asswage:
Spend that you cannot keepe; it is not best
That death should take his ayme from beauties rest.
Beautie (faire Nymph), is womans golden crowne,
Mans conqueresse, and feminine renowne.   880
Not joynde with love, who deare yet ever solde it?
For Beautie's cheape, except Loves eie beholde it.
You have the beautie Faunus heart to move,
You have the body to reward his love.
Impart them both unto the longest liver,   885
It is a gift which will enrich the giver:
It seekes, it sues, it offers to be taken:
I sigh, I sue, and would not be forsaken.
If Beautie smile, then Faunus thinkes him blessed.
Then Melliflora with a smile expressed   890
How hard it is true love not to discover,
With that (not coy, nor lavish to her lover)
She said: who taught thee eloquence, and witte,
(Conceit was quickned, and his words made fitte,
She knew by love) whose force might wel perswade,   895

867 leyes, meadows

And make thee bragge the conquest of a maide?
Small were that boast, and smaller is my beautie,
The smallest praise deserving, and lesse dutie:
You talke of beauty (if the truth were knowne,)
Because so well acquainted with your owne: 900
For mine or any other excellence,
Were all imparted to me by your presence,
Which if I were, sole mistris of my mind,
I would repay, and be to you as kind:
But such a vow devoutly have I made   905
To die a virgin: scarce the halfe word said,
His wit and senses by desire set open:
Sweete Saint (quoth he) that vow must needes be broken,
It is not lawfull you should make a vow,
The which Religion cannot wel allow: 910
Our pure Precisians thinke themselves most wise,
Yet in this one point are they not precise:
No doubt, they marrie when they feele the motion;
Untimely timely subject to devotion
Are then your yeeres; to what end were you borne?   915
Remember but, and you wil be forsworne.
A cloister woman mewd up in a cell,
To die a maide, and then leade apes in hell,
A Votaresse, a Secluse, and a Nunne,
Nay you must be forsworne when all is done: 920
For, can you study, fast, and pray among?
No no, (faire nymph) your stomacke is too yong,
Your beautie will dispense with this decree,
You must be perjurde of necessitie.
If you but come your Orizons to say,   925
Dianaes Hunts-men will forget to pray,
Or rather leave before they do beginne.
Are you not then the Autresse of this sinne?
Or if her priests such fairenesse do espie,
They will be conquerd by your lookes, and die,   930
Committing murder, what wil follow then?
This odious name, The Murdresse of men,
Which is flat treason gainst all Deitie:
For murder is much worse than perjurie.
Save then my soule, and thousands more from spilling,   935

You get no praise (my Melliflore) by killing,
Such coy account, such nicenesse of an oath.
But they espide (not fully ended) both
Cleare Deiopeia comming from her sport:
Love saw his journey long, and time but short, 940
In fewer wordes he sealed up the match
And that though Argoes hundred eies did watch,
They should depart those Nymphs, and flie away.
Faunus kind entertainement spent the day:
So Melliflora in the tonguelesse night, 945
With snowie skinned Faunus tooke her flight.
Which when heav'n saw (what doth not heaven see?)
With raine of teares she shewes her dwellers be
Rapt with that sight, nor trees from mourning keepe,
But every twig with dropping teares do weepe. 950
Such beauties past them, then the clowdes gave place,
That heaven might freely smile upon her face:
The Moone at full was full prowd of that dutie,
That she might beare the torch to such rare beautie,
But to deprive the Moone of this her sight, 955
The Sun-set love-sicke, rose within the night:
With his approch, they both lay downe oppressed,
Whose length the earth in beauties livorie dressed:
Under an hill whose lifted bittle brow,
Would overlooke his prospect then below, 960
Whose prowd high Pines, unto this day are prowder,
They had the hap from summers sunne to shrowd her:
Now mong the Nymphes is Melliflora mist,
And also Faunus, whither they went none wist:
They seeke the hills, the valleys, and plaine ground, 965
And this they find, they were not to be found.
With eies, with teares, and tongue, their errand showne:
And this they knew, they were not to be knowne,
The more they thought, they knew not what to thinke,
But Deiopeia from the rest gan shrinke, 970
Thought she was gone with Faunus, was most likely,
(Rivalls in love wil be suspitious quickly.)
She offred incense to Dianaes shrine,
Even as sweete (   ) I offer unto thine.

959 bittle, beetle

277

But three daies rites and ceremonies ended, 975
Unto Diana she her journey tended,
With lowe obeisance to her deitie,
She told her Mellifloraes perjurie,
That she and Faunus, prince of Italie,
Were stolne away: at such impietie, 980
(Though Melliflore she loved dearely) wroth
And angrie was Diana with them both:
She sware her priests and huntsmen would not tarrie,
If thus her chastest Nymphes beganne to marrie.
No more they would, but then incontinent, 985
Her purest priests and all a wooing went:
But Deiopeia her selfe banished
Dianaes court, and in love languished.
  Faunus alone, with her alone required,
Alone with him, which she alone desired. 990
Yet now she feares to be with him alone,
Because no further in loves office gone:
He would have sealed with the cheefest armes
Of his desire, the waxe that Venus warmes.
But as she did the contrarie command, 995
He was afraide, durst not her words withstand.
Did not the boy therein a coward prove?
Nay rather valiant, to withstand such love.
The marriage was by one of Vestaes Nuns
Solemnized. She Faunus never shuns: 1000
He gives, she takes, and nothing is denide,
She his, he her love's force and valor tride.
And still they strive, but who obtainde the day,
Let him be judge that er'e fought such a fray:
But faint and breathlesse here the quarrell ends, 1005
Loves cause being righted, both againe are friends.
And Venus, to encrease their amitie,
Considering words against her deitie
Were spoke by Pycus: she incontinent,
In heate of rage her indignation spent: 1010
Transforming him into a bird of th'aire,
And where before, of al hee was most faire,
She makes him blackest, keeping nothing white,
But breast and bellie (for there dwelt delight)

And by her power divine she so hath framed,   1015
That by his owne name hee is ever named.
And seeming yet al women-kind to hate,
Over their houses alway he will prate:
And neare their poultrie build his nest and watch,
How he their chickens and their ducks may catch.   1020
Faunus and Melliflora now are gone,
To take possession of his fathers throne:
And being come, they find his mother dead,
For griefe her dearest sonne from court was fled.
Almost a yeare with mirth the time was spent,   1025
When chaste Diana on fell mischiefe bent
Entred the Court. (At that time Melliflore,
Grievd with the burden which her faire wombe bore.)
And put upon sterne Hecates attire
By magicke, meaning to explaine her ire: 1030
And so (to ease her hate which inly burned)
The faire child to a monster she hath turned:
His head was garded with two little hornes,
A beard he had, whose haires were sharpe as thornes,
Crooked his nose: his necke, his armes, and breast   1035
Were like a man, but like a goate the rest.
No sooner was the faire Nymphs wombe cut ope,
To give the monster largest roome and scope,
But out he flies, and to the wood doth runne,
(For there Diana pointed he should come)   1040
And tripping long time ore the leavie launes,
Joynd issue with the Satyres and the Faunes:
But Faunus changing Melliflores complection,
(Thus man to woman giveth all perfection:
And as our chiefe Philosophers will say,   1045
Woman by man is perfect made each way:
These virgins then of sound and upright carriage,
Are monsters plaine without the stay of marriage.)
At length begot Latinus, he Lavinia:
Æneas her from Turnus tooke away,   1050
Succeeding him, his sonne Ascanius,
And after him Æneas Silvius,
Him Brutus kild, and at our English Dover
Landed, and brought some Satyres with him over,

And nimble Faëries. As most writers graunt, 1055
London by Brute was named Troynovaunt.
The Faëries ofspring yet a long time went,
Among the woods within the wild of Kent,
Untill transformed both in shape and essence,
By some great power or heavenly influence, 1060
The Faëries proved full stout hardy knights,
In justs, in tilts, in turnaments, and fights,
As Spencer shewes. But Spencer now is gone,
You Faëry Knights, your greatest losse bemone.
    This boone Diana then did aske of Jove, 1065
(More to be venged on the Queene of Love,)
That Faunus late transformed sonnes Satyres,
(So cald because they satisfide her ires)
Should evermore be utter enemies,
To lovers pastimes, sportfull veneries. 1070
Jove granted her this lawful just demand,
As we may see within our Faërie land:
The Satyres jerking sharp fang'd poesie,
Lashing and biting Venus luxurie,
Gauling the sides of foule impiety, 1075
Scourging the lewdnesse of damnd villany,
Shooting out sharp quills in each angry line,
Through heapt-up vices like the porcupine.
If this praise-worthy be, then first of all
Place I the Satyre Academicall, 1080
His Satyres worthy are (if any one)
To be ingrav'd in brasse, and marble stone:
Detracting nothing from the excellencie,
Of the Rhamnusian Scourge of Villanie,
But I was borne to hate your censuring vaine, 1085
Your envious biting in your crabbed straine.
Now let us shew the Satyres enmitie,
Which Brutus left behind in Italie.

1080 Satyre Academicall, Bk. II of Joseph Hall's *Virgidemiarum*
1084 Scourge of Villanie, by John Marston

SALMACIS AND HERMAPHRODITUS

Francis Beaumont

(1602)

My wanton lines doe treate of amorous love,
Such as would bow the hearts of gods above:
Then Venus, thou great Citherean Queene,
That hourely tripst on the Idalian greene,
Thou laughing Erycina, daygne to see   5
The verses wholly consecrate to thee;
Temper them so within thy Paphian shrine,
That every Lovers eye may melt a line;
Commaund the god of Love that little King,
To give each verse a sleight touch with his wing,   10
That as I write, one line may draw the tother,
And every word skip nimbly o're another.
    There was a lovely boy the Nymphs had kept,
That on the Idane mountaines oft had slept,
Begot and borne by powers that dwelt above,   15
By learned Mercury of the Queene of love:
A face he had that shew'd his parents fame,
And from them both conjoynd, he drew his name:
So wondrous fayre he was, that (as they say)
Diana being hunting on a day,   20
Shee saw the boy upon a greene banke lay him,
And there the virgin-huntresse meant to slay him,
Because no Nymphes did now pursue the chase:
For all were strooke blind with the wantons face.
But when that beauteous face Diana saw,   25
Her armes were nummed, & shee could not draw;
Yet did she strive to shoot, but all in vaine,
Shee bent her bow, and loos'd it streight againe.

Then she began to chide her wanton eye,
And fayne would shoot, but durst not see him die.   30
She turnd and shot, and did of purpose misse him,
She turnd againe, and did of purpose kisse him.
Then the boy ran: for (some say) had he stayd,
Diana had no longer bene a mayd.
Phoebus so doted on this rosiat face,   35
That he hath oft stole closely from his place,
Where he did lie by fayre Leucothoes side,
To dally with him in the vales of Ide:
And ever since this lovely boy did die,
Phoebus each day about the world doth flie,   40
And on the earth he seekes him all the day,
And every night he seekes him in the sea:
His cheeke was sanguine, and his lip as red
As are the blushing leaves of the Rose spred:
And I have heard, that till this boy was borne,   45
Roses grew white upon the virgin thorne,
Till one day walking to a pleasant spring,
To heare how cunningly the birds could sing,
Laying him downe upon a flowry bed,
The Roses blush'd and turnd themselves to red.   50
The Rose that blush'd not, for his great offence,
The gods did punish, and for impudence
They gave this doome that was agreed by all;
The smell of the white Rose should be but small.
His haire was bushie, but it was not long,   55
The Nymphs had done his tresses mighty wrong:
For as it grew, they puld away his haire,
And made abilliments of gold to weare.
His eyes were Cupids: for untill his birth,
Cupid had eyes, and liv'd upon the earth,   60
Till on a day, when the great Queene of love
Was by her white doves drawn from heaven above,
Unto the top of the Idalian hill,
To see how well the Nymphs their charge fulfill,
And whether they had done the goddesse right,   65
In nursing of her sweet Hermaphrodite:
Whom when she saw, although complete & full,
Yet she complaynd, his eyes were somewhat dull:
282

And therefore, more the wanton boy to grace,
She puld the sparkling eyes from Cupids face, 70
Fayning a cause to take away his sight,
Because the Ape would sometimes shoot for spight.
But Venus set those eyes in such a place,
As grac't those cleare eyes with a clearer face.
For his white hand each goddesse did him woo: 75
For it was whiter then the driven snow:
His legge was straighter then the thigh of Jove:
And he farre fairer then the god of love.
    When first this wel-shapt boy, beauties chiefe king,
Had seene the labour of the fifteenth spring, 80
How curiously it paynted all the earth,
He 'gan to travaile from his place of birth,
Leaving the stately hils where he was nurst,
And where the Nymphs had brought him up at first:
He lov'd to travaile to the coasts unknowne, 85
To see the regions farre beyond his owne,
Seeking cleare watry springs to bathe him in:
(For he did love to wash his ivory skinne)
The lovely Nymphes have oft times seene him swimme,
And closely stole his clothes from off the brim, 90
Because the wanton wenches would so fayne
See him come nak'd to aske his clothes againe.
He lov'd besides to see the Lycian grounds,
And know the wealthy Carians utmost bounds.
    Using to travaile thus, one day he found 95
A cristall brooke, that tril'd along the ground,
A brooke, that in reflection did surpasse
The cleare reflection of the clearest glasse.
About the side there grew no foggy reedes,
Nor was the fount compast with barren weedes: 100
But living turfe grew all along the side,
And grasse that ever flourisht in his pride.
Within this brook a beauteous Nymph did dwell,
Who for her comely feature did excell;
So faire she was, of such a pleasing grace, 105
So straight a body, and so sweet a face,
So soft a belly, such a lustie thigh,
    99 foggy, marshy

283

So large a forehead, such a cristall eye,
So soft and moyst a hand, so smooth a brest,
So faire a cheeke, so well in all the rest, 110
That Jupiter would revell in her bowre,
Where he to spend againe his golden showre:
Her teeth were whiter then the mornings milke,
Her lip was softer then the softest silke,
Her haire as farre surpast the burnisht gold, 115
As silver doth excell the basest mold:
Jove courted her for her translucent eye,
And told her, he would place her in the skye,
Promising her, if she would be his love,
He would ingrave her in the heaven above, 120
Telling this lovely Nymph, that if he would,
He could deceive her in a showre of gold,
Or like a Swanne come to her naked bed,
And so deceive her of her maiden-head:
But yet, because he thought that pleasure best, 125
Where each consenting joynes each loving brest,
He would put off that all-commaunding crowne,
Whose terrour strooke th'aspiring Giants downe,
That glittering crown, whose radiant sight did tosse
Great Pelion from the top of mighty Osse, 130
He would depose from his world-swaying head,
To taste the amorous pleasures of her bed:
This added he besides, the more to grace her,
Like a bright starre he would in heavens vault place her.

By this the proud lascivious Nymph was mov'd, 135
Perceiving by great Jove shee was belov'd,
And hoping as a starre she should ere long
Be sterne or gracious to the Sea-mans song,
(For mortals still are subject to their eye,
And what it sees, they strive to get as hie:) 140
Shee was contented that almighty Jove
Should have the first and best fruits of her love:
(For women may be likened to the yeere,
Whose first fruites still do make the dayntiest cheere.)
But yet Astræa first should plight her troth, 145
For the performance of Joves sacred oth.
(Just times decline, and all good dayes are dead,

When heavenly othes had need be warranted:)
This heard great Jupiter and lik'd it well,
And hastily he seekes Astræas cell,   150
About the massie earth searching her towre:
But she had long since left this earthly bowre,
And flew to heaven above, lothing to see
The sinfull actions of humanitie.
Which when Jove did perceive, he left the earth,   155
And flew up to the place of his owne birth,
The burning heavenly throne, where he did spy
Astræas palace in the glittering skie.
 This stately towre was builded up on hie,
Farre from the reach of any mortall eye;   160
And from the palace side there did distill
A little water, through a little quill,
The dewe of justice, which did seldome fall,
And when it dropt, the drops were very small.
Glad was great Jove when he beheld her towre,   165
Meaning a while to rest him in her bowre;
And therefore sought to enter at her dore:
But there was such a busie rout before;
Some serving men, and some promooters bee,
That he could passe no foote without a fee: 170
But as he goes, he reaches out his hands,
And payes each one in order as he stands;
And still, as he was paying those before,
Some slipt againe betwixt him and the dore.
At length (with much adoo) he past them all,   175
And entred straight into a spacious hall,
Full of darke angles and of hidden wayes,
Crooked Mæanders, infinite delayes;
All which delayes and entries he must passe,
Ere he could come where just Astræa was.   180
 All these being past by his immortall wit,
Without her doore he saw a porter sit,
An aged man, that long time there had beene,
Who us'd to search all those that entred in,
And still to every one he gave this curse,   185
None must see Justice but with emptie purse.
This man searched Jove for his owne private gaine,

To have the money which did yet remaine,
Which was but small: for much was spent before
On the tumultous rout that kept the dore.   190
When he had done, he brought him to the place
Where he should see divine Astræas face.
Then the great King of gods and men in went,
And saw his daughter Venus there lament,
And crying lowd for justice, whom Jove found   195
Kneeling before Astræa on the ground,
And still she cry'd and beg'd for a just doome
Against blacke Vulcan, that unseemely groome,
Whome she had chosen for her onely love,
Though she was daughter to great thundring Jove: 200
And though the fairest goddesse, yet content
To marrie him, though weake and impotent;
But for all this they alwayes were at strife:
For evermore he rayld at her his wife,
Telling her still, Thou art no wife of mine,   205
Anothers strumpet, Mars his concubine.
By this Astræa spyde almighty Jove,
And bow'd her finger to the Queene of love,
To cease her sute, which she would heare anon,
When the great King of all the world was gone.   210
     Then she descended from her stately throne,
Which seat was builded all of Jasper stone,
And o're the seat was paynted all above,
The wanton unseene stealths of amorous Jove;
There might a man behold the naked pride   215
Of lovely Venus in the vale of Ide,
When Pallas, and Joves beauteous wife and she
Strove for the prise of beauties raritie:
And there lame Vulcan and his Cyclops strove
To make the thunderbolts for mighty Jove: 220
From this same stately throne she down descended,
And sayd, The griefs of Jove should be amended,
Asking the King of gods what lucklesse cause,
What great contempt of state, what breach of lawes
(For sure she thought, some uncouth cause befell,   225
That made him visit poore Astræas cell)
Troubled his thought: and if she might decide it,

286

Who vext great Jove, he dearely should abide it.
Jove onely thankt her, and beganne to show
His cause of comming (for each one doth know   230
The longing words of Lovers are not many,
If they desire to be injoyd of any)
Telling Astræa, It might now befall,
That she might make him blest, that blesseth all:
For as he walk'd upon the flowry earth,   235
To which his owne hands whilome gave a birth,
To see how streight he held it and how just
He rold this massy pondrous heape of dust,
He laid him downe by a coole river side,
Whose pleasant water did so gently slide   240
With such soft whispering: for the brook was deepe,
That it had lul'd him in a heavenly sleepe.
When first he laid him downe, there was none neere him:
(For he did call before, but none could heare him)
But a faire Nymph was bathing when he wak'd,   245
(Here sigh'd great Jove, and after brought forth) nak'd,
He seeing lov'd, the Nymph yet here did rest,
Where just Astræa might make Jove be blest,
If she would passe her faithfull word so farre,
As that great Jove should make the mayd a starre.   250
Astræa yeelded: at which Jove was pleas'd,
And all his longing hopes and feares were eas'd.
    Jove tooke his leave, and parted from her sight,
Whose thoughts were ful of lovers sweet delight,
And she ascended to her throne above,   255
To heare the griefs of the great Queene of love:
But she was satisfide, and would no more
Rayle at her husband as she did before:
But forth she tript apace, because she strove,
With her swift feet to overtake great Jove;   260
She skipt so nimbly as she went to looke him,
That at the palace doore she overtooke him,
Which way was plaine and broad as they went out,
And now they could see no tumultuous rout.
Here Venus fearing, lest the love of Jove   265
Should make this mayd be plac'd in heaven above,
Because she thought this Nymph so wondrous bright.

That she would dazel her accustom'd light:
And fearing now she should not first be seene
Of all the glittring starres as shee had beene, 270
But that the wanton Nymph would ev'ry night
Be first that should salute eche mortall sight,
Began to tell great Jove, she griev'd to see
The heaven so full of his iniquity,
Complayning that eche strumpet now was grac'd, 275
And with immortall goddesses was plac'd,
Intreating him to place in heaven no more
Eche wanton strumpet and lascivious whore.
Jove mad with love, harkned not what she sayd,
His thoughts were so intangled with the mayd, 280
But furiously he to his Palace lept,
Being minded there till morning to have slept:
For the next morne, as soone as Phoebus rayes
Should yet shine coole, by reason of the seas,
And ere the parting teares of Thætis bed, 285
Should be quite shak't from off his glittring head,
Astræa promis'd to attend great Jove,
At his owne Palace in the heaven above,
And at that Palace she would set her hand
To what the love-sick god should her command: 290
But to descend to earth she did deny,
She loath'd the sight of any mortall eye;
And for the compasse of the earthly round,
She would not set one foot upon the ground.
Therefore Jove meant to rise but with the sunne, 295
Yet thought it long untill the night was done.
  In the meane space Venus was drawne along
By her white Doves unto the sweating throng
Of hammering Black-smithes, at the lofty hill
Of stately Etna, whose top burneth still: 300
(For at that burning mountaynes glittring top,
Her cripple husband Vulcan kept his shop)
To him she went, and so collogues that night
With the best straines of pleasures sweet delight,
That ere they parted, she made Vulcan sweare 305
By dreadfull Stix, an othe the gods do feare,

303 collogues, coaxes

If Jove would make the mortall mayd a starre,
Himselfe should frame his instruments of warre,
And tooke his othe by blacke Cocitus Lake,
He never more a thunder-bolt would make: 310
For Venus so this night his sences pleas'd,
That now he thought his former griefs were eas'd.
She with her hands the black-smiths body bound,
And with her Iv'ry armes she twyn'd him round,
And still the faire Queene with a pretty grace,   315
Disperst her sweet breath o're his swarty face:
Her snowy armes so well she did display,
That Vulcan thought they melted as they lay.
    Untill the morne in this delight they lay:
Then up they got, and hasted fast away   320
In the white Chariot of the Queene of love,
Towards the Palace of great thundring Jove,
Where they did see divine Astræa stand,
To passe her word for what Jove should command.
In limpt the Blacke-smith, after stept his Queene,   325
Whose light arrayment was of lovely greene.
When they were in, Vulcan began to sweare
By othes that Jupiter himselfe doth feare,
If any whore in heavens bright vault were seene,
To dimme the shining of his beauteous Queene,   330
Each mortall man should the great gods disgrace,
And mocke almightie Jove unto his face,
And Giants should enforce bright heaven to fall,
Ere he would frame one thunderbolt at all.
Jove did intreat him that he would forbeare.   335
The more he spoke, the more did Vulcan sweare.
Jove heard his words, and 'gan to make his mone,
That mortall men would plucke him from his throne,
Or else he must incurre this plague, he said,
Quite to forgoe the pleasure of the mayd: 340
And once he thought, rather then lose her blisses,
Her heavenly sweets, her most delicious kisses,
Her soft embraces, and the amorous nights,
That he should often spend in her delights,
He would be quite thrown down by mortal hands,   345
From the blest place where his bright palace stands.

But afterwards hee saw with better sight,
He should be scorn'd by every mortall wight,
If he should want his thunderbolts, to beate
Aspiring mortals from his glittering seate: 350
    Therefore the god no more did woo or prove her,
But left to seeke her love, though not to love her.
Yet he forgot not that he woo'd the lasse,
But made her twise as beauteous as she was,
Because his wonted love he needs would shew.   355
This have I heard, but yet scarce thought it true.
And whether her cleare beautie was so bright,
That it could dazel the immortall sight
Of gods, and make them for her love despaire,
I do not know; but sure the maid was faire.   360
    Yet the faire Nymph was never seene resort
Unto the savage and the bloudy sport
Of chaste Diana, nor was ever wont
To bend a bow, nor ever did she hunt,
Nor did she ever strive with pretie cunning,   365
To overgoe her fellow Nymphs in running:
For she was the faire water-Nymph alone,
That unto chaste Diana was unknowne.
It is reported, that her fellowes us'd
To bid her (though the beauteous Nymph refus'd)   370
To take, or painted quivers or a dart,
And put her lazy idlenesse apart.
Nor tooke she painted quivers, nor a dart,
Nor put her lazy idlenesse apart,
But in her cristall fountaine oft she swimmes,   375
And oft she washes o're her snowy limmes:
Sometimes she comb'd her soft dischevel'd hayre,
Which with a fillet tide she oft did weare:
But sometimes loose she did it hang behind,
When she was pleas'd to grace the Easterne wind: 380
For up and downe it would her tresses hurle,
And as she went, it made her loose hayre curle:
Oft in the water did she looke her face,
And oft she us'd to practise what quaint grace
Might well become her, and what comely feature   385
Might be best fitting so divine a creature.

Her skinne was with a thinne vaile overthrowne,
Through which her naked beauty clearely shone.
She us'd in this light rayment as she was,
To spread her body on the dewy grasse: 390
Sometimes by her owne fountaine as she walkes,
She nips the flowres from off the fertile stalkes,
And with a garland of the sweating vine,
Sometimes she doth her beauteous front in-twine:
But she was gathring flowres with her white hand, 395
When she beheld Hermaphroditus stand
By her cleare fountaine, wondring at the sight,
That there was any brooke could be so bright:
For this was the bright river where the boy
Did dye himselfe, that he could not enjoy 400
Himselfe in pleasure, nor could taste the blisses
Of his owne melting and delicious kisses.
Here did she see him, and by Venus law,
She did desire to have him as she saw:
　　But the fayre Nymph had never seene the place, 405
Where the boy was, nor his inchanting face,
But by an uncouth accident of love
Betwixt great Phoebus and the sonne of Jove,
Light-headed Bacchus: for upon a day,
As the boy-god was keeping on his way, 410
Bearing his Vine leaves and his Ivie bands,
To Naxos, where his house and temple stands,
He saw the Nymph; and seeing, he did stay,
And threw his leaves and Ivie bands away,
Thinking at first she was of heavenly birth, 415
Some goddesse that did live upon the earth,
Virgin Diana that so lively shone,
When she did court her sweet Endimion:
But he a god, at last did plainely see,
She had no marke of immortalitie. 420
Unto the Nymph went the yong god of wine,
Whose head was chaf'd so with the bleeding vine,
That now, or feare or terrour had he none,
But 'gan to court her as she sate alone:
　　Fayrer then fayrest (thus began his speech) 425
Would but your radiant eye please to inrich

My eye with looking, or one glaunce to give,
Whereby my other parts might feede and live,
Or with one sight my sences to inspire,
Far livelier then the stole Promethean fire;   430
Then might I live, then by the sunny light
That should proceed from thy thrise-radiant sight,
I might survive to ages; but that missing,
(At that same word he would have faine bin kissing)
I pine, fayre Nymph: O never let me dye   435
For one poore glaunce from thy translucent eye,
Farre more transparent then the clearest brooke.
　　The Nymph was taken with his golden hooke:
Yet she turn'd backe, and would have tript away;
But Bacchus forc't the lovely mayd to stay,   440
Asking her why she struggled to be gone,
Why such a Nymph should wish to be alone?
Heaven never made her faire, that she should vaunt
She kept all beautie; it would never graunt
She should be borne so beauteous from her mother,   445
But to reflect her beauty on another:
Then with a sweet kisse cast thy beames on mee,
And Ile reflect them backe againe on thee.
At Naxos stands my Temple and my Shrine,
Where I do presse the lusty swelling Vine,   450
There with greene Ivie shall thy head be bound,
And with the red Grape be incircled round;
There shall Silenus sing unto thy praise,
His drunken reeling songs and tickling layes.
Come hither, gentle Nymph. Here blusht the maid,   455
And faine she would have gone, but yet she staid.
Bacchus perceiv'd he had o'recome the lasse,
And downe he throwes her in the dewy grasse,
And kist the helplesse Nymph upon the ground,
And would have stray'd beyond that lawful bound.   460
This saw bright Phœbus: for his glittering eye
Sees all that lies below the starry skye;
And for an old affection that he bore
Unto this lovely Nymph long time before,
(For he would ofttimes in his circle stand,   465
To sport himselfe upon her snowy hand)

He kept her from the sweets of Bacchus bed,
And 'gainst her wil, he sav'd her maiden-head.
    Bacchus perceiving this, apace did hie
Unto the Palace of swift Mercury: 470
But he did find him farre below his birth,
Drinking with theeves and catch-poles on the earth;
And they were drinking what they stole to day,
In consultation for to morrowes prey.
To him went youthfull Bacchus, and begun   475
To shew his cause of griefe against the Sunne,
How he bereft him of his heavenly blisses,
His sweet delights, his Nectar-flowing kisses,
And other sweeter sweetes that he had wonne,
But for the malice of the bright-fac't Sunne,   480
Intreating Mercury by all the love,
That had bene borne amongst the sonnes of Jove,
Of which they two were part, to stand his friend,
Against the god that did him so offend:
The quaint-tongu'd issue of great Atlas race,   485
Swift Mercury, that with delightfull grace,
And pleasing accents of his fayned tongue,
Hath oft reform'd a rude uncivill throng
Of mortals; that great messenger of Jove,
And all the meaner gods that dwell above: 490
He whose acute wit was so quicke and sharpe
In the invention of the crooked Harpe:
He that's so cunning with his jesting slights,
To steale from heavenly gods or earthly wights,
Bearing a great hate in his grieved brest,   495
Against that great commaunder of the West,
Bright-fac't Apollo: for upon a day,
Yong Mercury did steale his beasts away:
Which the great god perceiving, streight did shew
The pearcing arrowes and the fearefull bow   500
That kild great Pithon, & with that did threat him,
To bring his beasts againe, or he would beat him.
Which Mercury perceiving, unespide,
Did closely steale his arrowes from his side.
For this old grudge, he was the easlyer wonne   505
To helpe young Bacchus 'gainst the fierie Sunne.

And now the Sunne was in the middle way,
And had o'recome the one halfe of the day,
Scorching so hot upon the reeking sand,
That lies upon the neere Egyptian land,   510
That the hot people burnt e'ne from their birth,
Do creepe againe into their mother earth,
When Mercury did take his powerfull wand,
His charming Cadusæus in his hand,
And a thicke Bever which he us'd to weare,   515
When ought from Jove he to the Sunne did beare,
That did protect him from the piercing light,
Which did proceed from Phoebus glittring sight.
Clad in these powerfull ornaments he flies,
With out-stretcht wings up to the azure skies: 520
Where seeing Phoebus in his orient shrine,
He did so well revenge the god of wine,
That whil'st the Sun wonders his Chariot reeles,
The craftie god had stole away his wheeles.
Which when he did perceive, he down did slide,   525
(Laying his glittring Coronet aside)
From the bright spangled firmament above,
To seeke the Nymph that Bacchus so did love,
And found her looking in her watry glasse,
To see how cleare her radiant beauty was: 530
And, for he had but little time to stay,
Because he meant to finish out his day,
At the first sight he 'gan to make his mone,
Telling her how his fiery wheeles were gone;
Promising her, if she would but obtaine   535
The wheeles, that Mercury had stolne, againe,
That he might end his day, she should enjoy
The heavenly sight of the most beauteous boy
That ever was. The Nymph was pleas'd with this,
Hoping to reape some unaccustom'd blisse   540
By the sweet pleasure that she should enjoy,
In the blest sight of such a melting boy.
Therefore at his request she did obtaine
The burning wheeles, that he had lost, againe:
Which when he had receiv'd, he left the land,   545
And brought them thither where his Coach did stand,

And there he set them on: for all this space,
The horses had not stirr'd from out their place.
Which when he saw, he wept and 'gan to say,
Would Mercury had stole my wheeles away   550
When Phaeton, my hare-brain'd issue tride,
What a laborious thing it was to guide
My burning chariot, then he might have pleas'd me,
And of one fathers griefe he might have eas'd me:
For then the Steeds would have obayd his will,   555
Or else at least they would have rested still.
When he had done, he tooke his whip of steele,
Whose bitter smart he made his horses feele:
For he did lash so hard, to end the day,
That he was quickly at the Westerne sea,   560
And there with Thætis did he rest a space:
For he did never rest in any place
Before that time: but ever since his wheeles
Were stole away, his burning chariot reeles
Tow'rds the declining of the parting day: 565
Therefore he lights and mends them in the sea.
And though the Poets fayne, that Jove did make
A treble night for faire Alcmena's sake,
That he might sleepe securely with his love;
Yet sure the long night was unknowne to Jove: 570
But the Sunnes wheeles one day disordred more,
Were thrise as long amending as before.
    Now was the Sunne inviron'd with the Sea,
Cooling his watrie tresses as he lay,
And in dread Neptunes kingdome while he sleeps,   575
Faire Thætis clips him in the watry deeps,
The Mayre-maids and the Tritons of the West,
Strayning their voyces, to make Titan rest.
And while the blacke night with her pitchie hand,
Tooke just possession of the swartie land: 580
He spent the darkesome howres in this delight,
Giving his power up to the gladsome night:
For ne're before he was so truely blest,
To take an houre or one poor minutes rest.

580 swartie] swarsie

But now the burning god this pleasure feeles,   585
By reason of his newly crazed wheeles,
There must he stay untill lame Vulcan send
The fierie wheeles which he had tooke to mend.
Now al the night the Smith so hard had wrought,
That ere the Sunne could wake, his wheeles were brought.   590
Titan being pleas'd with rest, and not to rise,
And loth to open yet his slumbring eyes:
And yet perceiving how the longing sight
Of mortals wayted for his glittring light,
He sent Aurora from him to the skie,   595
To give a glimsing to each mortall eye.
Aurora much asham'd of that same place
That great Apollos light was wont to grace,
Finding no place to hide her shamefull head,
Paynted her chaste cheeks with a blushing red,   600
Which ever since remain'd upon her face,
In token of her new receiv'd disgrace:
Therefore she not so white as she had beene,
Lothing of ev'ry mortall to be seene,
No sooner can the rosie fingred morne   605
Kisse ev'ry flowre that by her dew is borne,
But from her golden window she doth peepe,
When the most part of earthly creatures sleepe.
     By this, bright Titan opened had his eyes,
And 'gan to jerke his horses through the skies,   610
And taking in his hand his fierie whip,
He made Æous and swift Æthon skip
So fast, that straight he dazled had the sight
Of faire Aurora, glad to see his light.
     And now the Sunne in all his fierie haste,   615
Did call to mind his promise lately past,
And all the vowes and othes that he did passe
Unto faire Salmacis, the beauteous lasse:
For he had promis'd her she should enjoy
So lovely faire, and such a well shap't boy,   620
As ne're before his owne all-seeing eye
Saw from his bright seate in the starry skye:
Remembring this, he sent the boy that way,
Where the cleare fountain of the fayre Nymph lay.

There was he comne to seeke some pleasing brooke.   625
No sooner came he, but the Nymph was strooke:
And though she hasted to imbrace the boy,
Yet did the Nymph awhile deferre her joy,
Till she had bound up her loose flagging haire,
And ordred well the garments she did weare,   630
Fayning her count'nance with a lovers care,
And did deserve to be accounted fayre.
And thus much spake she while the boy abode:
O boy, most worthy to be thought a god,
Thou mayst inhabit in the glorious place   635
Of gods, or maist proceed from humane race:
Thou mayst be Cupid, or the god of wine,
That lately woo'd me with the swelling vine:
But whosoe're thou art, O happy he,
That was so blest, to be a sire to thee;   640
Thy happy mother is most blest of many,
Blessed thy sisters, if her wombe bare any,
Both fortunate, and O thrise happy shee,
Whose too much blessed brests gave suck to thee:
If any wife with thy sweet bed be blest,   645
O, she is farre more happy then the rest;
If thou hast any, let my sport be sto'ne,
Or else let me be she, if thou hast none.
    Here did she pause awhile, and then she sayd:
Be not obdurate to a silly mayd.   650
A flinty heart within a snowy brest,
Is like base mold lockt in a golden chest:
They say the eye's the Index of the heart,
And shewes th'affection of eche inward part:
There love plays lively, there the little god   655
Hath a cleare cristall Palace of abode.
O barre him not from playing in thy heart,
That sports himselfe upon eche outward part.
Thus much she spake, & then her tongue was husht.
At her loose speach Hermaphroditus blusht: 660
He knew not what love was, yet love did shame him,
Making him blush, and yet his blush became him:
Then might a man his shamefast colour see,
Like the ripe apple on the sunny tree,

Or Ivory dide o're with a pleasing red, 665
Or like the pale Moone being shadowed.
    By this, the Nymph recover'd had her tongue,
That to her thinking lay in silence long,
And sayd: Thy cheeke is milde, O be thou so,
Thy cheeke saith I, then do not answere no, 670
Thy cheeke doth shame, then doe thou shame, she sayd:
It is a mans shame to deny a mayd.
Thou look'st to sport with Venus in her towre,
And be belov'd of every heavenly powre.
Men are but mortals, so are women too, 675
Why should your thoughts aspire more then ours doo?
For sure they doe aspire: Else could a youth,
Whose count'nance is so full of spotlesse truth,
Be so relentlesse to a virgins tongue?
Let me be woo'd by thee but halfe so long; 680
With halfe those tearmes, doe but my love require,
And I will easly graunt thee thy desire.
Ages are bad, when men become so slow,
That poore unskilfull mayds are forc't to woo.
    Her radiant beauty and her subtill arte 685
So deepely strooke Hermaphroditus heart,
That she had wonne his love, but that the light
Of her translucent eyes did shine too bright:
For long he look'd upon the lovely mayd,
And at the last Hermaphroditus sayd: 690
How should I love thee, when I doe espie
A farre more beauteous Nymph hid in thy eye?
When thou doost love, let not that Nymph be nie thee;
Nor when thou woo'st, let that same Nymph be by thee:
Or quite obscure her from thy lovers face, 695
Or hide her beauty in a darker place.
By this, the Nymph perceiv'd he did espie
None but himselfe reflected in her eye,
And, for himselfe no more she meant to shew him,
She shut her eyes & blind-fold thus did woo him: 700
Fayre boy, thinke not thy beauty can dispence
With any payne due to a bad offence;
Remember how the gods punisht that boy

That scorn'd to let a beauteous Nymph enjoy 705
Her long wisht pleasure; for the peevish elfe,
Lov'd of all others, needs would love himselfe.
So mayst thou love, perhaps thou mayst be blest,
By graunting to a lucklesse Nymphs request:
Then rest awhile with me amid these weeds. 710
The Sunne that sees all, sees not lovers deeds;
Phoebus is blind when love-sports are begun,
And never sees untill their sports be done:
Beleeve me, boy, thy blood is very stayd,
That art so loth to kisse a youthfull mayd. 715
Wert thou a mayd, and I a man, Ile show thee,
With what a manly boldnesse I could woo thee:
Fayrer then loves Queene, thus I would begin,
Might not my over-boldnesse be a sinne,
I would intreat this favour, if I could, 720
Thy rosiat cheeke a little to behold:
Then would I beg a touch, and then a kisse,
And then a lower; yet a higher blisse:
Then would I aske what Jove and Læda did,
When like a Swan the craftie god was hid? 725
What came he for? why did he there abide?
Surely I thinke hee did not come to chide:
He came to see her face, to talke, and chat,
To touch, to kisse: came he for nought but that?
Yes, something else: what was it he would have? 730
That which all men of maydens ought to crave.
  This sayd, her eye-lids wide she did display:
But in this space the boy was runne away:
The wanton speeches of the lovely lasse
Forc't him for shame to hide him in the grasse.
When she perceiv'd she could not see him neere her, 735
When she had cal'd, and yet he could not heare her,
Looke how when Autumne comes, a little space
Paleth the red blush of the Summers face,
Tearing the leaves, the Summers covering,
Three months in weaving by the curious spring, 740
Making the grasse his greene locks go to wracke,
Tearing each ornament from off his backe;

So did she spoyle the garments she did weare,
Tearing whole ounces of her golden hayre:
She thus deluded of her longed blisse,   745
With much adoo at last she uttred this:
Why wert thou bashfull, boy? Thou hast no part
Shewes thee to be of such a female heart.
His eye is gray, so is the mornings eye,
That blusheth always when the day is nye.   750
Then his gray eye's the cause: that cannot be:
The gray-ey'd morne is farre more bold then he:
For with a gentle dew from heavens bright towre,
It gets the mayden-head of ev'ry flowre.
I would to God, he were the rosiat morne,   755
And I a flowre from out the earth new borne!
His face is smooth; Narcissus face was so,
And he was carelesse of a sad Nymphs woe.
Then that's the cause; and yet that cannot be:
Youthfull Narcissus was more bold then he,   760
Because he dide for love, though of his shade:
This boy nor loves himselfe, nor yet a mayd.
Besides, his glorious eye is wondrous bright:
So is the fierie and all-seeing light
Of Phœbus, who at ev'ry mornings birth   765
Blusheth for shame upon the sullen earth.
Then that's the cause; and yet that cannot be:
The fierie Sunne is farre more bold then he;
He nightly kisseth Thætis in the sea:
All know the story of Leucothoë.   770
His cheeke is red; so is the fragrant Rose,
Whose ruddie cheeke with over-blushing gloes:
Then that's the cause; and yet that cannot bee:
Eche blushing Rose is farre more bold then he,
Whose boldnesse may be plainely seene in this,   775
The ruddy Rose is not asham'd to kisse;
For alwayes when the day is new begun,
The spreading Rose will kisse the morning Sun.
     This sayd, hid in the grasse she did espie him,
And stumbling with her will, she fel down by him,   780
And with her wanton talke, because he woo'd not,

744 ounces, clusters   757 is] was

Beg'd that, which he poore novice understood not:
And, for she could not get a greater blisse,
She did intreat at least a sisters kisse;
But still the more she did the boy beseech,   785
The more he powted at her wanton speech.
At last the Nymph began to touch his skin,
Whiter then mountaine snow hath ever bin,
And did in purenesse that cleare spring surpasse,
Wherein Actæon saw th' Arcadian lasse.   790
Thus did she dally long, till at the last,
In her moyst palme she lockt his white hand fast:
Then in her hand his wrest she 'gan to close,
When through his pulses strait the warme bloud gloes,
Whose youthfull musike fanning Cupids fire,   795
In her warme brest kindled a fresh desire.
Then did she lift her hand unto his brest,
A part as white and youthfull as the rest,
Where, as his flowry breath still comes and goes,
She felt his gentle heart pant through his clothes.   800
    At last she tooke her hand from off that part,
And sayd: It panted like anothers heart.
Why should it be more feeble, and lesse bold?
Why should the bloud about it be more cold?
Nay sure, that yeelds, onely thy tongue denyes   805
And the true fancy of thy heart belyes.
Then did she lift her hand unto his chin,
And prays'd the prety dimpling of his skin:
But straight his chin she 'gan to overslip,
When she beheld the rednesse of his lip;   810
And sayd: Thy lips are soft, presse them to mine,
And thou shalt see they are as soft as thine.
Then would she faine have gone unto his eye,
But still his ruddy lip standing so nie,
Drew her hand backe; therefore his eye she mist,   815
'Ginning to claspe his necke, and would have kist;
But then the boy did struggle to be gone,
Vowing to leave her and that place alone.
But then bright Salmacis began to feare,
And sayd: Fayre stranger, I wil leave thee here   820
Amid these pleasant places all alone.

So turning back, she fayned to be gone;
But from his sight she had no power to passe;
Therefore she turn'd, and hid her in the grasse,
When to the ground, bending her snow-white knee,   825
The glad earth gave new coates to every tree.
  He then supposing he was all alone,
(Like a young boy that is espy'd of none)
Runnes here, and there, then on the bankes doth looke,
Then on the cristall current of the brooke,   830
Then with his foote he toucht the silver streames,
Whose drowzy waves made musike in their dreames,
And, for he was not wholy in, did weepe,
Talking alowd and babbling in their sleepe:
Whose pleasant coolenesse when the boy did feele,   835
He thrust his foote downe lower to the heele:
O'recome with whose sweet noyse, he did begin
To strip his soft clothes from his tender skin,
When strait the scorching Sun wept teares of brine,
Because he durst not touch him with his shine,   840
For feare of spoyling that same Iv'ry skin,
Whose whitenesse he so much delighted in;
And then the Moone, mother of mortall ease,
Would fayne have come from the Antipodes,
To have beheld him, naked as he stood   845
Ready to leape into the silver flood;
But might not: for the lawes of heaven deny,
To shew mens secrets to a womans eye:
And therefore was her sad and gloomy light
Confin'd unto the secret-keeping night.   850
  When beauteous Salmacis awhile had gaz'd
Upon his naked corps, she stood amaz'd,
And both her sparkling eyes burnt in her face,
Like the bright Sunne reflected in a glasse:
Scarce can she stay from running to the boy,   855
Scarce can she now deferre her hoped joy;
So fast her youthfull bloud playes in her vaynes,
That almost mad, she scarce her selfe contaynes.
When young Hermaphroditus as he stands,
Clapping his white side with his hollow hands,   860
Leapt lively from the land, whereon he stood,

Into the mayne part of the cristall flood.
Like Iv'ry then his snowy body was,
Or a white Lilly in a cristall glasse.
    Then rose the water-Nymph from where she lay,   865
As having wonne the glory of the day,
And her light garments cast from off her skin.
Hee's mine, she cry'd; and so leapt spritely in.
The flattering Ivy who did ever see
Inclaspe the huge trunke of an aged tree,   870
Let him behold the young boy as he stands,
Inclasp in wanton Salmacis's hands,
Betwixt those Iv'ry armes she lockt him fast,
Striving to get away, till at the last:
Fondling, she sayd, why striv'st thou to be gone?   875
Why shouldst thou so desire to be alone?
Thy cheeke is never fayre, when none is by:
For what is red and white, but to the eye?
And for that cause the heavens are darke at night,
Because all creatures close their weary sight;   880
For there's no mortall can so earely rise,
But still the morning waytes upon his eyes.
The earely-rising and soone-singing Larke
Can never chaunt her sweete notes in the darke;
For sleepe she ne're so little or so long,   885
Yet still the morning will attend her song,
All creatures that beneath bright Cinthia be,
Have appetite unto society;
The overflowing waves would have a bound
Within the confines of the spacious ground,   890
And all their shady currents would be plaste
In hollow of the solitary vaste,
But that they lothe to let their soft streames sing,
Where none can heare their gentle murmuring.
Yet still the boy, regardlesse what she sayd,   895
Struggled apace to overswimme the mayd.
Which when the Nymph perceiv'd, she 'gan to say:
Struggle thou mayst, but never get away.
So graunt, just gods, that never day may see
The separation twixt this boy and mee.   900
    The gods did heare her pray'r and feele her woe;

And in one body they began to grow.
She felt his youthfull bloud in every vaine;
And he felt hers warme his cold brest againe.
And ever since was womens love so blest,   905
That it will draw bloud from the strongest brest.
Nor man nor mayd now could they be esteem'd:
Neither, and either, might they well be deem'd,
When the young boy Hermaphroditus sayd,
With the set voice of neither man nor mayd: 910
Swift Mercury, thou author of my life,
And thou my mother, Vulcans lovely wife,
Let your poore offsprings latest breath be blest,
In but obtayning this his last request,
Grant that who e're heated by Phoebus beames,   915
Shall come to coole him in these silver streames,
May nevermore a manly shape retaine,
But halfe a virgine may returne againe.
    His parents hark'ned to his last request,
And with that great power they the fountaine blest.   920
And since that time who in that fountaine swimmes,
A mayden smoothnesse seyzeth halfe his limmes.

VENUS AND ANCHISES: BRITTAIN'S IDA

Phineas Fletcher

(1628)

A NOTE ON THE TEXT

Brittain's Ida was first published by Thomas Walkley who attributed it with mild protestation to 'that Renowned Poët, Edmond Spencer.' How and where Walkley obtained his copy is unknown, but Fletcher, who at the time of its publication was serving as a rector in Norfolk, seems not to have countered the attribution. In 1923 Miss Ethel Seaton discovered a manuscript version of the poem, together with other Fletcher items, in the Sion College Library and was able to confirm Fletcher's authorship. The provenance and date of the manuscript are unknown; first recorded in a library catalogue in 1658, it was very likely earlier than the printed text of *Brittain's Ida* or other of Fletcher's works, many of which were in print by 1633.[1] On the basis of its secretary hand and the 'paucity and nature of the corrections,' Miss Seaton concludes that it was the work of a copyist.

The relationship of the manuscript version to Walkley's printed text is puzzling, and its superiority over the printed text seems debatable.[2] Miss Seaton, however, feels that it is nearer to Fletcher's draft than the printed text. Among her reasons she cites, first of all, the 'less happy' title of *Brittain's Ida*, which in the manuscript is simply *Venus and Anchises*. But

---

[1] For a full discussion of attribution, date, etc., see Miss Seaton's introduction to her edition of the manuscript, *Venus and Anchises* (Oxford University Press, 1926).

[2] In the first flush of enthusiasm with which he greeted the discovery, Dr. F. S. Boas asserted that the manuscript must henceforth be 'the primary authority' for the text, *TLS*, 29 March 1923, p. 216.

it seems likely that the two should be conflated to read *Venus and Anchises: Brittain's Ida*, with Drayton's similar linking of the central figures and the locale in his *Endimion and Phœbe: Ideas Latmus* affording a precise parallel. Secondly, she notes the omission in the printed text of four stanzas present in the manuscript. These include two introductory stanzas in which the poet, using his pen name Thirsil, asserts he has been prompted by the 'fayre Eliza' to 'tune his noates unripe' on the banks of the river Cam. Taken in conjunction with the concluding stanza, they provide a personal framework for the narrative. Such a personal framework, together with the localizing of the scene, accords with the mode Lodge had established in *Scillaes Metamorphosis*, where the poet encounters Glaucus on the banks of the Isis. Why then were they omitted from the printed text? One possibility is that Walkley suppressed them since his readers would be expecting the name of Colin Clout instead of Thirsil. Still, if Walkley had pirated the work, as has been suggested, would he have scrupled at altering *Thirsil* to *Colin*? The alternative, and perhaps simpler, explanation is that these stanzas (and perhaps the two later omissions as well)[1] were simply not in Walkley's copy. The 1628 octavo collates A⁴ (first leaf missing), B–C⁸ which suggests that had he had the stanzas, Walkley would have included them. Finally, Miss Seaton cites the fact that the manuscript does not have the divisions into cantos or the introductory quatrains found in the printed text. These might have been added (?by Walkley) for their Spenserian flavour; however, there is the parallel within the genre of the very influential Marlowe–Chapman poem with its divisions into sestiads and introductory stanzas.

More importantly, what of the textual variants? Miss Seaton finds them chiefly 'misreadings by the copyist or the printer' with few 'genuine author's variants.' However, the misreadings of the copyist are more conspicuous than those of the compositor (e.g., '*three-hand* pastures' for '*three-leav'd* Pastures,'I.3.4; *Proud* for *Prov'd*, III.4.2; *lowlie* for *lovely*, IV.3.1; *mount* for *moove*, IV.7.4), especially if one excludes such common printer's errors as the dropping of a letter (*Cupio* for *Cupido*), the

---

[1] Stanza 43 (V.3 in this edition), the second of three stanzas linked by a motif, appears recast, as Miss Seaton notes, in the third *Piscatory Eclogue*.

dropping of a word (II.6.8 and III.8.3), and, possibly, eye transpositions (II.5.5, V.5.5, and VI.9.8). Most of the variants represent minor changes in diction (*Chinne* becomes *cheeke*, I.4.5; *snowy* becomes *Ivory*, I.6.1; *frame* becomes *forme*, V.10.1) and suggest no rationale other than that of taste. Others however, reinforce the artifice of the poem, which is characterized by antitheses and heavy alliterative and assonantal effects. Thus,

So [thinking] seeking to revive, more wounds his feeble sprite (IV.3.8) [MS reading in brackets]

And swearing gentle patience, [Closelie] gently smil'd (V.9.2)

The [thick-lac'd] thicke-lockt bowes shut out the tell-tale Sunne (II.3.1).

Some of the variants seem to indicate revision: *view'd*, necessitated by the rime, for *spide* (II.1.3) and reductions of hypermetrical lines (III.1.1 and st. 19; III.7.4 and st. 25; III.10.8 and st. 28). Other changes also seem intentional in that they echo phraseology within the poem ('*thousand* sheppeardes' becomes '*hundred* Shepheards,' I.3.3, picked up in line 5, '*hundred* sportings'; '*Careles* swaines' becomes '*Shepheards* boyes,' I.3.5, repeated in V.6.4; '*babbling* eccho' becomes '*blabbing*,' II.9.4, used also in II.3.2 and VI.11.3; 'fearefull *joye* and *wished* feare' becomes 'fearefull *hope*, and *wishing* feare,' II.6.1; *hope* and *feare* are again used together in II.9.7 and V.7.2; 'heartes *lowest* Center' becomes 'hearts *low* center,' IV.5.6, repeated in VI.11.5).

Thus it seems far from definite that the manuscript is closer to Fletcher's draft than Walkley's printed version, although the four additional stanzas in the manuscript must be reckoned with as well as a few manuscript readings which seem superior. Consequently, I have followed the 1628 text, although adopting certain of the manuscript readings, recorded in the textual notes. These readings, together with the omitted stanzas (I.1, 2; V.3; and VI.8), are reprinted here from Miss Seaton's edition by the kind permission of the President and Court of Governors of Sion College and the Royal Society of Literature.

CANTO I

The youthly Shepheards wonning here,
And Beauties rare displayd appeare:
What exercise hee chiefe affects,
His Name, and scornefull love neglects.

I

Thirsil (poore ladd) whose Muse yet scarcely fledge
Softlie for feare did learne to sing and pipe,
And sitting lowe under some Covert hedge
With Chirping noyse ganne tune his noates unripe,
Sighing those sighs which sore his heart did gripe,
   Where lovelie Came doeth lose his erring waye
   While with his bankes the wanton waters playe,
   Which still doe staye behind, yet still doe slippe away;

2

Thirsil hidde in a willowes shaddowing
(Nor higher durst his dastard thoughtes aspire)
Thus ganne to trye his downie Muses wing,
For soe the fayre Eliza deign'd desire.
Hir wishes were his lawes, hir will his fire,
   And hiding neerer Came his stranger name
   He thought with song his raging fire to tame,
   Fond boye that fewell sought to hide soe great a flame.

3

In Ida Vale (who knowes not Ida Vale?)
When harmelesse Troy yet felt not Græcian spite:
A hundred Shepheards woon'd, and in the Dale,
While their faire Flockes the three-leav'd Pastures bite:
The Shepheards boyes, with hundred sportings light,
   Gave winges unto the times to speedy hast:
   Ah foolish Lads, that strove with lavish wast,
   So fast to spend the time, that spends your time as fast.

3.4 three-leav'd, clover

4

Among the rest that all the rest excel'd,
A dainty Boy there wonn'd, whose harmelesse yeares,
Now in their freshest budding gently sweld;
His Nimph-like face ne're felt the nimble sheeres,
Youth's downy blossome through his cheeke appeares:
  His lovely limbes (but love he quite discarded)
  Were made for play (but he no play regarded,)
  And fit love to reward, and with love be rewarded.

5

High was his fore-head, arch't with silver mould,
(Where never anger churlish rinkle dighted)
His auburne lockes hung like darke threds of gold,
That wanton aires (with their faire length incited)
To play among their wanton curles delighted.
  His smiling eyes with simple truth were stor'd:
  Ah! how should truth in those thiefe eyes be stor'd.
  Which thousand loves had stol'n, and never one restored.

6

His lilly-cheeke might seeme an Ivory plaine,
More purely white than frozen Apenine:
Where lovely bashfulnesse did sweetely raine,
In blushing scarlet cloth'd, and purple fine.
A hundred hearts had this delightfull shrine,
  (Still cold it selfe) inflam'd with hot desire,
  That well the face might seeme, in divers tire,
  To be a burning snow, or else a freezing fire.

7

His cheerfull lookes, and merry face would proove,
(If eyes the index be where thoughts are read)
A dainty play-fellow for naked love;
Of all the other parts enough is sed,
That they were fit twins for so fayre a head:

6.3 raine; raigne *MS*, a homonymic spelling. Other interesting examples are
III.9.1 (beauties bearing; beautie baring *MS*); v.10.6 (limb'd; limned); VI.4.2
(straight; strait *MS*).

Thousand boyes for him, thousand maidens dy'de,
Dye they that list, for such his rigorous pride,
He thousand boyes (ah foole) and thousand maids deni'd.

8

His joy was not in musiques sweete delight,
(Though well his hand had learnt that cunning arte)
Or dainty songs to daintier eares indite,
But through the plaines to chace the nimble Hart
With well-tun'd hounds; or with his certaine dart
    The tusked Boare, or savage Beare to wound;
    Meane time his heart with monsters doth abound,
    Ah foole to seeke so farre what neerer might be found!

9

His name (well knowne unto those Woody shades,
Where unrewarded lovers oft complaine them)
Anchises was; Anchises oft the glades
And mountaines heard Anchises had disdain'd them;
Not all their love one gentle looke had gain'd them,
    That rockey hills, with echoing noyse consenting,
    Anchises plain'd; but he no whit relenting,
    (Harder then rocky hils) laught at their vaine lamenting.

CANTO II

Diones Garden of delight,
With wonder holds Anchises sight;
While from the Bower such Musique sounds,
As all his senses neere confounds.

I

One day it chanc't as hee the Deere persude,
Tyred with sport, and faint with weary play,
Faire Venus grove not farre away he view'd,
Whose trembling leaves invite him there to stay,
And in their shades his sweating limbes display:
    There in the cooling glade he softly paces,
    And much delighted with their even spaces,
    What in himselfe he scorn'd, hee praisd their kinde imbraces.

310

2

The Woode with Paphian mirtles peopled,
(Whose springing youth felt never Winters spiting)
To laurels sweete were sweetely married,
Doubling their pleasing smels in their uniting,
When single much, much more when mixt delighting:
   No foote of beast durst touch this hallowed place,
   And many a boy that long'd the woods to trace,
   Entred with feare, but soone turn'd back his frighted face.

3

The thicke-lockt bowes shut out the tell-tale Sunne,
(For Venus hated his all blabbing light,
Since her knowne fault which oft she wisht undone)
And scattered rayes did make a doubtfull sight,
Like to the first of day, or last of night:
   The fittest light for Lovers gentle play;
   Such light best shewes the wandring lovers way,
   And guides his erring hand: Night is loves holly-day.

4

So farre in this sweete Labyrinth he stray'd,
That now he viewes the Garden of delight;
Whose breast with thousand painted flowers array'd,
With divers joy captiv'd his wandring sight;
But soone the eyes rendred the eares their right:
   For such strange harmony he seem'd to heare,
   That all his senses flockt into his eare,
   And every faculty wisht to be seated there.

5

From a close Bower this dainty Musique flow'd,
A bower appareld round with divers Roses
Both red and white; which by their liveries show'd
Their Mistris faire, that there her selfe reposes:
Seem'd they would strive with those rare Musique clozes,
   By spreading their faire bosomes to the light,
   Which the distracted sense should most delight;
   That, raps the melted eare; this, both the smel & sight.

5.5 they] *MS*; that *1628*

6

The Boy 'twixt fearefull hope, and wishing feare,
Crept all along (for much he long'd to see
The Bower, much more the guest so lodged there)
And as he goes, he markes how well agree
Nature and arte, in discord unity:
   Each striving who should best performe his part,
   Yet arte now helping nature, nature arte:
   While from his eares unwares a voyce thus stole his heart.

7

Fond men, whose wretched care the life soone ending,
By striving to increase your joy, do spend it;
And spending joy, yet find no joy in spending:
You hurt your life by striving to amend it,
And seeking to prolong it, soonest end it:
   Than while fit time affords thee time and leasure,
   Enjoy while yet thou mayst thy lifes sweet pleasure:
   Too foolish is the man that starves to feed his treasure:

8

Love is lifes end (an end but never ending)
All joyes, all sweetes, all happinesse awarding:
Love is lifes wealth (nere spent, but ever spending)
More rich, by giving, taking by discarding:
Love's lifes reward, rewarded in rewarding,
   Than from thy wretched heart fond care remoove;
   Ah should thou live but once loves sweetes to proove,
   Thou wilt not love to live, unlesse thou live to love.

9

To this sweete voyce, a dainty musique fitted
It's well-tuned strings; and to her notes consorted:
And while with skilfull voyce the song she dittied,
The blabbing Echo had her words retorted;
That now the Boy, beyond his soule transported,
   Through all his limbes feeles run a pleasant shaking,
   And twixt a hope & feare suspects mistaking,
   And doubts he sleeping dreames, & broad awake feares waking.

6.8 unwares] *MS*; om. *1628*   8.3 lifes] *MS*; life *1628*

CANTO III

Fair Cythareas limbes beheld,
The straying Lads heart so inthral'd:
That in a Trance his melted spright,
Leaves th'sences slumbring in delight.

1

Now to the Bower hee sent his theevish eyes,
To steale a happy sight; there doe they finde
Faire Venus, that within halfe naked lyes;
And straight amaz'd (so glorious beauty shin'd)
Would not returne the message to the minde:
  But full of feare, and superstitious awe,
  Could not retire, or backe their beames with-draw,
  So fixt on too much seeing made they nothing saw.

2

Her goodly length, stretch't on a Lilly-bed;
(A bright foyle of a beauty farre more bright,)
Few Roses round about were scattered,
As if the Lillies learnt to blush for spite,
To see a skinne much more then Lilly-white:
  The bed sanke with delight so to be pressed,
  And knew not which to thinke a chance more blessed,
  Both blessed so to kisse, and so agayne be kissed.

3

Her spacious fore-head like the clearest Moone,
Whose full-growne Orbe begins now to be spent,
Largely display'd in native silver shone,
Giving wide roome to beauties Regiment,
Which on the plaine with love tryumphing went:
  Her golden haire a rope of pearle imbraced,
  Which with their dainty threds oft times enlaced,
  Made the eie think the pearle was there in gold inchased.

4

Her full large eye, in jetty-blacke array'd,
Prov'd beauty not confin'd to red and white,

But oft her selfe in blacke more rich display'd;
Both contraries did yet themselves unite,
To make one beauty in different delight:
   A thousand loves sate playing in each eye,
   And smiling mirth kissing faire courtesie,
   By sweete perswasion wan a bloodlesse victory.

5

The whitest white set by her silver cheeke,
Grew pale and wan like unto heavy lead:
The freshest Purple fresher dyes must seeke,
That dares compare with them his fainting red:
On these Cupido winged armies led,
   Of little loves, that with bold wanton traine
   Under those colours, marching on the plaine,
   Force every heart, and to low vasselage constraine.

6

Her lips, most happy each in others kisses,
From their so wisht imbracements seldome parted,
Yet seem'd to blush at their so wanton blisses;
But when sweete words their joyning sweet disparted,
To th'eare a dainty musique they imparted:
   Upon them fitly sate delightfull smiling,
   A thousand soules with pleasing stealth beguiling:
   Ah that such shew's of joyes should be all joyes exiling.

7

The breath came slowly thence, unwilling leaving
So sweet a lodge, but when she once intended,
To feast the aire with words, the heart deceiving,
More fast it thronged so to be expended;
And at each word a hundred loves attended,
   Playing ith'breath, more sweete then is that firing,
   Where that Arabian onely bird expiring,
   Lives by her death, by losse of breath more fresh respiring.

6.3 their so] *MS*; such their *1628*

8

Her chin, like to a stone in gold inchased,
Seem'd a faire jewell wrought with cunning hand,
And being double, doubly the face it graced.
This goodly frame on her round necke did stand,
Such pillar well such curious worke sustain'd
   And on his top the heavenly spheare up rearing,
   Might well present, with daintier appearing,
   A lesse but better Atlas, that faire heaven bearing.

9

Lower two breasts stand all their beauties bearing,
Two breasts as smooth and soft; but ah alas!
Their smoothest softnes farre exceedes comparing:
More smooth and soft; but naught that ever was,
Where they are first, deserves the second place:
   Yet each as soft and each as smooth as other;
   And when thou first tri'st one & then the other,
   Each softer seemes then each, & each then each seemes
                                smoother.

10

Lowly betweene their dainty hemisphæres,
(Their hemisphæres the heav'nly Globes excelling,)
A path, more white then is the name it beares,
The lacteall path, conducts to the sweet dwelling,
Where best delight all joyes sits freely dealing;
   Where hundred sweetes, and still fresh joyes attending;
   Receive in giving, and still love dispending,
   Grow richer by their losse, and wealthy by expending.

11

But stay bold shepheard, here thy footing stay,
Nor trust too much unto thy new-borne quill,
As farther to those dainty limbes to stray;
Or hope to paint that vale, or beautious hill,
Which past the finest hand and choycest skill:

8.3 it] *MS*; om. *1628*   11.2 new-borne] *MS*; now-borne *1628*

But were thy Verse and Song as finely fram'd,
As are those parts, yet should it soone be blam'd,
For now the shameles world of best things is asham'd.

12

That cunning Artist that old Greece admir'd,
Thus farre his Venus fitly portrayed;
But there he left, nor farther ere aspir'd:
His Dædale hand, that Nature perfected
By arte, felt arte by nature limitted.
 Ah! well he knew, though his fit hand could give
 Breath to dead colours, teaching marble live,
 Yet would these lively parts his hand of skill deprive.

13

Such when this gentle boy her closly view'd,
Onely with thinnest silken vaile o'er-layd,
Whose snowy colour much more snowy shew'd,
By being next that skin; and all betray'd,
Which best in naked beauties are aray'd:
 His spirits melted with so glorious sight,
 Ran from their worke to see so splendent light,
 And left the fainting limbes sweet slumbring in delight.

CANTO IV

The swonding Swaine recovered is
By th'Goddesse; his soule rapting blisse:
There mutuall conference, and how
Her service she doth him allow.

I

Soft-sleeping Venus waked with the fall,
Looking behind, the sinking Boy espies,
With all she starts, and wondereth withall,
She thinkes that there her faire Adonis dyes,
And more she thinkes the more the Boy she eyes:
 So stepping neerer, up begins to reare him;
 And now with love himselfe she will confer him,
 And now before her Love himselfe she will preferre him:

2

The Lad soone with that dainty touch reviv'd,
Feeling himselfe so well, so sweetly seated,
Begins to doubt whether he yet here liv'd,
Or else his flitting soule to heav'n translated
Was there in starry throne, and blisse instated:
  Oft would he dye, so to be often saved;
  And now with happy wish he closly craved,
  For ever to be dead, to be so sweet ingraved.

3

The Paphian Princesse (in whose lovely breast,
Spitefull disdaine could never find a place)
When now she saw him from his fit releast,
(To Juno leaving wrath and scolding base)
Comforts the trembling Boy with smiling grace,
  But oh! those smiles (too full of sweete delight)
  Surfeit his heart, full of the former sight;
  So seeking to revive, more wounds his feeble sprite.

4

Tell me, faire Boy (sayd she) what erring chance,
Hither directed thy unwary pace:
For sure contempt, or pride durst not advance
Their foule aspect in thy so pleasant face:
Tell me, what brought thee to this hidden place?
  Or lacke of love, or mutuall answering fire,
  Or hindred by ill chance in thy desire:
  Tell me, what ist thy faire and wishing eyes require?

5

The Boy (whose sence was never yet acquainted
With such a musique) stood with eares arected;
And sweetly with that pleasant spell enchanted,
More of those sugred straines long time expected,
Till seeing she his speeches not rejected,
  First sighes arising from his hearts low center,
  Thus gan reply; when each word bold would venter
  And strive the first, that dainty labyrinth to enter.

6

Faire Cyprian Queene (for well that heavenly face
Prooves thee the mother of all conquering Love)
Pardon I pray thee my unweeting pace,
For no presumptuous thoughts did hither moove
My daring feete, to this thy holy Grove;
    But lucklesse chance (which if you not gaine-say,
    I still must rue) hath caus'd me here to stray,
    And lose my selfe (alas) in losing of my way.

7

Nor did I come to right my wronged fire,
Never till now I saw what ought be loved,
And now I see, but never dare aspire
To moove my hope, where yet my love is mooved;
Whence though I would, I would it not remooved:
    Onely since I have plac't my love so high,
    Which sure thou must, or sure thou wilt deny,
    Grant me yet still to love, though in my love to dye.

8

But shee that in his eyes Loves face had seene,
And flaming heart, did not such suite disdaine
(For cruelty fits not sweete beauties Queene)
But gently could his passion entertaine,
Though she Loves Princesse, he a lowly Swaine:
    First of his bold intrusion she acquites him;
    Then to her service (happy Boy) admits him;
    And like another Love, with Bow and quiver fits him.

9

And now with all the loves he grew acquainted,
And Cupids selfe, with his like face delighted.
Taught him a hundred wayes with which he daunted
The prouder hearts, and wronged lovers righted,
Forcing to love, that most his love despited.
    And now the praçtique Boy did so approove him,
    And with such grace and cunning arte did moove him,
    That all the pritty loves, and all the Graces love him.

CANTO V

The Lovers sad despairing plaints,
Bright Venus with his Love acquaints;
Sweetly importun'd he doth shew,
From whom proceedeth this his woe.

1

Yet never durst his faint and coward heart,
(Ah foole! faint heart faire Lady ne're could win)
Assaile faire Venus with his new-learnt arte,
But kept his love, and burning flame within,
Which more flam'd out, the more he prest it in:
   And thinking oft, how just shee might disdaine him;
   While some coole mirtle shade did entertaine him,
   Thus sighing would he sit, & sadly would he plain him:

2

Ah fond and haplesse Boy! nor know I whether,
More fond, or haplesse more, that all so high
Hast plac't thy heart, where love and fate together,
May never hope to end thy misery,
Nor yet thy selfe dare wish a remedy.
   All hindrances (alas) conspire to let it;
   Ah fond and haplesse Boy! if canst not get it,
   In thinking to forget, at length learne to forget it.

3

Happelesse but fonder boye soe vainelie thinking
Whoe ever Could by learning learne forgetting?
Cann'st thow forgett a song by often singing
Or dittie canst unlearn by oft repeating?
Whoe ever thought to blunt an edge by whetting?
   Allsoe the thought of what thow shouldst oppresse
   By thinking more doeth more it self encrease,
   Soe must thow much more learne by thy forgettfulnes.

4

Ah farre too fond, but much more haplesse Swaine!
Seeing thy love can be forgotten never.

Serve and observe thy love with willing paine;
And though in vaine thy love thou doe persever,
Yet all in vaine doe thou adore her ever.
　　No hope can crowne thy thoughts so farre aspiring,
　　Nor dares thy selfe desire thine owne desiring,
　　Yet live thou in her love, and dye in her admiring:

5

Thus oft the hopelesse Boy complayning lyes;
But she that well could guesse his sad lamenting,
(Who can conceale love from Loves mothers eyes?)
Did not disdaine to give his love contenting:
Cruell the soule that feedes on loves tormenting:
　　Nor did she scorne him though not nobly borne,
　　(Love is nobility) nor could she scorne,
　　That with so noble skill her title did adorne.

6

One day it chanc't, thrice happy day and chance!
While loves were with the Graces sweetly sporting,
And to fresh musique sounding play and dance;
And Cupids selfe with Shepheards boyes consorting,
Laught at their pritty sport, and simple courting:
　　Faire Venus seates the fearefull Boy close by her,
　　Where never Phœbus jealous lookes might eye her,
　　And bids the Boy his Mistris, and her name descry her.

7

Long time the youth bound up in silence stood,
While hope and feare with hundred thoughts begun
Fit Prologue to his speech; and fearefull blood
From heart and face, with these post-tydings runne,
That eyther now he's made, or now undone:
　　At length his trembling words, with feare made weake,
　　Began his too long silence thus to breake,
　　While from his humble eies first reverence seem'd to speake:

5.5 loves] *MS*; soules *1628*. Cf. *Sicelides* III, 5: "Too cruell she that makes her
hearts contenting,/To see a heart languish in loves tormenting." (Seaton, p. 106)

320

8

Faire Queene of Love, my life thou maist command,
Too slender price for all thy former grace,
Which I receive at thy so bounteous hand;
But never dare I speake her name and face;
My life is much lesse-priz'd than her disgrace:
  And for I know if I her name relate,
  I purchase anger, I must hide her state,
  Unlesse thou sweare by Stix I purchase not her hate.

9

Faire Venus well perceiv'd his subtile shift,
And swearing gentle patience, gently smil'd:
While thus the Boy persu'd his former drift:
No tongue was ever yet so sweetely skil'd,
Nor greatest Orator so highly stil'd;
  Though helpt with all the choisest artes direction,
  But when he durst describe her heav'ns perfection,
  By his imperfect praise, disprais'd his imperfection.

10

Her forme is as her selfe, perfect Cælestriall,
No mortall spot her heavenly frame disgraces:
Beyond compare: such nothing is terrestriall:
More sweete then thought or pow'rfull wish embraces,
The map of heaven; the summe of all the Graces.
  But if you wish more truely limb'd to eye her
  Than fainting speech, or words can well descry her,
  Look in a glasse, & there more perfect you may spy her.

Canto VI

The Boyes short wish, her larger grant,
That doth his soule with blisse enchant:
Whereof impatient uttering all,
Inraged love contrives his thrall.

I

Thy crafty arte (reply'd the smiling Queene)
Hath well my chiding, and hot rage prevented,

1.2 hot] not *1628*; my *MS*

Yet might'st thou thinke, that yet 'twas never seene,
That angry rage and gentle love consented:
But if to me thy true love is presented,
   What wages for thy service must I owe thee?
   For by the selfe same vow, I here avow thee,
   What ever thou require, I frankly will allow thee.

2

Pardon (replies the Boy) for so affecting,
Beyond mortallity; and not discarding,
Thy service was much more than my expecting;
But if thou (more thy bounty-hood regarding)
Wilt needes heape up reward upon rewarding;
   Thy love I dare not aske, or mutuall firing,
   One kisse is all my love, and prides aspiring,
   And after starve my heart, for my too much desiring.

3

Fond Boy! (sayd she) too fond that askt no more;
Thy want by taking is no whit decreased,
And giving spends not our increasing store:
Thus with a kisse, his lips she sweetly pressed;
Most blessed kisse; but lippes more than most blessed,
   The Boy did thinke heaven fell while thus he joy'd;
   And while joy he so greedily enjoy'd,
   He felt not halfe his joy by being over-joyed.

4

Why sighst, faire Boy? (sayd she), dost thou repent thee
Thy narrow wish in such straight bonds to stay?
Well may I sigh (sayd he) and well lament me,
That never such a debt may hope to pay:
A kisse (sayd she) a kisse will backe repay:
   Wilt thou (reply'd the Boy too much delighted)
   Content thee, with such pay to be requited?
   She grants; & he his lips, heart, soule, to payment cited.

2.6 firing] *MS*; fixing *1628*   3.5 lippes] *MS*; hope *1628*

5

Looke as a Ward, long from his Lands detain'd,
And subject to his Guardians cruel lore,
Now spends the more, the more he was restrain'd,
So he; yet though in laying out his store,
He doubly takes; yet findes himselfe grow poore:
   With that, he markes, and tels her out a score,
   And doubles them, and trebles all before:
   Fond Boy! the more thou paist, thy debt still grows the more.

6

At length, whether these favours so had fir'd him,
With kindly heate, inflaming his desiring;
Or whether those sweete kisses had inspir'd him;
Hee thinkes that some thing wants for his requiring;
And still aspires, yet knows not his aspiring:
   But yet though that hee knoweth, so she gave
   That he presents himselfe her bounden slave;
   Stil his more wishing face seem'd some what else to crave.

7

And boldned with successe and many graces,
His hand, chain'd up in feare, he now releast:
And asking leave, courag'd with her imbraces;
Againe it prison'd in her tender breast;
Ah blessed prison! prisners too much blest!
   There with those sisters long time doth he play;
   And now full boldly enters loves high way;
   While downe the pleasant vale, his creeping hand doth stray.

8

At length into the haven he arrives
Where safe from storme the love-beate vessel rides,
And as a shippe that now the port atcheives
With thundrye shotte the angrie Neptune Chides
And with a thowsand joyes, past feares derides,
   Soe th'happie boye in this faire haven blest
   Meanes here sometime his joyfull bark to rest,
   And mocke those dangerous waves that late his boat opprest.

9

She not displeased with this his wanton play,
Hiding his blushing with a sugred kisse;
With such sweete heat his rudenesse doth allay,
That now he perfect knowes what ever blisse
Elder love taught, and he before did misse:
     That moult with joy, in such untri'd joyes trying,
     He gladly dies, and death new life applying,
     Gladly againe revives, that oft he may be dying.

10

Long thus he liv'd, slumbring in sweete delight,
Free from sad care, and fickle worlds annoy;
Bathing in liquid joyes his melted sprite;
And longer mought, but he (ah foolish Boy!)
Too proud, and to impatient of his joy,
     To woods, and heav'n, and earth his blisse imparted;
     That Jove upon him downe his thunder darted,
     Blasting his splendent face, and all his beauty swarted.

11

Such be his chance, that to his love doth wrong,
Unworthy he to hold so worthy place,
That cannot hold his peace and blabbing tongue:
Light joyes float on his lips, but weightie grace
Sinckes deepe, and th'hearts low center doth imbrace:
     Might I enjoy my love till I unfold it,
     I'de lose all favours when I blabbing told it:
     He is not fit for love, that is not fit to hold it.

9.6 moult, melted   9.8 revives] *MS*; he dyes *1628*
11.2 hold] *MS*; have *1628*   11.4 weightie] *MS*; rightly *1628*

NARCISSUS OR THE SELF-LOVER

James Shirley

(1646)

1

Faire Eccho rise, sick-thoughted Nymph awake,
Leave thy green Couch and Canopie of Trees,
Long since the quiristers o'th'wood did shake
Their wings, and sing to the bright Suns uprise:
   Day hath wept o're thy Couch, and progressed,
   Blusheth to see faire Eccho still in bed.

2

If not the Birds, who 'bout the Coverts flie,
And with their warbles charm the neighboring aire,
If not the Sun, whose new Embroiderie,
Makes rich the leaves that in thy Arbors are,
   Can make thee rise; yet Love-sick Nymph away,
   Thy young Narcissus is abroad to day.

3

See not farre off Cephisus sonne appeares,
No Nymph so faire in all Diana's traine,
When like a huntresse she for chace prepares;
His Bugle-horne, tyed in a silken chaine,
   And mounted on a comely Steed, which knowes
   What weight he carries, and more proudly goes.

4

Pursue him timerous Maid, he moves apace,
Favonius waits to play with thy loose haire,

And helpe thy flight; see how the drooping grasse
Courts thy soft tread, thou child of Sound and Aire.
   Attempt and over-take him, though he be
   Coy to all other Nymphs, he'll stoop to thee.

5

If thy face move not, let thy eyes expresse,
Some Rhetorick of thy teares to make him stay;
He must be a Rock, that will not melt at these,
Dropping their native Diamonds in his way:
   Mistaken he may stoop at them, and this
   (Who knowes how soon?) may helpe thee to a kisse.

6

If neither love, thy beautie, nor thy teare,
Invent some other way to make him know,
He need not hunt, that can have such a Deere.
The Queen of Love did once Adonis woe.
   But hard of soule, with no perswasions won,
   He felt the curse of his disdaine too soone.

7

In vaine I counsell her to put on wing,
Eccho hath left her solitarie Grove,
And in a Vale, the Palace of the spring,
Sits silently attending for her love;
   But round about to catch his voice with care,
   In every shade and Tree, she hid a snare.

8

Now doe the Hunts-men fill the aire with noise,
And their shrill hornes chafe her delighted eare,
Which with loud accents give the wood a voice,
Proclaiming Parley to the fearefull Deere:
   Shee heares the jolly tunes, but every straine,
   As high and musicall, she returnes againe.

5.4 their] (sugg. R. Armstrong); these

9

Rous'd is the game, pursuit doth put on wings,
The Sun doth shine, and guild them out their way:
The Deere into an o're-growne Thicket springs,
Through which he quaintly steales his shine away.
   The Hunters scatter; but the Boy o're-throwne
   In a darke part o'th'wood complaines alone.

10

Him, Eccho lead by her affection found,
Joy'd (you may ghesse) to reach him with her eye;
But more, to see him rise without a wound,
Who yet obscures her selfe behinde some Tree:
   He vext exclaimes, and asking, where am I?
   The unseen Virgin answers, *here am I*.

11

Some guide from hence; will no man heare? he cries,
She answers in her passion: *O man heare*.
I dye, I dye, say both; and thus she tries
With frequent answers to entice his eare
   And person to her Court, more fit for love,
   He tracts the sound, and findes her odorous Grove.

12

The way he trod was pav'd with Violets,
Whose azure leaves doe warme their naked stalks,
In their white double Ruffes the Dazies jet,
And Primroses are scattered in the walkes:
   Whose pretty mixture in the ground declares
   Another Galaxie emboss'd with starres.

13

Two rows of Elmes ran with proportion'd grace,
Like natures Arras to adorne the sides,
The friendly Vines their loved Barks embrace,
While folding tops the checkerd ground-work hides.
   Here oft the tired Sun himselfe would rest,
   Riding his glorious Circuit to the West.

14

From hence delight conveyes him unawares
Into a spacious green, whose either side
A Hill did guard, whilst with his Trees like haires,
The Clouds were busie binding up his head:
    The flowrs here smile upon him as he treads,
    And but when he looks up, hang downe their heads.

15

Not far from hence, neare an harmonious Brook,
Within an Arbour of conspiring Trees,
Whose wilder Boughes into the streame did look,
A place more sutable to her distresse,
    Eccho suspecting that her love was gone,
    Her selfe had in a carefull posture throwne.

16

But Time upon his wings had brought the Boy
To see this lodging of the aëry Queen,
Whom the dejected Nymph espyes with joy,
Through a small Window of sweet Eglantine;
    And that she might be worthy his embrace,
    Forgets not to new dresse her blubber'd face.

17

With confidence she sometimes would go out,
And boldly meet Narcissus in the way:
But then her feares present her with new doubt,
And chide her over-rash resolve away.
    Her heart with over-charge of love must break,
    Great Juno will not let poore Eccho speak.

18

Ungentle Queen of heaven, why was thy curse
So heavy on this Virgin? Jove comprest
Not her, and must her Destinie be worse
Then theirs that met his flame? thy angry breast
    Holds not in all the list a blacker doome,
    Better transforme the maid, then make her dumbe.

16.4 sweet] (Dyce); om.   18.4 his] (Dyce); her

JAMES SHIRLEY

19

Thy jealousie was sinne, above what she
Was guilty of: But she is wife to Jove,
For that in heav'n must there no Justice be?
Or didst thou finde this cruelty, for her love
    To this coy Lad, whom in the Book of Fate
    Thou didst fore-see thy selfe shouldst love too late?

20

Thou tedious to thy selfe, not being faire,
To whom thy wakefull jealousie succeeds
A greater curse; when mortalls jealous are,
They're cur'd to know their faith abus'd, what seeds
    For some act worse than hers, grow up in thee,
    At once to doubt, and know Joves perjurie?

21

But still this Nymph was innocent, reverse
Thy rash decree, repentance is no sinne
In heavenly natures; but I vaine rehearse
The story of thy hate: it is not in
    Poore Eccho's pow'r to Court the Boy, with more
    Than smiles or teares, and his last breath restore.

22

Narcissus now collects his scattered sence,
He findes himselfe at losse, drawne thither by
Imagin'd answers to his griefe, from whence
That he may find some surer guide, he'll try
    His Bugle-horne, whose sound was understood,
    But drew no great compassion from the wood.

23

Onely, so soon as he dispatch'd the aire,
At her owne Bow'r Eccho receiv'd the noice;
Every thing help'd to bring the message neare,
And the winde proud to wait upon the voice;
    When she return'd a cheerefull answer, knew
    The way agen, and with loud musick flew.

21.4 The] (Dyce); Thy

329

24

Narcissus glad that such returne was made,
And flattred by his over-busie eare,
Was soon directed to the Virgins shade,
Without a thought to finde a faire Nymph there:
    Nor did he see the maid, for she, so soone
    As he appear'd, found passage to be gone.

25

The Boy inquisitive looks round with feare,
But could see none to make addresses to,
Nor observes any print of foot-step there,
The flow'rs unprest his modest forehead view,
    And court his stay; the trees and every thing
    Give him a silent welcome to the spring.

26

Amazed what this solitude should meane,
And wondring at the sound that did invite him
So late to that faire desert, a new scene,
With a most curious Arbor doth delight him,
    Who now to please his late surprized eyes;
    Whilst they doe gaze, downe on a banke he lies.

27

And now does every object shew what spell
It hath upon his sences, too much sight
Deprives him of his eyes, a mist doth dwell
About 'em, and by soft degrees invite
    The Boy to slumber, which glad Eccho spies,
    And while he dreames, keeps centry with her eyes.

28

In silence she approaches where he lay,
With his armes chained crosse upon his breast;
His silken Bonnet sliding, did betray
A face, which all the Nymphs did call the best.
    A Banke his Pillow was, the flowers his sheet,
    His Blanket aire, the trees his Coverlet.

29

Sometimes the winde befriends a tender bough,
Part of his leavie Canopie, which hides
The subject of all wonder, his white brow,
And helpes it nearer to obtaine a kisse:
    Which once enjoy'd, away the twig doth skip,
    Not daring to be taken at his lip.

30

While taller boughes hover about his head,
And justle one another for their view;
The humble branches are enamoured,
And have their short carresses with him too.
    Thus all conspire, him severall waies to woe,
    For whose love onely they delight to grow.

31

Eccho at every look feeles new desires,
And wishes that he were Endymion,
For whom in her most glorious star attires,
Oft in her night-Gown came the Love-sick Moon,
    To Latmos sacred Hill, when for his sake,
    Whilst he did sleep, she'd ever wish to wake.

32

But this she soon revokes, her love will beare
No rivall thoughts, no competition.
The Queen of heaven must have no interest here;
This Beauties Empire must be all her owne:
    Thus while she all embraceth, her desires
    Conspire but to enlarge her Funerall fires.

33

Her eye takes in more flame now, than before,
Gazing improves her loves perfection,
Whose every part riseth a silent woer,
And the most taking presence doth put on;
    Sweetly enticing her delighted sence,
    To lose her selfe in every excellence.

34

One while shee thinks all but a cozening dream,
And him but some phantastick mockerie:
'Tis too much happinesse if he be the same,
And she the Nymph that she was wont to be:
    If she sleep not, who blessed more than she:
    Yet if she dreame, awake she'd never be.

35

How could his haire, so many finest threds
Of gold, but make a net to catch her sight?
How could she trace his brow? or see those lids,
Whose either Ivorie box shut up a light
    To travellers, more chearefull, than the starre
    That ushers in the day, but brighter farre?

36

She with her danger doth these parts admire,
But loves 'em more; anothers flame and art
May praise, her love belongs to her owne fire,
And is the office proper to her heart.
    But Eccho has not done, for she pursues
    Dangers, above what she at distance views.

37

Sh'as yet but exercis'd her wondring eye
Upon his wealthy cheek, his brow, his haire,
Another sense the Nymph will satisfie;
She thinks his heavenly lips forgotten are:
    Which now she boldly tastes, and at first kisse,
    Concludes, there is no other heaven but this.

38

The lips that will not open to praise his
She wishes may be clos'd eternally.
These freely touch'd, are able to entice
The soule to lose its immortality.
    The Gods may boast Ambrosia alone,
    But she feeds on a dew above their owne.

39

Oft doth she kisse, as often doth she see,
A fresher blush dye o're his Corall gate,
Whose close enjayles his tongue, and seems to be
Asham'd, the maid is so insatiate.
    But speake he cannot, though she doe him wrong,
    Her doore, and his doe double bar his tongue.

40

But stay rash Eccho, see what thou hast done;
His lips, that kiss'd themselves like two Rose-leaves,
Grow pale o'th'suddaine, thy impression,
Them of their blushing modesty bereaves.
    His blood will be required of you, I feare;
    And see some drops upon your lip appeare.

41

And wilt thou still (forgetfull Nymph) pursue
Thy wanton touches? all the bloud is gone:
What of his cheek wilt thou be murtherer too?
Thinking the others Sanguine thither runne?
    Alas, there is but of its owne, a-part,
    Feare hath sent back the rest unto his heart.

42

Leave shamelesse Eccho, leave a little here,
Another time to enrich thy lip withall;
For thy owne sake this cruelty forbeare,
Dost thinke the guilt of such a bloud is small?
    But 'tis the last she feares, and cannot tell
    Better, than with a kisse to take farewell.

43

But use thy freedome, Ile not blame thee now,
Thou know'st his stubborne disposition,
Hasten thy kisses then, and take enow
To serve thee for an age, ere thou hast done:
    And when thou hast took all but one, fore-see
    Thou bee'st a taking that, eternally.

44

But Eccho needs no counsell to proceed,
Fearing too soon Narcissus should awake.
Shee plies his lips, as if to make them bleed
Were to restore the colour she did take.
    But marke what followes this offence! his eyes
    Ope by degrees, and she thence guilty flies.

45

It was a cowardise to steale away,
Not daring to avouch what she had done;
Fugitive Lover, thou hadst better stay,
The Boy's alone, and put fresh beautie on;
    Nor dost thou wisely maid, pursue thy choise:
    For Eccho seldome goes without a noise.

46

But she is gone, and the faire youth is risse,
Suspitious that he felt some person there;
Then busily he looks about the trees,
Whose boughs would guide him on the way to her;
    Directed by the winde, at last he found
    The beauteous Nymph laid carelesse on the ground.

47

Amaz'd that such a presence should remaine
In such an unfrequented place, as this:
He takes the wisest counsell of his braine,
In supposition she some goddesse is:
    And when he had devote submission paid
    To her, this with a trembling voice he said:

48

Celestiall dweller, sure thou art no lesse,
Such brightnesse never knew mortalitie:
Or if thou be'st a mortall, I may ghesse
There are no gods; nor heaven, if gods there be;
    Thou dost excell; and if a heaven, 'tis cleare,
    That here it is, because thou art not there.

49

Yet here it cannot be, for I am here
Conscious that I am wretched, and alone:
If this be heaven, I wish my selfe else-where;
All joyes inhabit heaven, but here are none;
    For if true joy exceed the name of things,
    We must deduce them from the higher springs.

50

Where am I then? alas I cannot tell,
Whether in earth or hell, if earth it be,
Then it is both; yet can it not be hell,
For that cannot be capable of thee.
    Beside, if Sages doe not hell bely,
    In hell, I sure should have more company.

51

But I doe walk this Labyrinth alone,
And this addes to the languish of my heart,
That in this sad confinement, I have none
Will joyne his misery, and take a part.
    I never yet provok'd the high heavens so,
    That they should marke me out alone to woe.

52

With many more, as late I hunting was
In this unlucky wood, I know not where
I lost my traine, ill fortune, and the place,
Conspiring with my horse to leave me there.
    Since when endeavouring my selfe to finde,
    I might as well o're-take, and stay the winde.

53

Faire goddesse, then informe me, where I am,
And with thy kinde and safe direction,
Convey a lost man thither, whence he came:
Or if not thither, to a place more knowne:
    Nay into any other wildernesse,
    There is a path from any place, but this.

54

Then shall the Nymphs, for they affect my name,
Build thee a glorious Temple for this deed,
Wherein they shall a stately Altar frame,
Which shall not with the tender first-lings bleed;
   They shall present fresh Chaplets, which their love
   Shall set on fire, and their sighes Incense prove.

55

Eccho who all the while attentive sate,
And heard the musick of his passion,
But held first pittie due to her owne fate,
Yet knew not with what art it should be done,
   Rallies her wiser thoughts, and while he staies
   Expecting answer, to her selfe she saies:

56

What shall poore Eccho doe ? I want a voice
To tell him what I am, how I have lov'd;
Juno, thy curse was an unhappy choice,
Some other punishment thou mightst have prov'd.
   Revoke this cruell doom, a power restore
   To my chain'd tongue, Ile never aske thee more.

57

Meane time, like a pale prisoner at the Bar,
Oppressed more with feare, than his own chaines,
(These of the feet, those the head troubles are)
Suspecting much her silence, he complaines
   In smother'd sighes, and 'cause they not prevaile,
   Look, and you'll see a teare is breaking jaile.

58

The Nymph in pitty of his griefe, put on
Her stock of smiles, and love in either eye,
Courts him to shine, the Majestie is gone
That frighted him; and now a fresher dye,
   Dawnes in his cheek, and his owne eye so neare,
   New burnisht, drew up the complaining teare.

59

Eccho now thinking she had won the prize,
Seeing all clouds cleare up, and in his brow
The milkie path of heaven agen, his eyes
Sparkling out heavenly fire, which even now
    Peep't through the brine of sorrow, came once more,
    Boldly to kisse her convert Paramour.

60

But Eccho mist her aime, for he went back,
And with his hand check'd her unruly one,
As such addresses did good manners lack,
She else perhaps might an embrace have stolne:
    Angry he was, a second knowledge now
    Appeares too plaine upon his rugged brow.

61

Look how some infant by the Parent beat,
For having plaid the wanton with her breast,
Afraid to crie looks pale, some pearly wet
Swelling to peep out of her watry nest,
    Shrinking his pretty lip, hangs downe the head,
    His red to pale, his pale converts to red.

62

So far'd poore Eccho in this extasie,
Whose trembling bloud although it had forsook
Her cheek, was ignorant yet where to be,
Feare had deflowr'd the beauty of each look,
    And had not some divine reliefe been sent,
    Shee had setled there her owne pale monument.

63

But unexpectedly her tongue release,
By Juno's owne compassion to the maid,
Whose sufferings in love her wrath appeas'd,
Gave Eccho a new life, who thought to have said
    Within her heart; proud boy, th'ast done thy worst;
    But found her voice, a cleare one, as at first.

63.3 appeas'd] (Dyce); appear'd

64

Then wisely fearing to have call'd him proud,
Could be no argument to make him kinde,
She thought to cure him with a Palinode,
Saying her heart was of another minde:
   And thought him gentle, yet some spirits gain'd;
   Unto the boy, thus she at last complain'd:

65

Mankinde, from henceforth must not nature call
An equall mother, fondly to bestow
Upon thee one, her beauties stock, her all,
And others by her empty hand undoe.
   For though not eldest, she hath made thee heire,
   And thou, above thy numerous brethren, faire.

66

But too much sweetnessse is ill plac'd upon
A stubborne heart: A Panther and a Dove,
Cruell and faire, were never meant for one:
Resigne thy beauty, or else put on love.
   Thou wert unkinde Narcissus, to deny,
   Thy selfe the office of a courtesie.

67

What was a kisse? the rape of such a Treasure
What Tyrant were he Judge, would call a sin?
Thou canst not loose thy lip, but finde a pleasure:
Come let us now, though late, loves warre begin;
   And meet me boldly, for one kisse of thine
   Ile give a thousand: Lov's Exchequers mine.

68

If thou bee'st scrupulous, I will not pay,
Thou shalt have halfe in earnest, if thou please:
Or if not so, I aske no longer day
To number the whole summe, before I cease:
   And at the totall, if thy lip repine,
   Ile trebble all, to have one more of thine.

69

But whither doth suspition draw thy eye?
Thou maist commit thy selfe to silent Groves,
The listning Trees grooms of my chamber be,
This Aire close Secretary to our loves.
    Be not too coy then to receive a kisse,
    Thou mightst have kist me twenty times 'ere this.

70

Come sit thee downe upon this banke a while,
And let us sport, as other lovers doe.
The heav'n in gold, the earth in green doth smile,
My heaven on earth, prethee doe thou so too.
    Unwreath thy armes, and with an amorous twine,
    Girdle my waste, whilst I in circle thine.

71

My shady Province, wall'd about with trees,
The wealthy currents that devide the Land,
Shall give up all their treasure to thy eyes:
Pleasure it selfe shall spread at thy command,
    Her most desired soule, and thou as free
    As aire, shalt move, and share all blisse with me.

72

If thou wilt hunt, the Lion and the Pard
Shall Every morne unto the Chace invite thee.
The Boare and Panther when thou art prepar'd,
Shall play before thy Speare, and never fright thee:
    Bleed any Beast, hunt what thou likest most,
    All wilde shall tame before thee as thou go'st.

73

See how the trees bow their exalted heads,
And not a shrub but signe of gladnesse beares,
Which else would shrink into their Earthy beds,
Or through their Barke break out in gummy teares;
    And for thy absence weep out all their Rinde,
    Proud if they have for thee their soule resign'd.

70.6 thine] (Dyce); shine

74

The Winde, thy Herald flies about the Groves,
Aloud proclaiming thee the wood-Nymphs King,
Snatching up odours as he whistling roves,
At thy hand to unlade them from his wing.
    The Silvans friske about, while Nymphs prepare
    A Rosie Garland to o're-top thy haire.

75

Shepheards shall all the day new pastimes spring,
A Maske of Satyrs shall beguile the night:
The choisest Birds shall to the Anticks sing,
The starres grow brighter to behold the sight:
    Yet these but shadowes of the mirth wee'll prove,
    If thou wilt stay, and be thy Eccho's love.

76

I have a Cloister over-looks the Sea,
Where every morning we secure from feare,
Will see the Porpise and the Dolphins play,
And all the wonders that inhabit there,
    Where many a Barke into the Clouds doth leap,
    While Surges caper round about the Ship.

77

Lovely Narcissus, prethee stay with me,
If thou doe thirst, from every Spring shall rise
Divinest Nectar, and thy food shall be
The glorious Apples of Hesperides:
    A Nymph shall be thy Hebe, if thou need
    Sha't have another for thy Ganimede.

78

Feele how my Pulses beate, my breasts swell high:
Come, come be not so modest, pretty one;
Why dost thou turne that heavenly cheek from me:
Who but thy selfe would such a blessing shun?
    Those frownes will discompose thy beauty quite,
    My lips doe blush in daring thee to fight.

79

Prethee unlock thy words sweet treasurie,
And rape me with the musick of thy tongue,
But let no accent touch upon Deny;
This will thy beauty, and my passions wrong.
    Ile rather praise thy silence; it may prove
    What Lovers use t'expound, consent to love.

80

The Boy seems pleas'd, and here begins to break
Into a language extasied the maid,
By her owne hearts dictamen he did speak:
And if she ask'd him love, he lov'd he said,
    She darts a glance, and he returnes a smile,
    She sees, and surfets on his lips the while.

81

But soon these Sun-beames vanish'd, all his smiles
Were feign'd, to get some knowledge how to quit
The wood, when she not moved with those wiles,
Told him all information was unfit
    Against her selfe; at this, swift as the winde,
    Away he flies, but leaves his frown behinde.

82

Eccho laments his absence, and in vaine
Calls him againe unto her amorous wars,
She hath too sure a proof of his disdaine:
She sighes and curses her malignant stars:
    And while she chides the Fate that gave her birth,
    Her eyes make poore themselves, t'enrich the earth.

83

Oh that I ne're had seen his face (quoth she)
That ignorant of the sweetnesse, I might rest
In supposition, what the blisse might be:
My knowledge has betraid me to the best;
    And by acquaintance with so much delight,
    I finde a new flame in my appetite.

84

Justice, thou dreadfull Queen Ramnusia,
Punish with sorrow my contemners pride,
And by some strange and most prodigious way,
Let him the weight of thy revenge abide.
    And since to me, his heart a Rock hath prov'd,
    Let him so love at last, and dye unlov'd.

85

Eccho hath spent her sting; Narcissus now
Hath got the top of an aspiring hill,
Whose site commands the Countrey round to view
Some tract, to lead him from the place, but still
    In vaine he does employ his searching eyes,
    Through thick embracing woods, no path he spies.

86

Wounded with objects that no comfort bring,
He might conclude his fortune at the worst,
Had he not seen hard by a goodly spring,
And thither he descends to quench his thirst.
    O doe not taste (Narcissus), hence will flow,
    What will thee more than thy past fate undoe.

87

Thy eyes betray thee, and are sorrowes spies,
Containe thy feet, thy danger is beneath,
Run not quick-sighted to a Precepice,
A blinde man cannot misse his way to death.
    Thy liberty was all thou lost before,
    The Nymphs too soon may thus thy death deplore.

88

Chuse any other fountaine: harke and feare,
The Birds are singing Dirges to thy death;
Does not a sooty Raven strike thine eare
From an high Oake tuning her fatall breath?
    A mighty cloud obscures the Suns bright eye,
    Not willing to behold thy Tragedy.

86.6 than] (Dyce); thou

89

And yet these move thee not: then reach the streame,
And meet thy blacker Destiny; the Sun
Is bright agen, wrath burnes in every beame,
And guilds the Scene of thy destruction:
    Each sullen winde is in his prison penn'd,
    Least with their murmure it the Spring offend.

90

No portion of a Birds forsaken nest,
Fell from the Bowes to interrupt the calme,
No wither'd leafe did in his fall molest
The stilnesse of it, smooth as setled balme,
    But Crystall lesse transparent. Such a mirrour,
    So form'd could onely shew disdaine his errour.

91

And now Narcissus humbled on the grasse,
And leaning with his breast upon the brinke,
Looks into th'water, where he spies a face,
And as he did incline his head to drinke;
    As faire a countenance seem'd to meet with his,
    Off'ring to entertaine him with a kisse.

92

Giving a little backe, he doth admire
The beauty of the face presented to him,
Thinking at first some water-Nymph was there,
And rising from her silver Couch to woe him:
    Yet Court she cannot whom she did surprise,
    Never from water did such flames arise.

93

His heart glowes in him. Punishment fulfills:
Love leaps into full age, at the first houre,
New wonders like the waves, with rouling hills
Follow his gazes: all that lov'd before,
    Have flung their gather'd flames into his breast,
    Fit him for Love, a Sacrifice and Priest.

94

But strucken with his owne, his burning eyes
Are onely thirsty now; he drinks apace
Into his soule the shadow that he sees,
And dotes on every wonder of the face.
   He stoops to kisse it, when the lips halfe way
   Meet, he retreats, and th'other steales away.

95

He, mov'd at the unkindnesse which he took
By his owne teaching, bowes himselfe againe,
The other meets him in the silent brook,
They spie agen, but he cannot refraine
   To Court whom he desires, and at his talke,
   The lips within the water seem to walke.

96

And every smile doth send his owne agen.
This cheeres him, but he cannot heare a sound
Break from the watrie prison, and he then
Complaines a fresh, that his unhappy wound
   Admits no cure, and as he beats his breast,
   The Conflict under water is exprest.

97

What e're thou art, come forth, and meet me here
He cries; why dost deceive me with a look?
What meanes that imitation? come neare,
Leape from the depth of thy imprisoning brook.
   Fold not thy armes like mine, or smile on me,
   Unlesse I may enjoy thy company.

98

But whether is my wiser reason fled?
It is the shadow of my selfe, I see,
And I am curst to be enamoured.
Where did I lose my soule? or where am I?
   What god shall pardon me this sin, if here,
   I must become my owne Idolater?

344

99

Thou fatall Looking-glasse, that dost present
My selfe to me, (my owne incendiarie.)
Oh let my eyes in love with their lament,
Weep themselves out, and prove a part of thee:
  This I shall gaine, either my shade may fleet,
  Or if it stay, I may want eyes to see't.

100

Under this burthen of my love I faint,
And finde I am with too much plenty poore:
Wealthy I am in nothing but my want;
I have, and yet (O gods) want nothing more:
  Mysteriously divided thus I stand,
  Halfe in the water, halfe upon the land.

101

But sure it cannot be my selfe I love;
How with my selfe despaire I to agree?
By one example both must gentle prove,
If I Narcissus love, can he hate me?
  It is no shade then doth my phansie flatter,
  But something that's divine doth blesse the water.

102

Essence of all that's faire, ascend to me;
To thy acceptance I present my heart:
Let not these elements our prisons be,
I in a fire, and thou in water art;
  O let a friendly kisse as we two meet,
  From thy coole water rise t'allay my heat.

103

This said, Narcissus doth his hold secure,
And with intention to receive a kisse,
His lip descends to meet the other there,
But hence his expectation cousned is;
  For touching but the superficies,
  Hee did too soon the frighted Image leese.

104

Th'offended water into Circles ran,
And with their motion so disturb'd the place,
The Lover could not see himselfe againe:
Then doth he call aloud unto this face;
    Thou bright-beam'd star, oh whither art thou gone?
    But newly shewne thy head, and set so soon?

105

Or if a Comet, thou hadst spent thy light,
(The matter gone, should feed thy flaming haire,)
Thou art mistaken; thy unnaturall flight
Is heaven: all Meteors to the earth repaire,
    Where I now mourne thy absence; But I feare,
    I have some way prophan'd the waters here.

106

What God soever doth this Fountaine owe,
Forgive me, and you Naiades that lave
Your tresses here, trust me I did not know
What sacred power, or President you have,
    My mother was a Nymph, Lyriope,
    Oh for her sake, some kinde one pitty me.

107

Forgive disturbed water, my rude touch,
'Twas not to rob thee of the smallest drop,
In penitentiall teares Ile pay as much
As there can hang upon my lips cold top:
    O calme thy brow then, let thy frownes declare
    Themselves at once finite, and Circular.

108

In thy smooth bosome once more let me pray
A sight of that sweet figure I adore,
Unlesse to heaven return'd some other way;
And if it be, 'tis not so farre before;
    But I can dye, and off this flesh Robe hurl'd,
    Ile overtake it in the other world.

109

Now doth each swelling Circle gently haste
To be dissolv'd, and spread themselves to aire;
No polish'd Marble seem'd more smooth, and fast;
The Boy takes this a fruit of his owne prayer,
    Yet e're he thank'd the gods, he thought it fit,
    To see his love, and seen, forgot them quite.

110

Fearing to be depriv'd agen, he woes,
As every sillable had bled a life,
A sigh, at every clamorous period goes,
With greater noise then it, but no reliefe.
    His aire of tongue, and breast, thus spent, a look
    Presents their stories, doubled in the brook.

111

But all in vaine, the face, he saw before,
Is in the same ill-shewing silence drest,
Chang'd to more sad, but not one accent more,
Deafe as the streame, and now he beats his breast,
    Condemn'd agen to his more haplesse thought,
    He had but all this while his shadow sought.

112

This multiplies his griefe into despaire,
Since his owne Image doth procure the fire,
And nothing left in nature to repaire
His vext affections, that now grow higher;
    That face, his owne, or whose so e're, was that
    Which took him first, to unlove is too late.

113

He beckens to the figure, that replies,
Taught by his posture how to call him thither;
To lift him from the water then he tries,
But when their white hands should have met together,
    A new distraction fell upon the streame,
    And his (because alone) thence weeping came.

114

When he to beare that company, lets fall
More teares than would have made another spring
Till griefe had not another drop to call,
Though to have cur'd his eyes, but will this bring
   The loved shade agen? No; every teare
   Was both his owne, and t'others murderer.

115

But more then this must be (Narcissus) borne,
As a revenge for many Nimphes that lov'd,
And dy'd upon the torture of thy scorne;
And see his eyes that once so charming mov'd
   Do loose their beames, and hasten to be dead
   In their owne hollowes, borne and buried.

116

See what a dotage on himselfe hath sent,
That brow that challeng'd late the snow, for white;
Veines that were made to shame the Firmament,
The cheek that so much wonder drew to it,
   The voice, when tun'd to love, might gods entice
   To change for earth their immortalities.

117

All, all is vanish'd, Nemesis have yet
Some pitty, let him live; he faints, he dies,
'Twere safer for the Boy himselfe to hate,
Then if he love, to pay so deare a price.
   He did but love himselfe, and if he die
   That loves, propose the haters destinie.

118

But Nemesis irrevocable doom,
Must be obey'd, though Eccho late repent,
Who with a murmuring pace unseen was come
To mourne for his, and her owne punishment.
   His groanes had thrild her soule, and at his death
   She comes to catch his fare-well taking breath.

119

And as a glimmering Taper almost spent,
Gasping for moisture to maintaine its fire,
After some darke contentions, doth present
A short-liv'd blaze, and presently expires:
  So he, collecting ebbing Nature, cryes,
  Oh youth, belov'd in vaine, farewell! and dyes.

120

Farewell, poore Eccho did repeat; and fled
With what wings sorrow lent, t'embalme the boy;
But looking carefully to finde the dead,
She miss'd the shadow of her livelesse joy:
  His body, vanish'd; by what mysterie
  Convey'd, not found by her inquiring eye.

121

But in the place where he did disappeare,
Out of the ground a lovely flower betrayes
His whiter leaves, and visibly did reare
His tufted head, with Saffron-colour'd rayes:
  Upon a smooth stemme all this beauty growes;
  This change to heaven the lost Narcissus owes.

122

Eccho with wonder turnes a Statue now,
Yet not an idle figure; for her eyes
From her darke swelling springs doe over-flow,
Having no pow'r to check them as they rise:
  She thus presents a fountaine, as she were
  Meant to refresh the new-borne Tulip there.

123

To which, after some truce with teares, she sayes:
Art thou a pledge for the sweet Boy I lov'd?
Oh, take a voice, tell by what aërie wayes,
The choisest flower of nature is remov'd.
  If in the blessed shades? I can make room,
  Through death to meet him in Elysium.

124

Assume the wings of love, Eccho, away
Unto the Stigian Lake, goe, follow him,
There thou maist finde him on a banke of Clay,
Eying himselfe upon the waters brim:
    The sooty gods enamoured on him are,
    And round about him on his beautie stare.

125

But since he was unkinde alive to me,
I must despaire to meet his love in death,
And this remaining flower, another He,
Shall be preserv'd with my best use of breath.
    And though the obstinate deserv'd to dye,
    I will be just, and love his memorie.

126

But since his curse, though just upon his pride,
Hath made him this example for his sin:
Never shall dreame ease my distracted head,
Sleep shall forget his office, and within
    Darke shades, shut up from all societie,
    In Rocks or Caves Ile undiscovered lye.

127

And to redeem the shame my folly had
Contracted, by preposterous woing man;
Whose bolder nature was in order made
To Court our Sex: Juno take back againe
    Thy gift; from henceforth Eccho will returne
    But their owne words, sent back againe in scorne.

128

This said, she walketh to the fountaines side,
Where she no sooner did the streame survey,
But her owne shadow in the glasse she spi'd,
And cryed, some other witch-craft did betray
    That heavenly boy; ô, perish in some wave!
    Be drown'd for ever, since thou wouldst not save.

129

It is not thee I seek; open thou streame,
And shew me where that fairer Strumpet is;
That from whose sight the Boies infection came,
And from poore Eccho did her soule entice,
    Will no charme call it back? poore Eccho then,
    Here cease to be the scorne of Gods and men.

130

With that impatient, she threw her weight
Into the tempting stream, where now we leave her;
Whom the proud waters did imprison strait,
Yet of her voice they did not quite bereave her,
    For when I ask'd aloud, is she not dead?
    Not dead, distinctly the Nymph answered;

    Of Eccho now no more remaines to tell,
    But that I her, and she bid me, farewell.

DATE DUE

MAR 1 '94			
JUL 1 1 '98			
GAYLORD			PRINTED IN U.S.A.